BREAKTHROUGH FRENCH 1

FOURTH EDITION

Stephanie Rybak

Brian Hill
General Editor
Head of the School of Languages
University of Brighton

If you are a teacher you can access resources on our website comprising tapescripts, teacher's notes and photocopiable exercise sheets. Site licences allowing free duplication of cassettes within an institution are available for this course – visit our website or call 01256 329242 x 3093 for more details. For Sales Enquiries call 01256 302866.

palgrave
macmillan

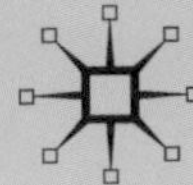

First edition published 1982 by Pan Books Ltd
First Palgrave Macmillan edition published 1988
Second edition 1992
Third edition 1996
Fourth edition 2003
First published 1982 by
PALGRAVE MACMILLAN
Palgrave Macmillan in the UK is an imprint of Macmillan Publishers Limited,
registered in England, company number 785998, of Houndmills, Basingstoke, Hampshire RG21 6XS.
Palgrave Macmillan in the US is a division of St Martin's Press LLC,
175 Fifth Avenue, New York, NY 10010.
Palgrave Macmillan is the global academic imprint of the above companies
and has companies and representatives throughout the world.
Palgrave® and Macmillan® are registered trademarks in the United States,
the United Kingdom, Europe and other countries.

ISBN–13 : 978–1–4039–1554–2 book
ISBN–10 : 1–4039–1554–7 book
ISBN–13 : 978–1–4039–1553–5 pack
ISBN–10 : 1–4039–1553–9 pack
ISBN–13 : 978–1–4039–1555–9 cassettes
ISBN–10 : 1–4039–1555–5 cassettes
ISBN–13 : 978–1–4039–1556–6 CDs
ISBN–10 : 1–4039–1556–3 CDs

A catalogue record for this book is available from the British Library.

Audio production for first to third editions Gerald Ramshaw, Max II; additional audio production for fourth edition Brian Hill
Voices: Philippe Monnet, Carolle Rousseau, Yves Aubert, Nicolas Levoy, Thierry Chenevat, Magalie Charrier, Christine Diamond, Micheline Maupoint, Marc Gaudry, Alban Clark

Design and typesetting design@djhunter

10 9 8
12 11 10

Printed in China

Acknowledgements

The author would like to thank the many French people who took part in the location recordings; all the colleagues who have worked on the publication of the course, in particular Helen Bugler, Philip Tye, Katie Lewis and Muriel Campbell; Guy Fontaine, Olive Rybak and Danielle Drinkwater

The author and publishers would like to thank the following for permission to use copyright material: Anjou Plaisance for an illustrated map from their brochure; Editions Gallimard for Jacques Prévert, 'Déjeuner du matin' in *Paroles*, copyright Editions Gallimard; N. Garinot for the reproduction of the 'palym hôtel' advertisement; SNCF Grandes Lignes for the reproduction of an annotated timetable.

The following photograph sources are acknowledged: Helen Beasley (middle & foot) pp. 11, 99; B. Bisson-Sygma p.224; Helen Bugler pp. 71, 117; Paul Carter p.19; D&J Hunter p.232; Roger-Viollet p.196. All other photographs were supplied by the author.

Every effort has been made to trace all the copyright holders but if any have been inadvertently overlooked the publishers will be pleased to make the necessary arrangement at the first opportunity

Contents

HOW TO USE THIS COURSE

Since the Breakthrough series was introduced in 1982, several million people world-wide have used the courses to learn a variety of languages. This is a completely revised edition: there are new recordings, new activities and new ways of presenting the material. We have talked to hundreds of learners about their 'Breakthrough' experiences and we have acted on what we were told to ensure the new course is even more enjoyable and useful.

Following this course will help you understand, speak and read most of the French you are likely to need on holiday or on business trips. The course is based on recordings made in France of ordinary French people in everyday situations. Step by step you will learn first to understand what they are saying and then to speak in similar situations yourself.

General hints to help you use the course

- Have confidence in us! Real language is complex and you will find certain things in every unit which are not explained in detail. Don't worry about this. We will build up your knowledge slowly, selecting only what is most important at each stage.
- Try to study regularly, but in short periods: 20–30 minutes each day is usually better than 3½ hours once a week.
- To help you learn to speak, say the words and phrases out loud whenever possible.
- If you don't understand something, leave it for a while. Learning a language is a bit like doing a jigsaw or a crossword: there are many ways to tackle it and it all falls into place eventually.
- Don't be afraid to write in the book and add your own notes.
- Do review your work frequently. It helps to get somebody to test you – and they don't need to know French.
- If you can possibly learn with somebody else you will be able to help each other and practise the language together.
- Learning French may take more time than you thought. Just be patient and above all don't get angry with yourself.

Suggested study pattern

Each unit of the course consists of approximately sixteen pages in the book and fifteen minutes of recording. The first page of each unit will tell you what you are going to learn and will give some hints on language learning. You should follow the material at first in the order in which it is presented. As you progress with the course you may find that you evolve a method of study which suits you better

– that's fine, but we suggest you keep to our pattern at least for the first two or three units or you may find you are not taking full advantage of all the possibilities offered by the material.

The book contains step-by-step instructions for working through the course: when to use the book on its own, when to use the recording on its own, when to use them both together and how to use them. On the recording our presenter will guide you through the various sections. Here is an outline of the pattern proposed:

Pronunciation notes

At the start of each unit there are some tips on pronunciation. One or two points are explained in the book, which are then picked up and practised on the recording. Remember that while good pronunciation of a foreign language is desirable, you will usually still be understood even if your accent is not quite accurate.

Conversations

Listen to each conversation, first without stopping the recording, and get a feel for the task ahead. Then go over it bit by bit in conjunction with the vocabulary and the notes. You should get into the habit of using the pause/stop and rewind buttons on your machine to give yourself time to think and to go over the conversation a number of times. Don't leave a conversation until you are confident that you have at least understood it.
Symbols used are:

 = listen to the recording;

▶ = key words which you should try and learn.

There are usually two or three conversations in each section, and three sets of conversations in a unit.

Practice

This section contains a selection of listening, reading and speaking activities which focus your attention on the most important language in the unit. To do them you will need to work closely with the book and often use your machine – sometimes you are asked to write the answers to an exercise and then check them on the recording, at others to listen first and then fill in answers in the book. Again, use your pause/stop and rewind buttons to give yourself time to think and to answer questions.

You will also find practice exercises for speaking the main words and phrases which you have already heard and had explained. The book gives only an outline of the exercises, so you are just listening to the recordings and responding. Usually you will be asked to take part in a conversation where you hear a question or statement in French, followed by a suggestion in English as to what to say. You then give your reply in French and listen to see if you were right. You will probably have to go over these spoken exercises a few times before you get them absolutely correct.

Grammar

At this stage in a unit things should begin to fall into place and you are ready for the grammar section. If you really don't like grammar, you will still learn a lot without studying this part, but most people quite enjoy finding out how the language they are using actually works and how it is put together. In each unit we have selected just one or two important things. At the end of the book is a straightforward summary of the main grammar points.

Key words and phrases

This is a list of the most important words and phrases used in the unit. Pause at this section to see how much you can remember. Look first at the French and find the English equivalent. Then try it the other way round, from English into French. If you find there are some groups of words you have forgotten (don't worry – it happens to everybody!), turn back and have another look at the conversations and notes. These key words and phrases are likely to crop up later in the course so it's worth getting to grips with them before you leave a unit.

Did you know?

In this section you will be given some practical background information on customs, culture and life in French-speaking countries.

Answers

The answers to all the exercises can be found on the last page of each unit, if they have not already been given on the recording.

If you haven't learned languages using a recording before, just spend five minutes on Unit 1 getting used to the mechanics: try pausing the recording and see how long the rewind button needs to be pressed to recap on different length phrases and sections. Don't be shy – take every opportunity you can to speak French to French people and to listen to real French. Try listening to French broadcasts on the radio or watch satellite television. It's even a good idea to talk to yourself in French as much as possible. Try describing what you see as you are travelling around, for instance. *Bon courage!*

At the back of the book

At the back of the book is a reference section which contains:

p. 233 the Review section, which recaps on each unit using speaking exercises.
p. 235 a short Grammar summary with definitions of grammatical terms (noun, adjective, etc.). The section also covers the main rules of French grammar for those who wish to study them in greater detail than the main part of the course provides.
p. 241 a French–English Vocabulary list containing all the words in the course.
p. 249 a brief Index to enable you to look things up in the book.

1 TALKING ABOUT YOURSELF

WHAT YOU WILL LEARN

- greeting people
- basic courtesies
- using the numbers 1–10
- understanding and answering simple questions about yourself
- the documentation you need in France
- some useful addresses for the tourist

BEFORE YOU BEGIN

Before you start, do read the introduction to the course on p. iv. This gives advice on studying alone and explains the study pattern suggested for this course.

Breakthrough French 1 will try to develop your ability to follow the gist of spoken French right from the start, so begin by listening to the first group of conversations on the recording without looking at your book. When you have listened to the conversations, you can look at the transcript of them in the book and read the notes explaining the language used. It is a good idea to listen to the conversations several times before you go on to the exercises in the Practice sections.

Pronunciation notes

Try to imitate as closely as you can the pronunciation of the native speakers on the recording. It may help you to avoid having a heavy foreign accent if you spend a few minutes speaking English with a French accent and then thinking about what it is that makes it sound French. Then, when you speak French, if you sound to yourself as though you are speaking with an exaggerated French accent, you are probably on the right lines!

CONVERSATIONS

Saying hello

LISTEN FOR...

- **bonjour** hello, good-day
- **Madame** literally, Madam
- **Monsieur** literally, Sir
- **Mademoiselle** Miss
- **Messieurs-dames** literally, Ladies and Gentlemen

Guy Bonjour, Madame.
Fleuriste Bonjour, Monsieur.

Guy Bonjour, Madame.
Pharmacien Bonjour, Monsieur.

Guy Bonjour, Mademoiselle.
Hôtesse Bonjour, Monsieur.

Guy Bonjour, Monsieur.
Commerçant Bonjour, Monsieur.

Réceptionniste Bonjour, Messieurs-dames.

bonjour

Fleuriste Florist
Pharmacien Pharmacist
Réceptionniste Receptionist
Commerçant Shopkeeper

The most important expressions are marked with a ▶. These are the ones you should try to learn by heart. They are listed again on p. 14.

▶ **Bonjour** good morning, good afternoon, hello. It translates literally as 'good-day'.

▶ **Madame** means Madam and
▶ **Monsieur** means Sir. We no longer call people Sir or Madam in ordinary conversation in English, but it is a matter of politeness to use **Monsieur** and **Madame** in French. They also mean Mr and Mrs and in writing are often abbreviated to **M.** and **Mme.**

▶ **Mademoiselle** (Miss) is used to a very young, unmarried woman. If in doubt, use **Madame.** The written abbreviation of **Mademoiselle** is usually **Mlle.**

▶ **Messieurs-dames** Ladies and Gentlemen. If you go into a small shop where there are other customers waiting, it is usual to say **Bonjour, Messieurs-dames** (or even just **Messieurs-dames**).

And when the evening comes...

LISTEN FOR...

bonsoir	hello, good evening
bonne nuit	good night

Michel	Bonsoir, Monsieur.
Christian	Bonsoir, Monsieur.
Stephanie	Bonsoir, Monsieur.
Luc	Bonsoir, Madame.
Bernadette	Bonne nuit.
Barbara	Bonne nuit.

- **bonsoir** good evening. Used for both hello and goodbye after about 5 p.m.

Thank you and goodbye

LISTEN FOR...

merci	thank you
au revoir	goodbye

Robert	Bon. Merci. Merci, Madame. Au revoir, Madame.
Réceptionniste	Au revoir, Monsieur.
Robert	Au revoir, Monsieur. Merci.
Julie	Merci.
Réceptionniste	Bonnes vacances!
Julie	Merci. Au revoir, Madame.

- **Bon** literally means 'good'. It is used here, as often, to wind up a conversation – we would say 'right' or 'OK'.

- **Bonnes vacances** (Have a) good holiday!

PRACTICE

The headphones symbol indicates that you will need to use the recording for this activity.

1 First of all, a chance to practise saying the words you have met so far. Carolle will say them on the recording for this exercise; repeat them after her, taking care to imitate her pronunciation as closely as you can. Notice in particular that the '**n**' in **bonjour** and **bonsoir** is not pronounced as an '**n**' – it just gives a nasal sound to the '**o**' which precedes it.

2 Next on the recording, you will hear a number of greetings addressed to you and your partner. After each one, there will be a pause for you to reply appropriately. For example, if you hear a man's voice saying **Bonjour, Messieurs-dames**, you should answer **Bonjour, Monsieur.** If you hear a woman's voice saying **Au revoir, Messieurs-dames**, you should reply **Au revoir, Madame.**

So that you can be sure what you have said is correct, Philippe will give correct versions after the pauses.

3 To help you remember the spellings of the words you have met, see if you can complete the grid.

CLUES

Across

1 Mrs (6)
3 Good-day (7)
4 Good, right, OK (3)
6 Goodnight (5, 4)
7 Goodbye (2, 6)
8 Ladies and Gentlemen (9-5)

Down

2 Thank you (5)
3 Good evening (7)
5 Mr (8)

ANSWERS P. 16

CONVERSATIONS

Please

LISTEN FOR...

- **s'il vous plaît** please
- **un café** one coffee
- **une bière** one beer

Garçon de café	S'il vous plaît, Monsieur?
Jacques	Un café et une bière, s'il vous plaît.

Garçon de café Waiter

▶ **S'il vous plaît** Please. Used here as a polite way to ask for the customer's order.

▶ **Un café et une bière** One coffee and one beer. **Un** and **une** both mean 'a' or 'one'. They are explained in the Grammar section on p. 12.

Counting 1 – 10

Anne	Tu sais compter?
Marie-Aimée	Oui. Un, deux, trois, quatre, cinq, six, sept, huit, neuf, dix.
Anne	Encore une fois!
Marie-Aimée	Un, deux, trois, quatre, cinq, six, sept, huit, neuf, dix.
Anne	Et maintenant, à l'envers!
Marie-Aimée	Dix, neuf, huit, sept, six, cinq, quatre, trois, deux, un, zéro.

Anne

Tu sais compter? Can you count? (literally, You know to count?) You do not need to learn this phrase (or others not marked with a ▶) for the moment.

▶ **oui** yes

▶ **un** 1, **deux** 2, **trois** 3, **quatre** 4, **cinq** 5, **six** 6, **sept** 7, **huit** 8, **neuf** 9, **dix** 10

Encore une fois! Once again! (literally, Again one time!)

▶ **et maintenant** and now

à l'envers backwards

▶ **zéro** zero

PRACTICE

4 Learn the numbers 1–10 by heart. Then play the counting conversation again, without looking at the book, and count aloud, forwards and backwards, with Marie-Aimée.

5 On the recording for this exercise, you will hear Yves saying the word **café** several times over. Notice how different the French pronunciation of it is from the English one: in French the stress is on the second syllable and the '**é**' does not end in a 'y' sound as it does in English. Repeat after Yves, doing your best to mimic his pronunciation.

Then you will hear him saying **bière**. Repeat it after him, trying to imitate the French '**r**', which is rather like a gargle at the back of the throat.

6 On the recording, Yves will give you a number of sums – all additions – on the model
deux et deux font ...
two and two make ...

See if you can say the correct answer in French before Carolle comes in with it.

CONVERSATIONS

 *Your name and address, please*

LISTEN FOR...

▶ **votre nom**	your (sur)name
▶ **votre prénom**	your forename
▶ **votre adresse**	your address

Réceptionniste	Votre nom, s'il vous plaît?
Nicole	Durand.
Réceptionniste	Et votre prénom?
Nicole	Nicole.
Réceptionniste	Et votre adresse, s'il vous plaît?
Nicole	6, avenue Général de Gaulle.

▶ **votre nom** your surname. Notice the pronunciation of **nom**, which is identical to that of **non**, meaning no.

It is a French tradition to greet people you know well with a kiss on both cheeks

Getting to know you

LISTEN FOR...

▶ **anglaise**	English (of a woman)
▶ **français**	French (of a man)
▶ **Londres**	London
▶ **votre travail**	your work
▶ **en vacances**	on holiday

Hervé	Vous êtes anglaise ou américaine?
Stephanie	Je suis anglaise. Et vous?
Hervé	Moi, je suis français. Vous habitez Londres?
Stephanie	Ah non, je suis de Milton Keynes. Et vous?
Hervé	Moi, je suis de Bruay la Buissière. Vous venez ici pour votre travail?
Stephanie	Non, je suis en vacances.
Hervé	Ah? Alors, bonnes vacances.
Stephanie	Merci.

▶ **Vous êtes anglaise ou américaine?** Are you English or American? (literally, You are English or American?) Putting a questioning intonation into the voice is enough to turn a statement into a question in French. French people do not usually distinguish between 'British' and 'English' in speech, but the correct word for British is

▶ **britannique.**

▶ **Je suis anglaise** I am English. A man would say **Je suis anglais.** The grammar section on p. 12 will explain this. For now, note that a man says **je suis écossais** (I am Scottish), **je suis gallois** (I am Welsh), **je suis irlandais** (I am Irish) or **je suis allemand** (I am German) but a woman says **je suis écossaise/ galloise/irlandaise/allemande.**

▶ **Et vous?** And you? A very useful way of returning a question. **Vous** is the normal word for 'you', whether you are talking to one or more persons.

▶ **français** French. A woman would say **Je suis française.**

▶ **Vous habitez Londres?** Do you live in London?

▶ **Ah non. Je suis de Milton Keynes.** Oh no. I am from Milton Keynes. If you were talking to a French person, you might want to say **Vous êtes de Paris?** (Are you from Paris?)

▶ **Moi, je suis de Bruay la Buissière.** I'm from Bruay la Buissière (a small town 40 km south-east of St Omer). **Moi, je** is literally 'Me, I', but it is used in French to stress the word 'I'.

▶ **Vous venez ici pour votre travail?** Are you here on business? (literally, You come here for your work?)

PRACTICE

7 This is a French identity card (**une carte d'identité**). Can you answer the questions about its owner?

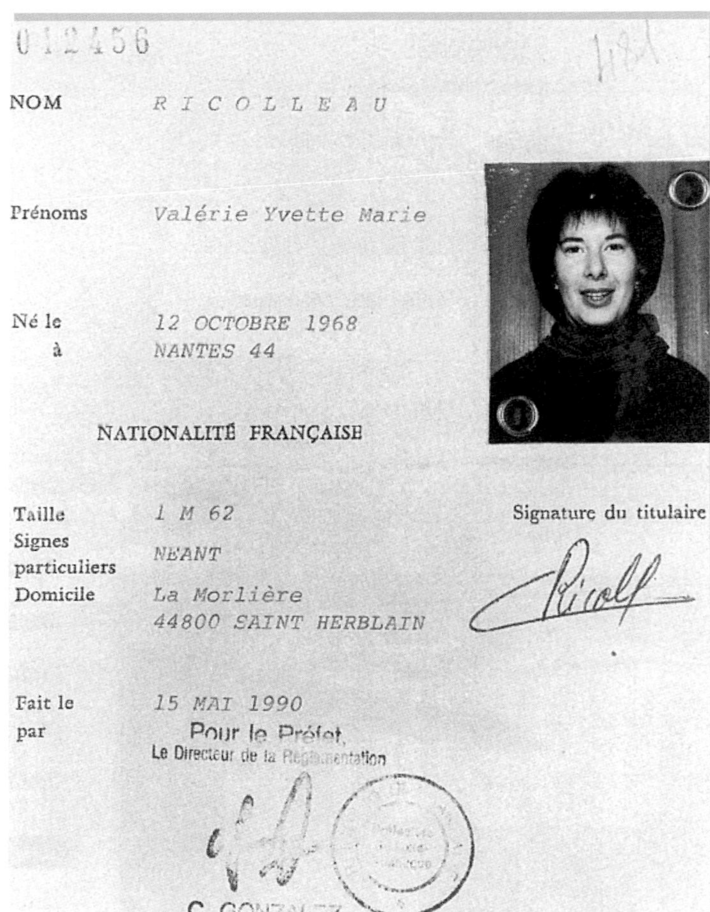

012456

NOM RICOLLEAU

Prénoms Valérie Yvette Marie

Né le 12 OCTOBRE 1968
à NANTES 44

NATIONALITÉ FRANÇAISE

Taille 1 M 62
Signes particuliers NEANT
Domicile La Morlière
44800 SAINT HERBLAIN

Signature du titulaire

Fait le 15 MAI 1990
par Pour le Préfet,
Le Directeur de la [illegible]

C. GON[illegible]

a. What is her surname?
b. What are her forenames?
c. What is her date of birth?
d. What is her nationality?

ANSWERS P. 16

8 Can you fill in your own particulars on the enrolment form below? New word: **la naissance**, birth.

a. Nom (M./Mme/Mlle) ______________________

b. Prénom ______________________

c. Date de naissance ______________________

d. Adresse ______________________

______________________ Code postal ______________

9 On the recording for this exercise, you will hear a conversation between a waitress and a customer. An incomplete transcript of it is given below, with the missing words jumbled up in the box. Listen to the recording as many times as you like and see if you can fill in the gaps.

êtes	s'il vous plaît	suis	vous	bonjour, Madame	en	merci, Madame	je	bonnes

Waitress Bonjour, Monsieur.

Customer ______________ Une bière, ______________

Waitress Oui, Monsieur. Une bière.

(*Brings it*) Votre bière, Monsieur.

Customer ______________ Vous êtes de Paris?

Waitress Non, je ______________ de Rouen.

Customer Vous ______________ française?

Waitress Oui – et ______________?

Customer Moi, ______________ suis américain.

Waitress Vous êtes ici ______________ vacances?

Customer Oui.

Waitress ______________ vacances, Monsieur!

Customer Merci, Madame!

ANSWERS P. 16

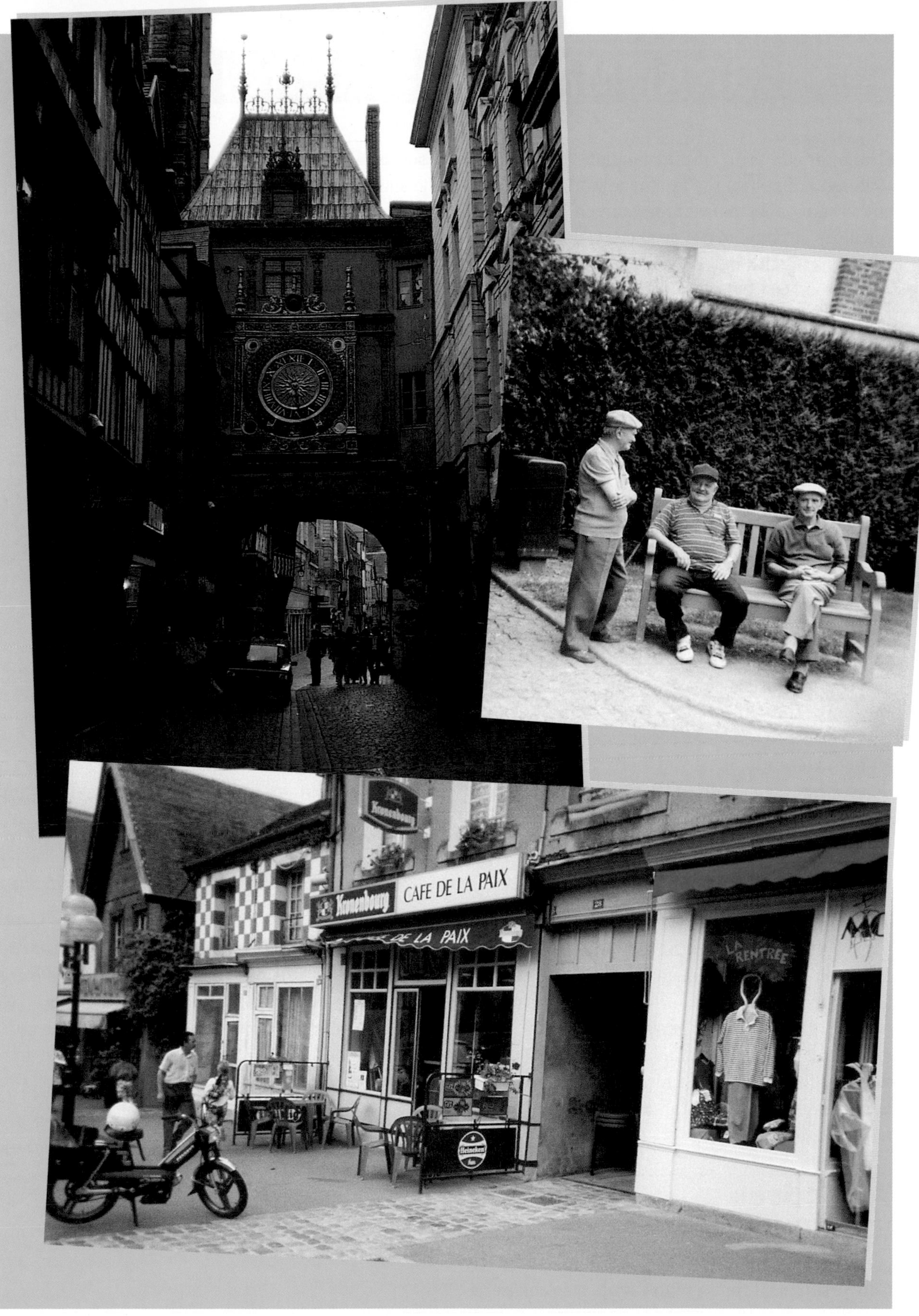

Kronenbourg
CAFE DE LA PAIX
LA RENTRÉE
Heineken

GRAMMAR AND EXERCISES

Grammar can seem off-putting, but understanding how the language works is a short-cut to being able to use it for yourself. It should certainly not inhibit you or make you afraid to open your mouth in case you make a mistake. Remember, MAKING MISTAKES DOES NOT MATTER AS LONG AS YOU MAKE YOURSELF UNDERSTOOD, but having an idea of the basics of grammar helps you to put words together.

Gender

All French nouns* belong to one of two groups called genders: masculine or feminine. Sometimes, it is a matter of common sense: **un Français** (a Frenchman) is obviously masculine and **une Française** (a Frenchwoman) is obviously feminine. However, the gender of most common nouns is not obvious: we can see nothing masculine about coffee (**un café**) or feminine about beer (**une bière**). You can tell the gender of most French nouns if they have the words for 'a' or 'the' in front of them. Get into the habit of noticing genders and trying to learn them as you learn new nouns, but don't worry about getting them wrong, because people will usually still understand you.

Un and *une*

The word for 'a' or 'an' in French is **un** in front of a masculine noun and **une** in front of a feminine noun. **Un** and **une** also mean 'one'. **Un café et une bière** could be translated as either 'A coffee and a beer' or 'One coffee and one beer'. Other examples: **un nom** (a surname), **un prénom** (a forename), **un soir** (an evening), **une adresse** (an address), **une nationalité** (a nationality) and **une nuit** (a night).

Adjectives

These are descriptive words such as big, blue, good, French. You will have noticed in Conversations 3 that a man says **je suis anglais, je suis américain** or **je suis français**, but a woman says **je suis anglaise, je suis américaine** or **je suis française.** This is because an adjective describing something masculine has a masculine form and one describing something feminine has a feminine form. So you say **un café français** (a French coffee) but **une bière française** (a French beer). All but the most common adjectives come after the noun in French. One that comes before the noun is **bon** (good): you say **un bon café** and **une bonne bière.**

The verb *être* to be

The verb 'to be' is as irregular in French as it is in English – and just as important. Here is the present tense. It is also given on the recording for Exercise 10, so that you know how to pronounce it.

je suis	I am	**nous sommes**	we are
tu es	you are	**vous êtes**	you are
il est	he/it is	**ils sont**	they are
elle est	she/it is	**elles sont**	they are

A few explanations:

- You will notice that there are two ways of saying 'you are'. In general, use **vous êtes** unless you are talking to a child or a good friend who uses the **tu** form when talking to you.
- Both **il est** and **elle est** can mean 'it is'. **Il** is used when 'it' refers to a masculine noun (like **un café**) and **elle** when 'it' refers to a feminine noun (like **une bière**). 'It is' is also often translated by **c'est** (literally 'this is' or 'that is'), e.g. **C'est un nom allemand** (It is a German name).
- The plural of **il** is **ils** and the plural of **elle** is **elles**. If 'they' refers to a mixture of masculines and feminines (e.g. a crowd of men and women) use **ils**.

* The definitions of grammatical terms such as noun, article and so on are given in the Grammar summary on pp. 235–240.

10 Working aloud with the recording, learn the verb **être** by heart, until you can say it with Carolle without looking at the book.

11 Cross out the incorrect option in each of the following:

a.	Madame Martin est	français. / française.		
b.	Janet, c'est	un / une	prénom	anglais. / anglaise.
c.	Haßler, c'est	un / une	nom	allemand. / allemande.
d.	Budweiser, c'est	un / une	bière	américain / américaine.
e.	L'Hôtel de France à Amiens, c'est	un bon / une bonne	adresse.	
f.	Bon / Bonne	nuit.		

ANSWERS P. 16

12 See if you can write out the French for the following:

a. I am English. (*said by a man*)

b. I am English. (*said by a woman*)

c. He is French.

d. She is French.

e. He is American.

f. She is American.

g. I am German. (*said by a man*)

h. I am German. (*said by a woman*)

ANSWERS P. 16

KEY WORDS AND PHRASES

Here are the most important words and phrases which you have met so far. Practise saying them aloud until you have learned them by heart.

bonjour	good morning, good afternoon, hello
bonsoir	good evening, hello
Monsieur	'Sir', Mr
Madame	'Madam', Mrs
Mademoiselle	Miss
Messieurs-dames	Ladies and Gentlemen
bonne nuit	goodnight
au revoir	goodbye
merci	thank you
s'il vous plaît	please
un café	a/one coffee
une bière	a/one beer
oui	yes
non	no
zéro	zero
un	one
deux	two
trois	three
quatre	four
cinq	five
six	six
sept	seven
huit	eight
neuf	nine
dix	ten
maintenant	now
votre nom et votre prénom	your surname and your forename
votre adresse	your address
Je suis anglais	I am English (*said by a man*)
Je suis anglaise	I am English (*said by a woman*)
Je suis britannique	I am British (*said by either*)
Je suis américain	I am American (*said by a man*)
Je suis américaine	I am American (*said by a woman*)
Vous êtes français?	Are you French? (*said to a man*)
Vous êtes française?	Are you French? (*said to a woman*)
Vous habitez (Londres)?	Do you live in (London)?
Je suis de (Milton Keynes)	I am from (Milton Keynes)
Moi, je suis de (Bruay)	I am from (Bruay)
Et vous?	And you?
Vous venez ici pour votre travail?	Do you come here on business?

Courtesy

It is easy to appear rude if you don't know the customs in a foreign country, so it is a good idea to use courtesy phrases (**merci, s'il vous plaît,** etc.) abundantly to make up for it. In French, it is polite to use **Monsieur, Madame** and **Mademoiselle** when you are speaking to someone, particularly with one-word utterances like **bonjour** or **merci**, which sound abrupt on their own. The French go on calling each other **Monsieur, Madame** or **Mademoiselle** long after the supposedly more reserved English-speaker has gone on to first-name terms. The French shake hands with friends or acquaintances every time they meet or say goodbye; it is considered rude not to do so. Kissing on both cheeks is also a common custom among family, close friends and young people.

Documents and laws

From the age of 18, everyone in France must have **une carte d'identité**. It contains a passport-type photograph, a signature and a fingerprint and is supposed to be carried everywhere. As a tourist, you are generally advised to carry your passport (or your identity card, if you are from an EU country which has them) at all times. If you are driving, you must always have your driving licence, your insurance certificate and your passport with you in the car. Be ready to produce them if a policeman asks for **vos papiers** (your papers). The 'green card' is no longer compulsory, but it is strongly recommended as without it your insurance cover is usually limited to third-party liability. Most insurance companies will issue a green card free of charge. If you hire a car in France, **la carte grise** (which is the vehicle registration document) should be with you in the car at all times. By law, you must also carry a full set of spare bulbs for your car. If your car does not have hazard lights, or if you are towing a caravan or trailer, you must also carry a red warning triangle in case of breakdown.

Travel to and from French-speaking countries

In addition to the AA, the RAC and travel agents, the following are good sources of information and brochures:

France The French Government Tourist Office, 178 Piccadilly, London W1J 9AL. Tel. 09068 244 123 (calls charged at 60p per minute); Fax 020 7493 6594; e-mail info@mdlf.co.uk; website www.franceguide.com. Their free annual reference guide *The Traveller in France* is a particularly good compendium of useful information and addresses.

Belgium The Belgian Tourist Office, 217 Marsh Wall, London E14 9FJ. Tel. 0906 302 0245 (calls charged at 50p per min); e-mail info@belgiumtheplaceto.be; website www.belgiumtheplaceto.be

Switzerland Switzerland Tourism, Swiss Centre, 10 Wardour Street, London W1D 6QF. Tel. 0207 851 1700; e-mail stlondon@switzerlandtourism.ch; website www.MySwitzerland.com

Quebec For information: Tel. 0870 5 561705 or www.Quebec4you.co.uk

AND FINALLY...

At the end of each unit of the course there is an opportunity to practise speaking, using the vocabulary you have met in the unit – particularly the Key words and phrases.

13

In the recording for this exercise, a guest is checking into a hotel. After each of the receptionist's greetings and questions, there will be a pause for you to give the client's response, which will be one of the words and phrases in the list below. When you have had a chance to speak, Yves will give a correct version.

Au revoir, Madame   Bonjour, Madame   Tom   Je suis américain   Smith

14

For this exercise, you are asked to play the part of an Englishwoman from York on holiday in France. On the recording, Yves will ask you some questions about where you are from and what you are doing in France. There will be a pause for you to answer in character, and then Carolle will say what you should have said.

In some ways, adults are better learners than children, because we have learned how to learn and we are often more motivated. What is not so good is our memory for new words, so we have to make more of a conscious effort to commit things to memory. Here are a few tips:

- Repeat new words aloud, many times over: you will remember them better than if you only hear and read them.
- Read the conversations and do the practice activities aloud.
- Write new words out; this will help to fix them in your mind.
- Look at new words to see if you can spot a link with English. For example, in this unit you have met the word for a forename, **un prénom**. Think of it as a 'pre-name' and it will be easier to remember.
- If there is no logical connection with English, it sometimes helps to invent an illogical one; for example, thinking of 'silver plates' may help you to remember **s'il vous plaît**!

ANSWERS

Exercise 3

					1 M	A	D	A	2 M	E			
									E				
			3 B	O	N	J	O	U	R				
			O						C				
	4 B	O	N				5 M		I				
			S				O						
		6 B	O	N	N	E	N	U	I	T			
			I				S						
	7 A	U	R	E	V	O	I	R					
							E						
							U						
8 M	E	S	S	I	E	U	R	S	D	A	M	E	S

Exercise 7

(a) Ricolleau **(b)** Valérie Yvette Marie **(c)** 12 October 1968 **(d)** French

Exercise 9

Bonjour, Madame/s'il vous plaît/Merci, Madame/suis/êtes/vous/je/en/Bonnes

Exercise 11

(a) Madame Martin est française. **(b)** Janet, c'est un prénom anglais. **(c)** Haßler, c'est un nom allemand. **(d)** Budweiser, c'est une bière américaine. **(e)** L'Hôtel de France à Amiens, c'est une bonne adresse. **(f)** Bonne nuit.

Exercise 12

(a) Je suis anglais. **(b)** Je suis anglaise. **(c)** Il est français. **(d)** Elle est française. **(e)** Il est américain. **(f)** Elle est américaine. **(g)** Je suis allemand. **(h)** Je suis allemande.

2 YOURSELF AND OTHERS

WHAT YOU WILL LEARN

- answering questions about your job, yourself and your family
- asking similar questions of others
- saying things are not so
- using numbers up to 20
- something about French-speaking countries around the world

BEFORE YOU BEGIN

A great deal of success in language learning depends on resisting the temptation to panic or despair when you are faced with a torrent of words you don't know, either in speech or in writing. If you keep your nerve and listen/look out for the words you do know, and then make some intelligent guesses, you may be surprised at how much of the gist you can understand. This is one reason why it is important to listen to the conversations the first time without looking at the book: it is a chance to practise this valuable skill of listening out for words you know. Similarly, there will be two reading exercises in this unit which are based on newspaper advertisements and announcements. You are not expected to understand all the words in them – you're only on Unit 2, after all! – but the practice of looking through them to pick out words you know or words which resemble English ones will be invaluable in preparing you for coping with the French documents which may come your way in real life.

Pronunciation notes

When someone speaks French with a heavy English accent, the most noticeable sounds are the vowels. In this unit we'll concentrate on the pronunciation of two of them: the '**é**', which you worked on in the word **café** in Unit 1, and the '**i**', which you will meet frequently in the conversations of this unit, for example in the word **Paris**.

CONVERSATIONS 

Do you work?

LISTEN FOR...

- **vous travaillez?** do you work?
- **je travaille** I work
- **à Paris** in Paris

Anna Vous travaillez?
Henri Ah oui, je travaille.
Anna A Paris?
Henri Oui. Et vous?
Anna Oui, moi aussi je travaille – à Paris également.

également too (lit. equally)

- **je travaille** I work. Notice that the ending of the verb is different with **je**. (See Grammar, p. 28.)
- **moi aussi** I too/me too
- **à Paris** in Paris. **A** can also mean 'at' or 'to'. (Note that it is not usual to put accents on capital letters in French – apart from **É**.)

Saying what your job is

LISTEN FOR...

A series of people saying what their jobs are. Listen to the recording and note the use of **je suis** (I am) before you look at the vocabulary.

Henri Je suis commerçant.
Fabienne Je suis secrétaire.
Claude Je suis comptable.
Georges Je suis homme d'affaires.
Brigitte Je suis dans l'enseignement – je suis professeur de gymnastique.
Lisette Je suis employée dans un établissement d'enseignement – je suis fonctionnaire.
Claude Heu – j'ai un emploi de bureau.

un commerçant a shopkeeper, tradesman
un/une secrétaire a secretary
un/une comptable an accountant

un homme d'affaires a businessman
un professeur a teacher (man or woman)
de of
(la) gymnastique gymnastics
un/une fonctionnaire civil servant, administrator

- **Je suis commerçant** I am (a) shopkeeper. In French, you don't use **un** or **une** when saying what somebody's job is.

- **Je suis homme d'affaires** I am (a) businessman. A businesswoman would say **Je suis femme d'affaires.** Some professions have different words for male and female practitioners; others use the same word for both, so that 'an engineer' is **un ingénieur** and 'a teacher' is **un professeur**, whether the person is a man or a woman.

Je suis dans l'enseignement I am in teaching.

employée employed. **Une employée** means a female employee. **Employé** (without a final **-e**) means 'employed' for a man. **Un employé** is a male employee.

un établissement d'enseignement a teaching establishment. The French like long words! In this case she means a school – the simpler word for a school is **une école.**

- **J'ai un emploi de bureau** I have an office job. **Un emploi** is a job; **un bureau** is an office.

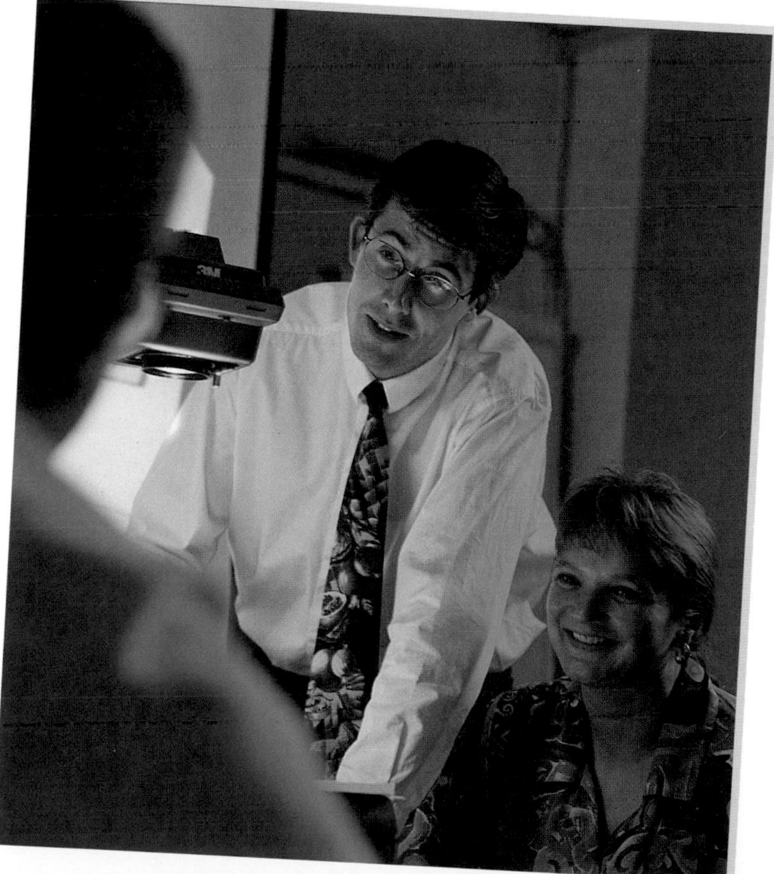

PRACTICE

Entreprise de bâtiment recherche **ÉLECTRICIEN.**
Téléphoner au 03.23.74.97.03

Recherche **PLOMBIER** pour le 1er septembre.
Tél. 05.34.56.67.81

Garage recherche **MÉCANICIEN AUTO**. Téléphoner pour rendez-vous au 05.56.87.10.23

Centre Hospitalier recrute
INFIRMIER/INFIRMIERE
6 mois minimum.
Tél. 02.98.56.87.24

Salon cherche
COIFFEUR/COIFFEUSE.
Tél 03.86.74.37.02

Hôtel *** recherche **RÉCEPTIONNISTE.**
Tél. 03.88.77.14.65

Urgent! Restaurant recherche
CUISINIER pour saison (juillet, août, septembre). Tél. 03.23.11.34.56

Vous êtes **MÉDECIN, DENTISTE, INGÉNIEUR ou TÉCHNICIEN**. Vous êtes prêt(e) à travailler 2 ans en Afrique … Téléphonez-nous au 04.74.56.12.09

1 Look at these advertisements from a newspaper. You won't understand all the words, but see if you can identify the names for the following jobs. (Writing out the French names should help you to memorise them.) The word **recherche** means 'seeks'.

a. Receptionist ______

b. Plumber ______

c. Electrician ______

d. Engineer ______

e. Car mechanic ______

f. Dentist ______

g. Doctor ______

h. Technician ______

i. Cook ______

j. Hairdresser (*male / female)* ______

k. Nurse (*male / female*) ______

The answers to this exercise are given on the recording with a pause for you to repeat them after Yves. Pay particular attention to your pronunciation of the sounds '**é**' and '**i**'. At the end of the list Yves will give you three more pieces of vocabulary:

à la retraite retired
une femme au foyer a housewife
au chômage unemployed

2

Select the correct job from the box below and under each of the drawings write in how each person would say what his/her job was. The first one has been done for you.

professeur de gymnastique	**comptable**	**secrétaire**
coiffeur	**plombier**	**réceptionniste**
dentiste	**médecin**	**à la retraite**

a. *Je suis professeur de gymnastique*

b. ______

c. ______

d. ______

e. ______

f. ______

g. ______

h. ______

i. ______

Carolle will give you the answers on the recording, with a pause after each for you to repeat it aloud. Notice that **je suis** includes the sound 'i', on which we are focusing in this unit.

CONVERSATIONS

A wedding anniversary

LISTEN FOR...

▶ **mariée** (f.)	married
trente-six ans	36 years
▶ **demain**	tomorrow
félicitations!	congratulations!
▶ **des enfants**	children

Stephanie	Vous êtes mariée?
Denise	Oui, nous sommes mariés depuis trente-six ans demain.
Stephanie	Félicitations! Et vous avez des enfants?
Denise	Six enfants.
Stephanie	Des garçons ou des filles?
Denise	Quatre filles et deux garçons.

▶ **Vous êtes mariée?** Are you married? If this had been addressed to a man, it would have been written **Vous êtes marié?** but the pronunciation would be exactly the same.

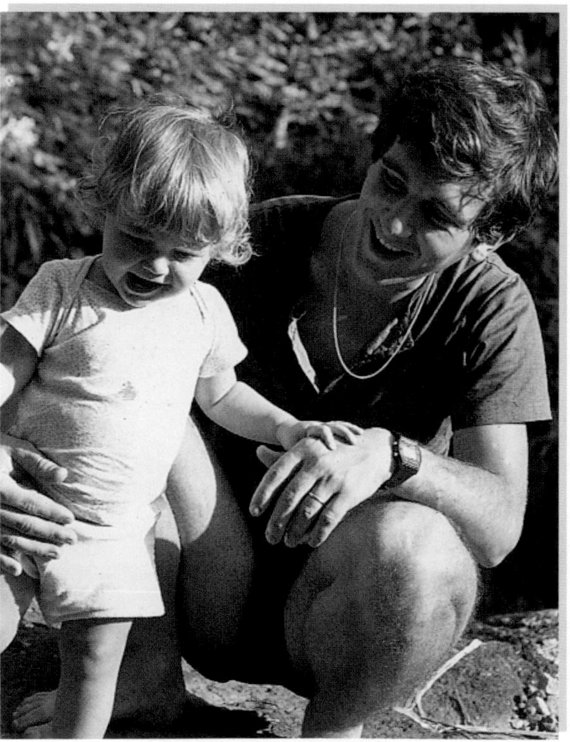

▶ **nous sommes mariés depuis trente-six ans demain** we have been married for thirty-six years tomorrow (literally, we are married since 36 years tomorrow). This construction shows that something which started in the past is still going on now: we have been married for 36 years – and we still are! Learn also: **Je suis marié(e) depuis un an.** I have been married for a year.
Mariés is spelt with an **s** here because the subject (**nous**) is plural.

▶ **vous avez des enfants?** do you have any children? **Des** means 'some' or 'any'.

▶ **Des garçons ou des filles?** Boys or girls? French nouns are almost always preceded by **des** (some), **les** (the), or some other article. The word **fille** means either 'girl' or 'daughter'. The word for 'a son' is
▶ **un fils**, which you will hear pronounced on the recording.

Family questions

LISTEN FOR...

je ne suis pas	I am not
célibataire	single
des frères et sœurs	brothers and sisters
votre père	your father
ma mère	my mother

Michel Vous êtes marié?
Christian Oui – et vous?
Michel Non, je ne suis pas marié – je suis célibataire. Et vous, avez-vous des enfants?
Christian Ah oui, j'ai trois filles: Claire, Isabelle et Céline.
Michel Avez-vous des frères et sœurs?
Christian Ah oui, j'ai ... trois frères et deux sœurs.
Michel Et votre père vit toujours?
Christian Ah oui, oui – et ma mère aussi.

Michel

- **je ne suis pas marié** I'm not married. **Ne** and **pas** either side of a verb make it negative. There are more examples in the next conversation and an explanation in the Grammar section of the unit.
- **célibataire** single. This can be an adjective or a noun, so **un célibataire** is a bachelor and **une célibataire** a single woman.
- **j'ai trois filles** I have three daughters.

Avez-vous des enfants? Do you have any children? This is the same as **Vous avez des enfants?** spoken with a questioning intonation.

Et votre père vit toujours? And is your father still alive? (Literally, And your father lives still?)

PRACTICE

Here is a family tree. Read the statements below it and listen to them being read on the recording. Then complete the vocabulary list for yourself.
You will need to understand **ils ont** (they have), which comes from the verb **avoir** (to have), which you will find set out on p. 28.

Danielle est la femme de Robert.
Ils ont trois filles: Brigitte, Michèle et Odette.
Claude est le mari de Brigitte, Pierre est le mari de Michèle et Philippe est le mari d'Odette.
Danielle et Robert ont trois petits-enfants: une petite-fille, Monique, et deux petits-fils, Bertrand et Jean-Luc.
Donc, les parents de Brigitte sont les grands-parents de Monique, de Bertrand et de Jean-Luc: Danielle est la grand-mère et Robert est le grand-père.

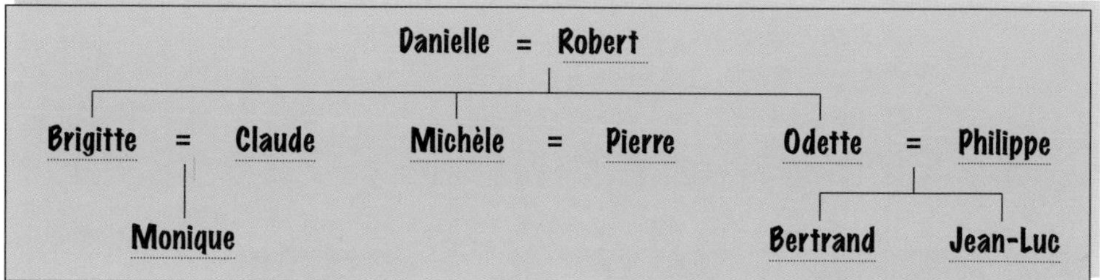

a. ______________________ grandmother

b. ______________________ grandfather

c. ______________________ grandparents

d. ______________________ granddaughter

e. ______________________ grandsons

f. ______________________ grandchildren

g. ______________________ wife

h. ______________________ husband

You will notice that, whereas in English we talk about 'grandchildren', in French, the word **grand** (big) is used of grandparents but **petit** (little) is used of grandchildren. It is actually rather more logical than English, when you think about it.

ANSWERS P. 32

4 This exercise is one of those that will give you practice at looking for words you can understand among lots of others that you can't.

Below are some announcements from the births and marriages columns of a newspaper.

i. **M. Jean-Jacques VARENNE**
et Mme, née Éliane Perraudin
ont la joie de vous annoncer
la naissance de leur fille
Hortense
Paris, le 6 mai 2003

ii. **Mme Inès CARNEAU-BÉZIEUX**
a la joie d'annoncer
la naissance de
son premier petit-enfant
Aymeric
chez
M. Félix FOUGEROLLE
et Mme, née Delphine
du Boisméry.
St Cloud, le 10 mai 2003

iii. **M. Alain du CRAY**
et Mme, née Virginie
Duboscq
ont l'honneur de vous faire part
de la naissance de leur fils
Thierry
frère de Laurent
Paris, le 8 mai 2003

iv. **M. et Mme René de CHATEAUVIEUX**
M. et Mme
Didier ROYAUX
sont heureux de vous
faire part du mariage
de leurs enfants
Aurélie et Olivier
en l'église St-Pierre
de Neuilly-sur-Seine.

a. Which one announces a wedding?

____

b. What is the maiden name of the woman who has just had a daughter?

____

c. Who has just had her first grandchild?

____

d. Who has just had a little brother?

____

ANSWERS P. 32

5 

On the recording, Philippe will prompt you to ask Carolle some questions about herself and her family. He will say in English what you should say in French; there will be a pause for you to speak (or to press the pause control on your machine to give yourself time to think) and then Yves will say what you should have said. Only after that will Carolle answer your question!

CONVERSATIONS 

Saying no

LISTEN FOR...

▶ **tu viens?**	are you coming? will you come?
▶ **au cinéma**	to the cinema
▶ **ce soir**	this evening
samedi	(on) Saturday

Nathalie Tu viens au cinéma avec moi ce soir?
Hervé Ah non, je ne peux pas ce soir.
Nathalie Heu, demain, alors?
Hervé Demain, je ne suis pas libre.
Nathalie Eh bien, samedi?
Hervé De toute façon, je n'aime pas le cinéma.

heu er
▶ **alors** then
▶ **libre** free
eh bien well then
de toute façon in any case

▶ **Tu viens au cinéma avec moi ce soir?** Will you come (literally, you are coming) to the cinema with me this evening? **Tu** is the word for 'you' that is used between friends, family and young people. To someone with whom you are on more formal terms, you would say
▶ **vous venez** instead of **tu viens.** (See Grammar, p. 74.)
Au = **à** + **le** (to the). This will be explained later on (Grammar, p. 42).

▶ **je ne peux pas** I can't. **Je peux** is 'I can'. To make it (or any other verb) negative, you put **ne** before it and **pas** after it.

▶ **je n'aime pas le cinéma** I don't like the cinema. **J'aime** is 'I like' – before a vowel, **je** shortens to **j'**. When **ne** is put before a verb beginning with a vowel, it too shortens: it becomes **n'**. (See Grammar, p. 28.) Note also
▶ **Vous aimez le cinéma?** Do you like the cinema?

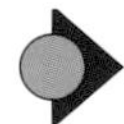

Numbers 1–20

Un, deux, trois, quatre, cinq, six, sept, huit, neuf, dix, onze, douze, treize, quatorze, quinze, seize, dix-sept, dix-huit, dix-neuf, vingt.

▶ **onze** 11, **douze** 12, **treize** 13, **quatorze** 14, **quinze** 15, **seize** 16, **dix-sept** 17, **dix-huit** 18, **dix-neuf** 19, **vingt** 20.

PRACTICE

6

Here is a partial transcript of the conversation in which Nathalie tries to persuade Hervé to go to the cinema. See if you can complete the gaps by listening to the recording again. The missing phrases are jumbled in the box. You can look back at the full transcript on p. 26 to check your answers when you have finished.

je ne suis pas libre	**je ne peux pas**	**je n'aime pas**	**avec moi**	**demain**

Nathalie Tu viens au cinéma ____________________ ce soir?

Hervé Ah non, ____________________ ce soir.

Nathalie Heu, ____________________, alors?

Hervé Demain, ____________________

Nathalie Eh bien, samedi?

Hervé De toute façon, ____________________ le cinéma.

7

French telephone numbers are said with the figures in pairs, so that, for example, 01.14.13.02.20 is said as **zéro un.quatorze.treize.zéro deux.vingt**. See if you can write out how the following numbers should be said:

a. 03.15.03.18.16 ____________________

b. 02.17.20.09.18 ____________________

c. 01.16.20.08.13 ____________________

d. 05.14.18.16.01 ____________________

e. 04.12.19.06.16 ____________________

The answers are given on the recording for this exercise. When you have checked them, cover up the first part of this exercise, listen to the recording again and see if you can write out the telephone numbers in figures below:

a. ____________________

b. ____________________

c. ____________________

d. ____________________

e. ____________________

GRAMMAR AND EXERCISES

Verbs

In English, we say 'I work' but 'he works'. In the same way – only rather more so – the endings of French verbs change. For example, you have already met **je travaille** and **vous travaillez**. They both come from the verb which has the infinitive **travailler**. (In English, the infinitive of a verb is the form which begins with 'to…', e.g. to work.)

Hundreds of French verbs – those with infinitives ending in **-er** – follow exactly the same pattern as **travailler**. Here is the present tense of it. It corresponds to two sorts of present tense in English, so that, for example, both 'I work' and 'I am working' are translated **je travaille**. You should learn the verb now – and the best way to do that is to listen to it on the recording and then say it aloud, over and over, until you know it by heart. Notice that **travaille, travailles** and **travaillent** all sound exactly the same.

TRAVAILLER

je travaille	I work I am working
tu travailles	you work you are working
il/elle travaille	he/she works he/she is working
nous travaillons	we work we are working
vous travaillez	you work you are working
ils/elles travaillent	they work they are working

Two of the verbs following this pattern are **aimer** (to like or to love) and **habiter** (to live). The only difference comes from the fact that **je** shortens to **j'** before a vowel sound, so **je** + **aime** is said and written as **j'aime**. You can hear the present tense of **aimer** on the recording. Most French words beginning with **h** are also treated as beginning with a vowel sound, so **je** + **habite** gives **j'habite**. All the other forms of the verbs (**tu aimes**, **elle habite** and so on) follow exactly the model of **travailler**.

The negative

In French, 'not' is expressed by putting **ne** before the verb and **pas** after it. 'I do not work' etc. are expressed:

je ne travaille pas
tu ne travailles pas
il/elle ne travaille pas
nous ne travaillons pas
vous ne travaillez pas
ils/elles ne travaillent pas

With verbs like **aimer** and **habiter**, which begin with a vowel sound, the **ne** abbreviates to **n'**:

je n'habite pas
tu n'habites pas
il/elle n'habite pas
nous n'habitons pas
vous n'habitez pas
ils/elles n'habitent pas

Avoir

Apart from **être**, the most common irregular verb is **avoir**, to have. You have already met some parts of the present tense. You should learn the whole of it now – it is on the recording.

AVOIR

j'ai	I have
tu as	you have
il/elle a	he/she has
nous avons	we have
vous avez	you have
ils/elles ont	they have

The negative goes like this:

je n'ai pas
tu n'as pas
il/elle n'a pas
nous n'avons pas
vous n'avez pas
ils/elles n'ont pas

8

Here is the beginning of a letter from a French girl introducing herself to her British pen-friend. There are one or two words which you have not met yet, but don't be fazed by them. See if you can put the correct verbs from the box into the gaps.

est n'habite pas ont sont aime est habite travaille

J' ______________ avec ma mère et mon frère à Nancy. Ma mère ______________ dans un grand hôtel: elle ______________ réceptionniste. Mes parents ______________ divorcés, alors mon père ______________ avec nous – il habite Metz avec sa nouvelle femme. Ils ______________ deux enfants. Mon père ______________ cuisinier dans un très bon restaurant. J' ______________ le cinéma et la gymnastique.

ANSWERS P. 32

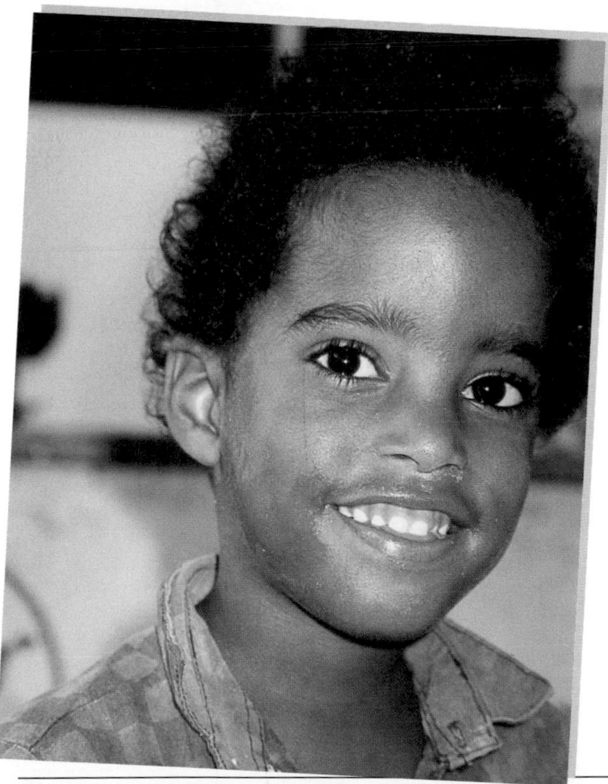

9

Now see if you can translate these sentences into French:

a. I work in London.

____

b. Do you (**vous**) work in Paris?

____

c. He doesn't like the cinema.

____

d. She is not married.

____

e. Do you (**vous**) have any children?

____

f. They have one son and two daughters.

____

g. They don't like the teacher.

____

h. (*To a little boy*) You're not English.

____

i. We live in London.

____

ANSWERS P. 32

PARTICIPER
je participe
tu participes
il/elle participe
nous participons
vous participez
ils profitent!

KEY WORDS AND PHRASES

Spend some time repeating these words and phrases aloud and then test yourself to see whether you can remember them.

Je travaille	I work
Vous travaillez	You work
Vous travaillez?	Do you work?
Moi aussi	I too/me too
A Paris	In Paris
J'ai (un emploi de bureau)	I have (an office job)
Je suis (professeur)	I am (a teacher)
Vous êtes marié?	Are you married? (*to a man*)
Vous êtes mariée?	Are you married? (*to a woman*)
Je ne suis pas marié(e)	I'm not married
Nous sommes mariés depuis trente-six ans	We have been married for thirty-six years
Vous avez des enfants?	Do you have any children?
des	some, any
Des garçons ou des filles?	Boys or girls?
J'ai trois filles et un fils	I have three daughters and a son
un mari	a husband
une femme	a wife, a woman
un frère	a brother
une sœur	a sister
un père	a father
une mère	a mother
célibataire	single
demain	tomorrow
alors	then
libre	free
Tu viens/vous venez au cinéma avec moi ce soir?	Will you come to the cinema with me this evening?
Je ne peux pas	I can't
Vous aimez le cinéma?	Do you like the cinema?
Oui, j'aime le cinéma	Yes, I like the cinema
Non, je n'aime pas le cinéma	No, I don't like the cinema
onze	eleven
douze	twelve
treize	thirteen
quatorze	fourteen
quinze	fifteen
seize	sixteen
dix-sept	seventeen
dix-huit	eighteen
dix-neuf	nineteen
vingt	twenty

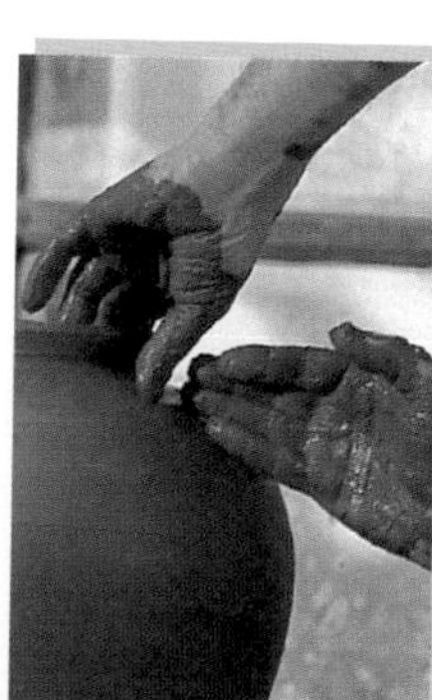

DID YOU KNOW?

La Francophonie

La Francophonie is the informal commonwealth of French-speaking people around the world.

French is an official language for some 220 million people, including:
70 million in Europe   120 million in Africa   30 million in America
400,000 in Asia and Oceania

Europe

As well as having 56 million speakers in France itself, French is an official language in:

- Belgium, where it is the mother tongue of two-fifths of the population. It is spoken mainly in the southern provinces (Hainaut, Liège, Luxembourg, Namur and the southern part of Brabant) and in Brussels.
- Switzerland, where it is the mother tongue of nearly a quarter of the population (predominantly the inhabitants of the western cantons of Vaud, Neuchâtel, Geneva and parts of Berne).
- Luxembourg and Monaco, which both have French as their official language.
- The valley of Aosta in Piedmont, Italy, where there are two official languages: French and Italian.

Africa

French is the official language of the island of Réunion, which is an Overseas French Department with a population of half a million. It is also the official language (or one of the official languages) in: Algeria, Benin, Burkina Faso, Burundi, Cameroon, the Central African Republic, Chad, the Congolese Republic, Dahomey, Djibouti, Gabon, Guinea, Ivory Coast, Madagascar, Mali, Mauritania, Mauritius, Mayotte, Morocco, Niger, Rwanda, Senegal, Togo, Tunisia and Zaïre.

America

- In Canada, French and English have equal rights as official languages, except in the province of Quebec, where French is now the sole official language. Over a quarter of Canadians are French-speaking. Most of these live in Quebec and the others chiefly in Ontario, New Brunswick and Manitoba.
- In Louisiana, French is no longer an official language, but it is still the mother tongue of half a million people.
- Martinique, Guadeloupe, French Guiana, Saint-Pierre-et-Miquelon and Haïti have French as their official language.

Asia and Oceania

- French is spoken by a small minority in the Khmer Republic, Vietnam and Laos, but it is no longer an official language.
- It is the official language of New Caledonia, French Polynesia and the Wallis and Fortuna Islands.

Sources

Peter Rickard, *A History of the French Language*, 2nd edn (London: Unwin Hyman, 1989), pp. 162–3.
Erik Gunnemark and Donald Kenrick, *A Geolinguistic Handbook*, 2nd edn (printed privately in Sweden by Erik Gunnemark, 1985), pp. 107, 178–9.

AND FINALLY...

10

For this activity, you are asked to play the part of a male dentist from Maidenhead. Carolle will ask you questions on the recording, Philippe will say in English what you should say in French and then there will be a gap for you to reply in character. After you have had a chance to speak, Yves will come in with what you should have said. Remember that what he says may not be the only correct version. For example, **J'habite Maidenhead** means much the same as **Je suis de Maidenhead**, so it doesn't matter if you say one and Yves says the other.

11

Spend a few minutes seeing how many sentences you can make up to describe your own family situation. Use the suggestions below to help you.

Je suis marié/mariée depuis X ans.
Je ne suis pas marié/mariée.
Je suis célibataire.
Je suis divorcé (m.)/divorcée (f.).
J'ai … enfants.
J'ai … filles et … garçons.
Je n'ai pas d'enfants. I don't have any children.
J'ai … frères et … sœurs.
Je n'ai pas de frères et sœurs.

When you have sorted out your sentences, turn on the recording for this exercise, where Yves will ask you a series of questions about yourself. Try to answer him using full sentences rather than just **oui** or **non**. Obviously, there are no correct answers for this exercise, because they depend on your own situation, but you should be able to produce appropriate answers on the basis of the list above.

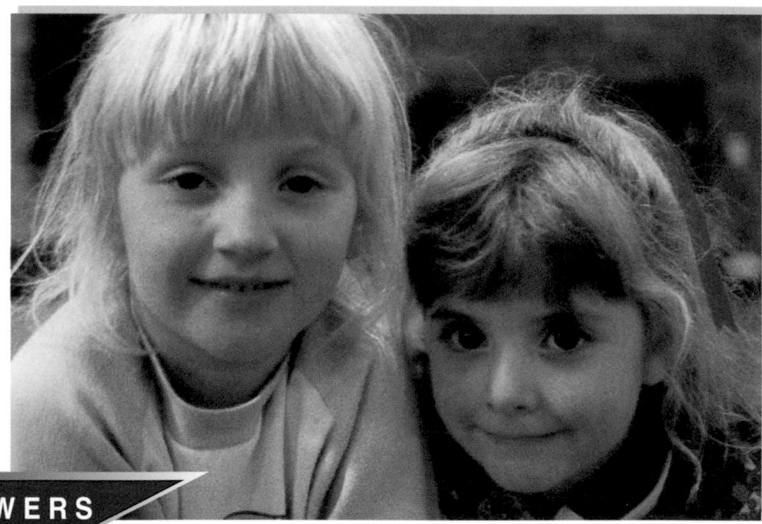

ANSWERS

EXERCISE 3

(a) grand-mère **(b)** grand-père **(c)** grands-parents **(d)** petite-fille **(e)** petits-fils **(f)** petits-enfants **(g)** femme **(h)** mari

EXERCISE 4

(a) iv **(b)** (Éliane) Perraudin **(c)** Mme Inès Carneau-Bézieux **(d)** Laurent (du Cray)

EXERCISE 8

habite/travaille/est/sont/n'habite pas/ont/est/aime

EXERCISE 9

(a) Je travaille à Londres. **(b)** Vous travaillez à Paris? **(c)** Il n'aime pas le cinéma. **(d)** Elle n'est pas mariée. **(e)** Vous avez des enfants? **(f)** Ils ont un fils et deux filles. **(g)** Ils n'aiment pas le professeur. **(h)** Tu n'es pas anglais. **(i)** Nous habitons Londres.

3 ORDERING DRINKS AND SNACKS

What you will learn

- asking and understanding what is available
- ordering breakfast, drinks, snacks and light meals
- something about typical drinks and snacks in France
- how to use a telephone in France
- the numbers 20–50

Before you begin

As you will find in this unit, many names for fast-food snacks are international. You will also learn some more specifically French vocabulary for things that you may wish to order. Perhaps even more importantly, you will learn how to ask what things are and what is available. Thought for the day: successful transactions in the foreign language depend on developing strategies for using the limited language you know in order to find out what you don't know.

CRÊPERIE - RESTAURANT
La Maison d'autrefois
29290 SAINT RENAN

Pronunciation notes

One of the most important things when you are learning a language is not to have hang-ups about making mistakes. Keep telling yourself that, as long as the other person understands what you are trying to say, you are doing well. However, it is satisfying to produce French that is better than that basic minimum. One aspect that needs conscious attention is pronunciation.

Conversations 1 include a number of examples of the vowel sound which is spelt '**é**', '**er**', '**ez**' or '**et**' in different words. Exercise 2 will help you to consolidate the work you have already done on this crucial sound.

In Conversations 2 there are several words containing one of the distinctively French nasal vowels – the one which is spelt '**en**' or '**an**'. Exercise 4 will give you practice at saying it.

CONVERSATIONS

Breakfast by telephone

LISTEN FOR...

- **un lait** one milk
- **chaud ou froid?** hot or cold?
- **d'accord** OK, agreed

Réceptionniste Oui? Alors deux petits déjeuners. Qu'est-ce que vous prenez? Alors un lait – chaud ou froid? Un lait chaud et un café-lait? Et tous les deux complets? D'accord.

- **deux petits déjeuners** two breakfasts. **Un déjeuner** is 'lunch' and **un petit déjeuner** (literally 'a little lunch') is breakfast.
- **Qu'est-ce que vous prenez?** What will you have? Literally, this means 'What is it that you are taking?' but it is more helpful to think of the whole expression **Qu'est-ce que ...?** as meaning 'What ...?'
- **un café-lait** a white coffee; **un café au lait** is the more usual expression.

tous les deux both of them (literally, all the two).

- **complets** full. This is shorthand: the receptionist is checking that the customer wants full continental breakfasts with the drinks. If you want continental breakfast with white coffee, ask for
- **un petit déjeuner complet avec du café au lait.**

Ordering breakfast

LISTEN FOR...

- **du thé** tea
- **citron** (with) lemon

Jeanne Bonjour, Monsieur.
Garçon Bonjour, Madame. Qu'est-ce que vous désirez?
Jeanne Heu ... Qu'est-ce que vous avez?
Garçon Pour le petit déjeuner nous avons du café, du café au lait, du lait, du chocolat et du thé.
Jeanne Un thé, s'il vous plaît.
Garçon Oui. Citron? Nature?
Jeanne Avec du lait froid.
Garçon Avec du lait froid. Parfait.
Jeanne Merci.

- **pour** for
- **un chocolat** a chocolate (eating or drinking)

parfait perfect, fine

Qu'est-ce que vous désirez? What would you like? (literally, What do you desire?)

- **Qu'est-ce que vous avez?** What do you have?

du café coffee. If you ask for **du café** or **un café**, you will be given just that: coffee, without milk. If you want to specify black coffee (worth doing at breakfast, which is the one time that people may assume that you want it white) ask for

- **un café noir.**

du some (in front of masculine nouns). 'Some' is often used in French where we wouldn't say anything in English (as in this list of drinks). There is more about **du** in the Grammar section.

- **citron? nature?** (with) lemon? on its own? French people usually drink tea without milk.

- **Avec du lait froid** With cold milk. It is worth specifying this in France as **un thé au lait** may well be served with hot milk!

PRACTICE

1 Listen to the recording for this activity (several times if necessary) and see if you can note down in English the five breakfast drinks ordered.

ANSWERS P. 46

2 On the recording for this activity, Yves will say a number of words and sentences which include the vowel sound which is most often spelt **'é'**. Repeat them after him in the pauses.

3 Now you are ordering breakfast for your party. Philippe will tell you on the recording what people want to drink with their continental breakfast: you order for them. Each time, after you have had a chance to speak, Carolle will give a correct version of what you should have said.

CONVERSATIONS 2

Ordering beer and soft drinks

LISTEN FOR...

- **comme bière** in the way of beer
- **de la pression** draught

Jeanne	Qu'est-ce que vous avez comme bière, s'il vous plaît?
Garçon	Comme bière nous avons de la pression et de la Kronenbourg en bouteilles.
Jeanne	Bon ... heu ... deux pressions, s'il vous plaît.
Garçon	Deux pressions? Des petits? Des grands ...?
Jeanne	Des petits.
Garçon	Des petits – d'accord.
Jeanne	Merci. Et pour les enfants, qu'est-ce que vous avez?
Garçon	Pour les enfants: Orangina, Coca-Cola, Schweppes – heu – du lait, lait-fraise et tout ça.
Jeanne	Ben ... deux Orangina, s'il vous plaît.
Garçon	Deux Orangina.
Jeanne	Merci.

- **en** in
- **petit** small
- **grand** large

un Orangina trade name of an orangeade
du lait-fraise strawberry milk-shake
un Schweppes tonic water

- **Qu'est-ce que vous avez comme bière?** What have you got in the way of beer? A very useful construction. Another example: **Qu'est-ce que vous aimez comme musique?** What do you like in the way of music?

Des petits, des grands ...? Small ones, large ones ...? This refers to small and large glasses of beer. A glass is **un verre.**

et tout ça and all that.

Bon and **ben** (correctly **Bon** and **bien**) are just noises that people make while they are making up their minds.

Ordering an apéritif

LISTEN FOR...

- **Qu'est-ce que c'est que ...?** What is ...?
  le cocktail maison the house cocktail
- **du champagne** champagne
- **je vais prendre ça** I'll have that

Guy	Qu'est-ce que c'est que le cocktail maison, s'il vous plaît?
Serveuse	C'est de la crème de cassis avec du champagne.
Guy	Ah, ça a l'air pas mal. Je vais prendre ça.
Jeanne	Tiens, moi aussi.
Serveuse	D'accord: deux cocktails maison.

- **Qu'est-ce que c'est?** means What is it?
- **Qu'est-ce que c'est que le cocktail maison?** What is the house cocktail?
  The last **que** is optional in this construction: you can equally well say **Qu'est-ce que c'est, le cocktail maison?**
  You can also use **Qu'est-ce que c'est...?**, with or without the **que** on the end, if you don't understand what something is. For example, if you want to know what **crème de cassis** means, you can ask **Qu'est-ce que c'est (que) la crème de cassis?**

- **C'est** It is
  de la crème de cassis avec du champagne blackcurrant liqueur with champagne. The usual name for this mix is **un kir royal**. With white wine rather than champagne, it is simply **un kir**.

  ça a l'air pas mal that sounds all right (literally, that has the appearance not bad).
- **pas mal**, depending on the tone of voice, can mean everything from a grudging 'not bad' to 'very good indeed'!

- **Je vais prendre ça** I'll have that (literally, I am going to take that).

- **Tiens, moi aussi** Mm, me too. The **tiens** is untranslatable. Here the tone of voice implies 'That's a good idea!'

PRACTICE

4 A little work on pronunciation, this time spotlighting the nasal sound which is spelt **en**, **an** or **am**. It has occurred in Conversations 2 in the words: **Kronenbourg**, **en**, **grands**, **enfants**, **Orangina**, **champagne**, **prendre**. On the recording for this activity, Carolle says a number of phrases and sentences using these words. Repeat them after her, imitating her pronunciation as closely as you can.

5 Read through this menu. **Un flacon** is another word for **une bouteille**. **L'eau minérale** (mineral water) can be **plate** (still) like Coralie or **gazeuse** (fizzy) like Perrier. **Anisé** means 'aniseed-based'. Listen to the recording for this exercise and put a ✔ on the menu beside the drinks that are actually ordered.

Answers p. 46

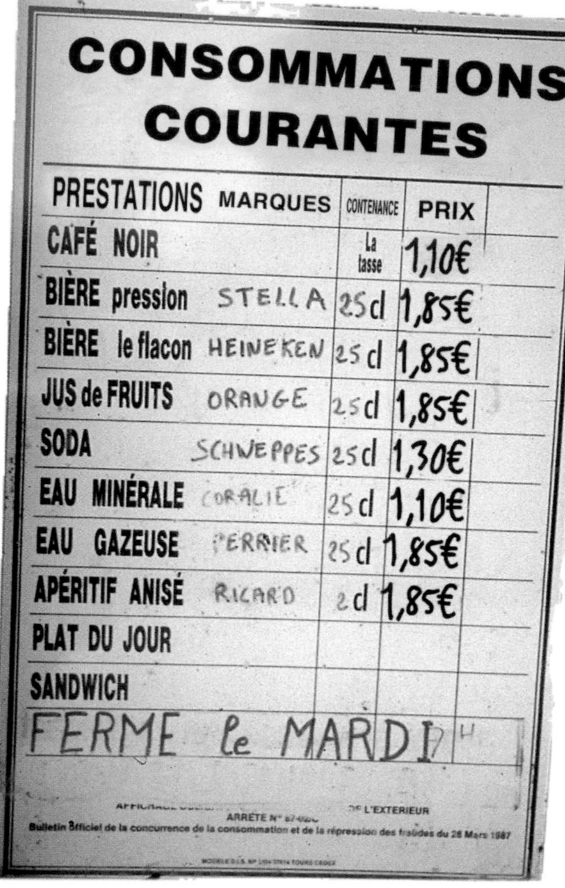

CONSOMMATIONS COURANTES
PRESTATIONS
MARQUES
CONTENANCE
PRIX
CAFÉ NOIR
La tasse
1,10€
BIÈRE pression
STELLA
25cl
1,85€
BIÈRE le flacon
HEINEKEN
25cl
1,85€
JUS de FRUITS
ORANGE
25cl
1,85€
SODA
SCHWEPPES
25cl
1,30€
EAU MINÉRALE
CORALIE
25cl
1,10€
EAU GAZEUSE
PERRIER
25cl
1,85€
APÉRITIF ANISÉ
RICARD
2cl
1,85€
PLAT DU JOUR
SANDWICH
FERME le MARDI

6 Look back at Conversations 2 and make sure you know how to ask a bartender

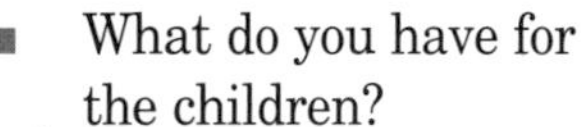

- What do you have for the children?
- What do you have in the way of apéritifs?
- What is the house cocktail?

Then turn on the recording for this exercise, where Philippe will prompt you to ask these questions and to order some drinks, one of which will be **un whisky** – no translation needed here! Yves will say what you should have said after the pauses.

CONVERSATIONS 3

Ordering savoury pancakes

LISTEN FOR...

- **trois galettes** three savoury pancakes
- **au jambon** with ham
- **au fromage** with cheese
- **boire** to drink
- **quelque chose** something
- **du cidre** cider
- **une grande bouteille** a large bottle

Serveuse Madame, vous désirez?
Danielle Trois galettes, s'il vous plaît: une galette au jambon et au fromage, une galette à la saucisse et une galette aux œufs et au jambon.
Serveuse Et vous voulez boire quelque chose?
Danielle Oui – du cidre, s'il vous plaît.
Serveuse Une grande bouteille, une petite …?
Danielle Une grande bouteille, je pense, s'il vous plaît.
Serveuse Très bien, Madame.

Crêpes au Blé Noir (salées)

Crêpe beurre	3,00€
Crêpe Jambon (épaule)	4,80€
Jambon œuf	7,20€
Jambon champignons	7,20€
Crêpe Fromage	4,80€
Fromage jambon	7,20€
Fromage champignons	7,20€
Crêpe œuf	4,80€
Œuf fromage	7,10€
Crêpe complète (jambon,œuf, fromage)	8,00€
Complète tomates	8,40€
Complète champignons	8,40€
Complète oignons	8,40€
Crêpe gourmet (complète, champignons, tomates, oignons)	12,50€

je pense I think

- **très bien** very well, certainly

- **galettes** are savoury pancakes made from buckwheat flour, a Breton speciality. The general word for a pancake (sweet or savoury) is
- **une crêpe.**

- **une galette au jambon et au fromage** a ham and cheese pancake.

- **une galette à la saucisse** a sausage pancake.

- **une galette aux œufs et au jambon** an egg(s) and ham pancake. **Au, à la** and **aux** will be explained in the Grammar section on p. 42.

Vous voulez boire quelque chose? Would you like something to drink? Literally, (Do) you want to drink something?

- **du cidre** cider, the traditional accompaniment to **galettes.** It is usually served in an earthenware bowl (**un bol**).

Numbers 20–50

LISTEN FOR...

- **vingt** twenty
- **trente** thirty
- **quarante** forty

Vingt, vingt et un, vingt-deux, vingt-trois, vingt-quatre, vingt-cinq, vingt-six, vingt-sept, vingt-huit, vingt-neuf.

Trente, trente et un, trente-deux, trente-trois, trente-quatre, trente-cinq, trente-six, trente-sept, trente-huit, trente-neuf.

Quarante, quarante et un, quarante-deux, quarante-trois, quarante-quatre, quarante-cinq, quarante-six, quarante-sept, quarante-huit, quarante-neuf, cinquante.

PRACTICE

7

rillettes potted meat, like fibrous pâté
saucisson sec dry salami
saucisson à l'aïl salami with garlic (correctly spelt with two dots, to show that it is pronounced as two syllables)
beurre butter

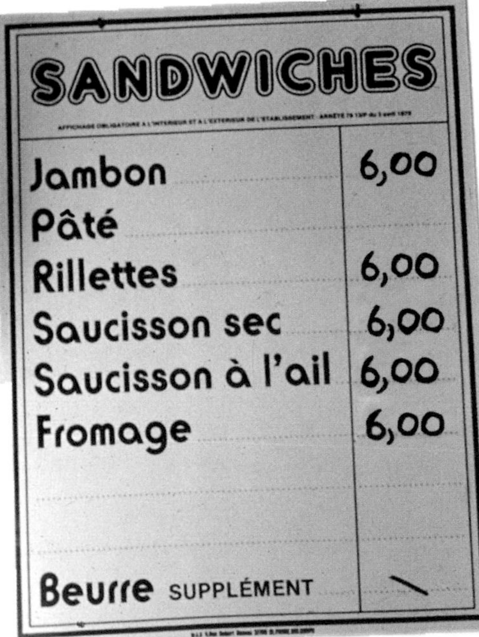

SANDWICHES	
Jambon	6,00
Pâté	
Rillettes	6,00
Saucisson sec	6,00
Saucisson à l'ail	6,00
Fromage	6,00
Beurre SUPPLÉMENT	\

Study this sandwich menu and then listen to the recording, where you will hear Carolle ordering drinks and snacks. She starts by asking

- **Qu'est-ce que vous avez à manger?** What do you have to eat? In addition to sandwiches, the barman offers her **hot dogs** and **pizzas**. Less obvious is
- **un croque-monsieur** a toasted cheese and ham sandwich, and
  un croque-madame the same thing with an egg on the top.

(**Croque-monsieur** and **croque-madame** don't have an **s** in the plural.) Here is an incomplete transcript of the conversation Carolle has with the barman. Can you fill in the gaps, using the menu to help you?

Barman	S'il vous plaît, ______________________________?
Carolle	Qu'est-ce que vous avez à manger, ______________________________?
Barman	Nous ______________________________ des pizzas, des hot dogs, des croque-monsieur, ______________________________ croque-madame et des ______________________________
Carolle	Bon. Alors, un ______________________________
Barman	Oui…
Carolle	Un sandwich aux ______________________________
Barman	Oui …
Carolle	Un sandwich au ______________________________
Barman	Oui …
Carolle	Et un sandwich au ______________________________
Barman	Vous ______________________________ du camembert ou du gruyère?
Carolle	Du ______________________________, s'il vous plaît.
Barman	D'accord.
Carolle	Et ______________________________ limonades, s'il vous plaît.
Barman	Parfait.

ANSWERS P. 46

8 Now you order from the sandwich menu in the previous exercise, following Philippe's prompts on the recording. Remember to say **un sandwich *au* jambon, un sandwich *au* pâté, un sandwich *aux* rillettes, un sandwich *au* saucisson sec, un sandwich *au* saucisson à l'aïl** and **un sandwich *au* fromage.**

9 **a.** See if you can write down in figures the numbers which Yves says on the recording for this exercise.

______________________________ ______________________________

______________________________ ______________________________

______________________________ ______________________________

____

ANSWERS P. 46

b. Read those numbers aloud in French. Then wind back and play the recording again, saying the numbers with Yves.

À 300 mètres du conservatoire botanique
Blé Noir
CRÊPERIE
SALADERIE
SALON DE THÉ
OUVERT TOUS LES JOURS
SERVICE CONTINU de 12 h à 21 h 30.

GRAMMAR AND EXERCISES

Le, la, l', les

In French, there are three words for 'the'. Before a masculine singular noun it is **le**, e.g. **le citron** (the lemon). Before a feminine singular noun it is **la**, e.g. **la galette** (the savoury pancake). If the noun begins with a vowel, both **le** and **la** are shortened to **l'**, e.g. **l'aïl** (garlic). Before a plural noun, masculine or feminine, 'the' is **les**, e.g. **les crêpes, les enfants.**

Unfortunately, there is no overall rule to tell you which words are masculine and which are feminine: you just have to learn the gender with each new noun. Foreign learners make lots of mistakes over genders, but French people usually understand anyway. In dictionaries and in the vocabulary at the back of this book, gender is indicated by (m.) or (f.).

Du, de la, de l', des

Du is used before a masculine singular noun to mean 'some', e.g. **du cidre** (some cider). Before a feminine singular noun, 'some' is **de la**, e.g. **de la bière** (some beer). If a singular noun, masculine or feminine, begins with a vowel, 'some' is **de l'**, e.g. **de l'Orangina**. The plural of all these forms is **des**, e.g. **des œufs** (some eggs).

Note that **du, de la, de l'** and **des** are used in French where 'some' would not be needed in English. For example, in Conversations 1 the waiter said **Pour le petit déjeuner nous avons du café, du café au lait, du lait, du chocolat et du thé.** In English, we would say 'For breakfast we have black coffee, white coffee, milk, chocolate and tea' (leaving out the 'some').

Au, à la, à l', aux

These words follow exactly the same pattern as **du, de la** and so on. On the recording, Philippe tells you how to pronounce the following extra vocabulary, which illustrates **au** being used before a masculine, singular noun:

une glace au chocolat	a chocolate ice-cream
un sorbet au cassis	a blackcurrant sorbet

and **à la** before a feminine singular noun:

une glace à la vanille	a vanilla ice-cream
un sorbet à la framboise	a raspberry sorbet

Before a singular noun (masculine or feminine) beginning with a vowel sound, use **à l'** – you have already met **du saucisson à l'aïl.** Before a plural noun, the form is **aux** – you have already met **un sandwich aux rillettes.**

But **au, à la, à l'** and **aux** are even more useful than this as they can also mean 'to the', 'at the' or 'in the'. So **Nous travaillons au bureau** is 'We are working in the office' and **Nous sommes à la crêperie** 'We are at the pancake house'.

The verb *prendre*

Most French verbs follow a regular pattern. However, some of the most frequently used ones are irregular. One of these is **prendre** (to take) – you need to learn it by heart:

je prends	I take I am taking
tu prends	you take you are taking
il/elle prend	he/she takes he/she is taking
nous prenons	we take we are taking
vous prenez	you take you are taking
ils/elles prennent	they take they are taking

Remember that **prendre** is used rather than **avoir** when ordering food and drink: **Je prends un café** I'll have a coffee.

The verbs **comprendre** (to understand) and **apprendre** (to learn) follow exactly the same pattern as **prendre: Vous comprenez? Oui, je comprends.**

10

Can you complete the table below with **le/la/l'** as appropriate in the left-hand column and **un** or **une** in the right-hand one?

'The'	'A'
Example:	
la galette	une galette
le sandwich	__________ sandwich
__________ crêpe	une crêpe
la glace	__________ glace
__________ sorbet	un sorbet
le cidre	__________ cidre
__________ bière	une bière
le thé	__________ thé
__________ restaurant	un restaurant
la crêperie	__________ crêperie
__________ œuf	un œuf
le café	__________ café

ANSWERS P. 46

11

Cross out the incorrect words in each set of brackets. If you need to check the genders of some of the nouns, you can use the vocabulary at the back of the book.

a. Je vais prendre [le/la/l'/les] cocktail maison.
b. Je n'aime pas [le/la/l'/les] bière.
c. Et moi, je n'aime pas [le/la/l'/les] aïl.
d. Vous aimez [le/la/l'/les] crêpes?
e. Vous prenez [du/de la/de l'/des] café?
f. Un thé avec [du/de la/de l'/des] lait froid, s'il vous plaît.
g. Et pour moi, [du/de la/de l'/des] eau minérale, s'il vous plaît.
h. Une galette [au/à la/à l'/aux] saucisse, s'il vous plaît.
i. Moi, je vais prendre une galette [au/à la/à l'/aux] œufs.
j. Et moi, un sandwich [au/à la/à l'/aux] jambon.

ANSWERS P. 46

12

Two different ways of answering each of these questions are suggested below. The first one has been given in full; can you write out the others?

a. Vous prenez du café?

Oui, je prends du café.

Oui, nous ______________________________

b. Vous apprenez le français?

Oui, j' ______________________________

Oui, nous ______________________________

c. Vous comprenez le français?

Oui, je ______________________________

Oui, nous ______________________________

Now see if you can translate:

d. They don't understand French

____

____

e. They don't learn French.

____

____

f. He doesn't understand English.

____

____

g. She isn't learning English.

____

____

(Remember that in French there is no distinction between 'She isn't learning' and 'She doesn't learn'.)

ANSWERS P. 46

KEY WORDS AND PHRASES

à manger	to eat/for eating
à boire	to drink/for drinking
pour le petit déjeuner	for breakfast
un lait	a milk
chaud ou froid?	hot or cold?
un café au lait	a white coffee
un café noir	a black coffee
un chocolat	a chocolate (eating or drinking)
un thé	a tea
citron	(with) lemon
nature	on its own
avec du lait froid	with cold milk
un petit déjeuner complet	continental breakfast
avec du café au lait	with white coffee
c'est	it is
Qu'est-ce que c'est?	What is it?
Qu'est-ce que c'est que (le cocktail maison)?	What is (the house cocktail)?
Qu'est-ce que vous avez pour les enfants?	What have you got for the children?
Qu'est-ce que vous avez comme bière?	What have you got in the way of beer?
Je vais prendre ça	I'll have that
Tiens, moi aussi	Mm, me too
une galette/une crêpe	a pancake
au jambon et au fromage	with ham and cheese
à la saucisse	with sausage
aux œufs et au jambon	with eggs and ham
du cidre	cider
une grande bouteille	a large bottle
une petite bouteille	a small bottle
un sandwich au fromage	a cheese sandwich
un croque-monsieur	a toasted cheese and ham sandwich
très bien	very well, certainly
d'accord	OK, agreed

The numbers 20–50 are also key language for this unit.

DID YOU KNOW?

Un petit déjeuner complet usually consists of a pot of black coffee, a pot of hot milk, croissants, bread, butter and jam. In most of the big hotels, American-style buffets are served, with cheese, ham, eggs and fruit juice in addition to basic breakfast fare. Since the prices quoted for hotel accommodation are per room rather than per person, they usually exclude the cost of breakfast.

There is very little difference between a bar and a café in France. Both stay open from early morning till late at night. They serve all sorts of cold drinks (alcoholic and non-alcoholic), hot drinks and sometimes snacks as well. In summer, popular drinks are **un panaché** (a shandy), **un citron pressé** (freshly squeezed lemon juice, served with cold water, ice and sugar to taste) and **un diabolo-menthe** (lemonade mixed with bright green peppermint cordial and served with ice). **Un Schweppes** means a tonic water! Drinks are cheaper if you stand at the counter inside than if you sit at a table or outside on the **terrasse**. Having a drink on the **terrasse** of somewhere as fashionable as Fouquet's on the Champs-Élysées can be very expensive indeed – but fun if you are feeling extravagant.

Telephones

A café is also a likely place to find a phone box (**une cabine téléphonique**). Call-boxes take coins or phone cards (**cartes téléphoniques/télécartes**), which you can buy from a post office, at a railway station, in a **tabac** or at a France Télécom commercial agency.

To dial abroad from France:

- Listen for the dialling tone.
- Insert money or **télécarte.**
- Dial the international code (**l'indicatif international**), which is about to change from 19 to 00.
- Wait. In most, but not all, areas of France there will then be a second dialling tone.
- Dial the country code, e.g.
  44 for the United Kingdom (**le Royaume-Uni**)
  353 for the Republic of Ireland or
  1 for the United States.
- Dial the area code, leaving out the first 0 (e.g. for Brighton dial 1273 instead of 01273).
- Dial the rest of the number.
- A signal will indicate when you need to insert more money.

Cheap rate for foreign calls from France is 7 p.m.–8 a.m and weekends.

Since 1996 French telephone numbers have been ten digits, beginning 01 in Paris, 02 in the North-West, 03 in the North-East, 04 in the South-East and 05 in the South-West. When dialling from abroad, omit the 0.

If you call long-distance from a post office, a telephonist will usually dial the number for you and then tell you which booth (**cabine**) to go to. You pay when the call is finished.

Site touristique exceptionnel !

RESTAURANT
Situé au sommet du château d'eau

Salle panoramique du château d'eau
BAR - CRÊPERIE
GLACIER
Restaurant pour groupes
29830
PLOUDALMEZEAU
✆ 02 98 48 15 88

AND FINALLY...

13 Follow Philippe's prompts on the recording as you order in a **crêperie**. Yves will come in with a correct version after each of the pauses. As always, you can give yourself more time to think by using the pause control on your cassette player.

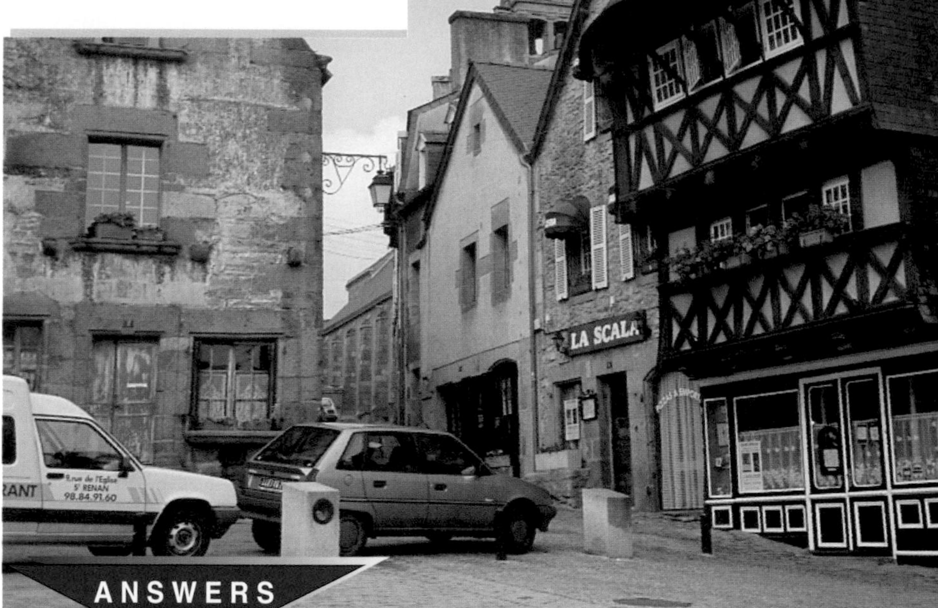

ANSWERS

Exercise 1
White coffee, black coffee, chocolate, lemon tea and tea with cold milk.

Exercise 5
Bière pression/Café noir/Jus de fruits/Schweppes

Exercise 7
Madame/s'il vous plaît/avons/des/sandwiches (also spelt sandwichs)/croque-monsieur/rillettes/jambon/fromage/désirez/gruyère/quatre

Exercise 9
42/39/21/47/28/50/31

Exercise 10
un sandwich/la crêpe/une glace/le sorbet/un cidre/la bière/un thé/ le restaurant/une crêperie/l'œuf/un café

Exercise 11
(**a**) le (**b**) la (**c**) l' (**d**) les (**e**) du (**f**) du (**g**) de l' (**h**) à la (**i**) aux (**j**) au

Exercise 12
(**a**) Oui, nous prenons du café. (**b**) Oui, j'apprends le français./Oui, nous apprenons le français. (**c**) Oui, je comprends le français./Oui, nous comprenons le français. (**d**) Ils ne comprennent pas le français. (**e**) Ils n'apprennent pas le français (**f**) Il ne comprend pas l'anglais. (**g**) Elle n'apprend pas l'anglais.

4 GETTING SOMEWHERE TO STAY

What you will learn

- asking questions
- booking in at hotels and camp-sites
- asking where things are
- coping with numbers up to 100
- the alphabet in French
- something about French hotels and camp-sites

Before you begin

Notice that similarity to English words often gives a clue to the meaning of French words, even when the meaning is not exactly the same in the two languages. In this unit you will come across the verb **rester**, which means to stay or remain (not 'to rest') and the verb **quitter**, which means 'to leave' or (on the telephone) 'to hang up'. You will meet the word **le camping**, used for a camp-site, the word **la place**, used here for 'space' and, in other contexts, for a seat at a theatre or a square in a town. **Une chambre** generally means a bedroom, though it does translate as 'chamber' in such expressions as **la Chambre de Commerce.**

Pronunciation notes

Pronunciation practice in this unit will concentrate on the sound '**ou**'. You will hear it in the first recording of Conversations 1 in the words **vous**, **pour**, **jours**, **voulez** and **pouvez**. To sensitise your ear before you listen, say aloud – very slowly – the English sound 'oo' (as in 'who', 'shoe', 'do', 'moo'). Notice how the sound alters in the middle as your lips come closer together. In the French '**ou**', the lips do not move and the sound does not waver.

CONVERSATIONS

Booking in at a camp-site

LISTEN FOR...

- **pour deux personnes** for two persons
- **combien de jours?** how many days?
- **trois semaines** three weeks

Réceptionniste	Bonjour, Madame. Que désirez-vous?
Marie-Claude	Est-ce qu'il reste encore des places pour deux personnes?
Réceptionniste	Combien de jours vous voulez rester?
Marie-Claude	Trois semaines (je pense).
Réceptionniste	Trois semaines. Bon. Je vais regarder ... Bon, d'accord. Trois semaines – c'est d'accord. Est- ce que vous pouvez me donner votre nom et votre adresse, s'il vous plaît?
Marie-Claude	Oui, bien sûr.

encore (*here*) still

- **le jour** day
- **la semaine** week
- **bien sûr** certainly

Que désirez-vous? How can I help you? (literally, What do you desire?)
This means the same as **Qu'est-ce que vous désirez?**, which you have already met.

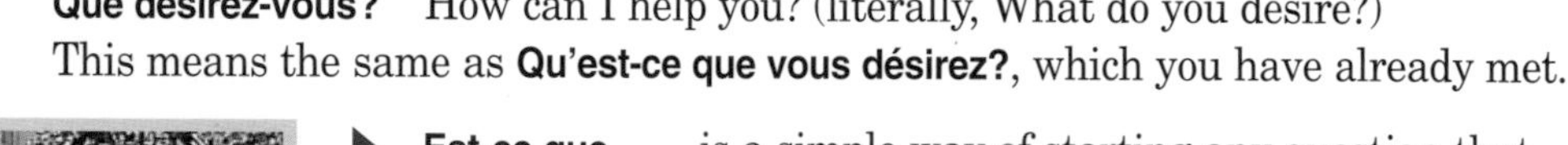

- **Est-ce que ...** is a simple way of starting any question that can be answered by 'yes' or 'no'. (See Grammar section, p. 58.)

il reste there remains or there remain (e.g. **Il reste une place**; **il reste deux places.**)

- **Est-ce qu'il reste encore des places?** Are there any spaces left? **Places** is also the word you use when booking seats for a cinema, theatre or concert (**Deux places à vingt euros, s'il vous plaît** Two seats at 20 euros, please).

- **Combien de jours vous voulez rester?** How many days do you want to stay? **Combien de ...?** is a very useful phrase meaning 'How much ...?' or 'How many ...?'. A hotel or camp-site receptionist will often also ask
- **C'est pour combien de nuits?** How many nights is it for?
- **C'est pour combien de personnes?** How many people is it for?

Je vais regarder I'll have a look (literally, I'm going to look).

Est-ce que vous pouvez me donner ...? Can you give me ...?

Booking hotel rooms

LISTEN FOR...

- **des chambres** rooms
- **pour ce soir** for this evening
- **avec salle de bains** with bathroom
- **deux lits séparés** two separate beds

ENCLOS PAROISSIAUX

Auberge Saint Thégonnec

02.98.79.61.18

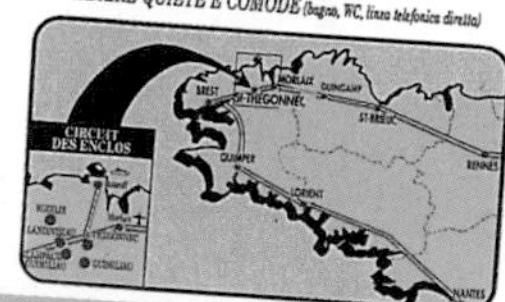

HOTEL ★★

CHAMBRES CALMES & CONFORTABLES
(bains, WC, TV, téléphone direct)
PEACEFUL AND COMFORTABLE ROOMS
RUHIGE, KOMFORTABLE ZIMMER
CAMERE QUIETE E COMODE

Guy	Bonjour, Madame.
Réceptionniste	Bonjour, Monsieur.
Guy	Est-ce que vous avez des chambres pour ce soir?
Réceptionniste	Oui, Monsieur.
Guy	J'aurais besoin d'une chambre d'une personne ...
Réceptionniste	Oui.
Guy	... avec salle de bains ...
Réceptionniste	Oui.
Guy	... et d'une chambre de deux personnes avec salle de bains aussi.
Réceptionniste	D'accord. Et la chambre pour deux personnes ... voulez-vous un grand lit ou deux lits séparés?
Guy	Deux lits séparés, s'il vous plaît.
Réceptionniste	Deux lits séparés. D'accord. Je vais donc prendre votre nom pour faire la réservation ...
Guy	Monsieur Fontaine.
Réceptionniste	Monsieur Fontaine. D'accord, c'est noté.

donc then

▶ **Est-ce que vous avez des chambres pour ce soir?** Do you have any rooms for tonight?

J'aurais besoin d'une chambre d'une personne I'd need a room for one person. **J'aurais besoin de** is a polite formula using the conditional (would) tense. You do not need to learn to use it yet. However, you should note the simpler

▶ **J'ai besoin de** I need (literally, I have need of). **De** changes to **d'** before a vowel (just as **je** changes to **j'** and **ne** to **n'**).

▶ **avec salle de bains** with bathroom. Note also

▶ **sans salle de bains** without bathroom. (Don't pronounce the final **s** of **sans**: the word rhymes with **en**.)

▶ **avec douche** with shower

▶ **sans douche** without shower

une chambre de deux personnes a room for (literally of) two people.

▶ **une chambre *pour* deux personnes** is the more usual expression.

voulez-vous do you want?

▶ **un grand lit ou deux lits séparés** a double bed or two separate beds. You do not need to add the word **séparés.**

Je vais donc prendre votre nom I'll take your name then (literally, I am going then to take your name).

pour faire la réservation to make the reservation.

Monsieur Fontaine It is far more acceptable in French than in English to say your title (**Monsieur**, **Madame**, etc.) when you give your name.

c'est noté that's noted.

PRACTICE

1 First some pronunciation practice, which will also help you to memorise the language you have met. Repeat after Yves a series of phrases all including the sound '**ou**'.

2 Look at this card from a hotel in Saint-Malo.

a. Does the hotel serve breakfast?

____

b. Do all the rooms have private facilities?

____

c. Do you get a colour television?

____

d. And a direct-dial telephone?

____

e. Does the hotel have a restaurant? ______________________________

f. Can you spot on the card the word for 'lift' (in which you *ascend*)?

____

g. What about the word for 'hair-drier'? (Oddly enough, there is a clue in **du saucisson sec**, which you met in the last unit!)

ANSWERS P. 62

____

3 Now you can practise booking a room yourself. First prepare the phrases you will need:

- Have you (got) any rooms for this evening?
- A double-bedded room with bathroom.

Then turn on the recording and follow Philippe's prompts. Carolle will give correct versions after the pauses.

CONVERSATIONS 2

The alphabet

A B C D E F G H I J K L M N O P Q R S T U V W X Y Z.

The tricky letters are

- **E** and **I** (it is the **I** which is pronounced something like 'ee')
- **G** and **J** (which are pronounced the other way round in French)
- **W** (which is double-V rather than double-U as in English)
- **Y** (**i grec** means 'Greek i')

The Palym Hotel receptionist takes a telephone booking

LISTEN FOR...

le 18 septembre	18th September
▶ **avec cabinet de toilette**	with washing facilities
▶ **confirmer par lettre**	confirm by letter

Réceptionniste Allo, Palym Hôtel ... Bonjour ...Le 18 septembre, oui, ne quittez pas ... oui heu ...Avec cabinet de toilette, oui, d'accord. A quel nom? ... Rodriguez ...Vous pouvez me confirmer par lettre? ... Non, P-A-L-Y-M ...Oui, 4, rue Emile-Gilbert, dans le douzième ... G-I-L-B-E-R-T : Voilà ...C'est ça. C'est entendu.

entendu agreed

▶ **Allo** (also spelt **allô**) hello (used only on the telephone).

le 18 septembre 18th September. You will be learning how to say dates in Unit 6.

ne quittez pas hold on (literally, don't leave) – telephone jargon.

▶ **avec cabinet de toilette** with washing facilities. This means there will be a wash-basin and possibly a bidet en suite. It does not mean there will be a private lavatory.

A quel nom? In what name?

Vous pouvez me confirmer par lettre? Can you confirm for me by letter? Hotels may also ask for **des arrhes** (a deposit).

dans le douzième (literally, in the twelfth). Paris is divided into twenty numbered **arrondissements** (districts).

Voilà (*here*) that's it.

▶ **C'est ça** That's right.

Full up!

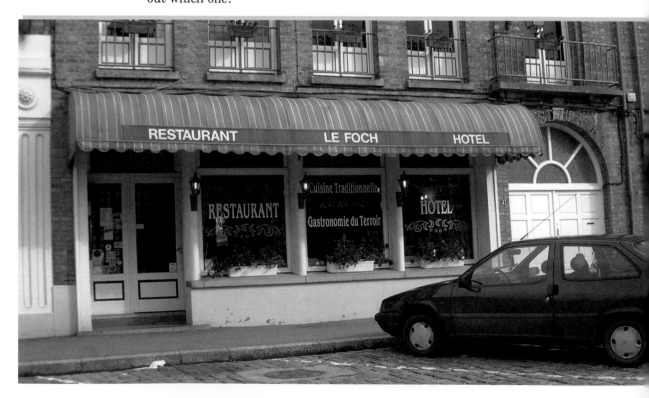

Réceptionniste	Allo, Palym Hôtel ... Bonjour ... Ah non, nous sommes complets, Monsieur ... Oui ... Au revoir.

nous sommes complets we are full up. You met **complet** meaning 'full' in **un petit déjeuner complet** (a full breakfast).

PRACTICE

4 You'll hear the alphabet again in the recording for this exercise. Play it through several times, repeating the letters after Yves. Then play it again and see if you can say them *with* him.

palym hôtel**
(Face à la gare de Lyon)

TÉL. 01 43 43 24 48 et 01 43 45 26 60
FAX. 01 43 41 69 47

4, RUE ÉMILE-GILBERT
75012 PARIS

5 'The Palym Hotel receptionist takes a telephone booking' was one side of a telephone conversation. Opposite are two versions of what the caller may have said in each of the gaps, but in each case only one of the lines makes sense in the context. Can you work out which one?

Réceptionniste	Allo, Palym Hôtel.
Client	**a.** Bonsoir, Madame. ☐
	b. Bonjour, Madame. ☐
Réceptionniste	Bonjour.
Client	**c.** Que désirez-vous? ☐
	d. Est-ce que vous avez des chambres pour le 18 septembre? ☐
Réceptionniste	Le 18 septembre, oui, ne quittez pas … oui, heu …
Client	**e.** J'ai besoin d'une chambre avec salle de bains. ☐
	f. J'ai besoin d'une chambre pour une personne avec cabinet de toilette. ☐
Réceptionniste	Avec cabinet de toilette, oui, d'accord. A quel nom?
Client	**g.** Rodriguez. ☐
	h. Anglais. ☐
Réceptionniste	Rodriguez. Vous pouvez me confirmer par lettre?
Client	**i.** Oui. Palym, c'est P-A-L-I-M-E? ☐
	j. Oui. Palym, c'est P-A-L-Y-M? ☐
Réceptionniste	Non, P-A-L-Y-M.
Client	**k.** Vous pouvez me donner votre adresse, s'il vous plaît? ☐
	l. Est-ce que vous pouver me donner votre nom, s'il vous plaît? ☐
Réceptionniste	Oui, 4, rue Émile-Gilbert, dans le douzième …
Client	**m.** Le douzième? ☐
	n. Gibère? ☐
Réceptionniste	G-I-L-B-E-R-T.
Client	**o.** G-I-L-B-E-R-T? ☐
	p. G-I-B-E-R-E? ☐
Réceptionniste	Voilà.
Client	**q.** Alors, vous êtes complets. ☐
	r. Je vais donc vous confirmer par lettre. ☐
Réceptionniste	C'est ça. C'est entendu.

ANSWERS P. 62

6

When you have checked the answers you gave in the last exercise, you will find it helpful to put a line through the incorrect versions as you will be using that text as a script for this exercise. Carolle will read the receptionist's lines. There will be no English prompts this time – just pauses for you to stop the recording and read the caller's lines. Then Yves will give correct versions of your part.

CONVERSATIONS

Finding out where things are in the hotel

LISTEN FOR...

première (f.)/**premier** (m.)	first
à gauche	on the left
A quel étage?	On which floor?

Jeanne	Où sont les toilettes, s'il vous plaît?
Réceptionniste	Heu – première porte ici à gauche.
Jeanne	Bon, merci. Et ma chambre est à quel étage?
Réceptionniste	Alors, votre chambre est au troisième étage.
Jeanne	Et il y a des toilettes là?
Réceptionniste	Oui, oui, oui. A l'étage il y a des toilettes.
Jeanne	Et la douche?
Réceptionniste	La douche – alors, il y a une douche au deuxième étage, hein.
Jeanne	D'accord. Et on est au premier?
Réceptionniste	Non, nous sommes au rez-de-chaussée.

- **première** (f.)/**premier** (m.) first
- **ici** here
- **là** there

hein meaningless filler word

- **Où sont les toilettes?** Where are the toilets? **Les toilettes** (plural) is generally used instead of **la toilette**, even when there is only one. As well as **Où sont...?** (Where are...?) you should learn
- **Où est...?** Where is...? e.g. **Où est la salle de bains?** Where is the bathroom?

Première porte ici à gauche First door on the left here.

- **ma chambre est à quel étage?** my room is on which floor?

votre chambre est au troisième étage your room is on the third floor. All ordinal numbers apart from **premier/première** are formed by adding **-ième** to the number, e.g.

- **deuxième** second
- **troisième** third
- **quatrième** fourth
- **cinquième** (because, as in English, a **q** cannot be followed by any letter other than a **u**)
- **sixième, septième, huitième,**
- **neuvième** (notice that the **f** of **neuf** becomes a **v** in **neuvième**),
- **dixième** (pronounced as though the **x** were a **z**).

These are often written **6**[e], **7**[e], **8**[e], etc.

- **il y a** there is, there are. (See Grammar section, p. 58.)

  on est au premier? we're on the first floor, aren't we? (literally, one is on the first?) The word **étage** is understood. **On** is used very frequently in French to mean 'people' or 'we'.

- **nous sommes au rez-de-chaussée** we are on the ground floor.

Danielle wants to change her traveller's cheques

LISTEN FOR...

- **des chèques de voyage** traveller's cheques

Danielle Pardon, Monsieur – où peut-on changer des chèques de voyage, s'il vous plaît?
Homme Excusez-moi, Madame, je ne comprends pas – je suis anglais.

- **l'homme** the man
- **excusez-moi** sorry, excuse me
- **Pardon** Excuse me, sorry. Used here as a polite way of addressing a stranger. It is also the word to use if you are trying to make your way through a crowd or if you want to apologise (for example, for bumping into someone). An interesting difference between French and English usage is that, if you stand back to allow a French person to go through a door in front of you, s/he will say **Pardon** rather than **Merci**.

- **où peut-on changer des chèques de voyage?** where can one change traveller's cheques? These are often called simply **traveller's** (with the stress on the final syllable).

- **Excusez-moi, Madame, je ne comprends pas – je suis anglais** I'm sorry, Madame, I don't understand – I'm English. A very useful set of phrases to know! If you are a woman, remember to say **je suis anglaise** (or **écossaise, galloise, irlandaise, américaine, allemande** or whatever).

Numbers 50–100

50–59
Cinquante, cinquante et un, cinquante-deux, cinquante-trois, cinquante-quatre, cinquante-cinq, cinquante-six, cinquante-sept, cinquante-huit, cinquante-neuf.

60–69
Soixante, soixante et un, soixante-deux, soixante-trois, soixante-quatre, soixante-cinq, soixante-six, soixante-sept, soixante-huit, soixante-neuf.

70–79

Soixante-dix, soixante et onze, soixante-douze, soixante-treize, soixante-quatorze, soixante-quinze, soixante-seize, soixante-dix-sept, soixante-dix-huit, soixante dixneuf.

80–89

Quatre-vingts, quatre-vingt-un, quatre-vingt-deux, quatre-vingt-trois, quatre-vingt-quatre, quatre-vingt-cinq, quatre-vingt-six, quatre-vingt-sept, quatre-vingt-huit, quatre-vingt-neuf.

90–100

Quatre-vingt-dix, quatre-vingt-onze, quatre-vingt-douze, quatre-vingt-treize, quatre-vingt-quatorze, quatre-vingt-quinze, quatre-vingt-seize, quatre-vingt-dix-sept, quatre-vingt-dix-huit, quatre-vingt-dix-neuf … cent.

soixante-dix … quatre-vingt-dix-neuf 70 … 99 (literally, sixty-ten … four score-nineteen). No, this is not a joke – the French really do express the numbers 70–100 in this cumbersome way! The Swiss and the Belgians have been more rational and call 80 **huitante** (in Switzerland) and **octante** (in Belgium); they both use **nonante** for 90. However, unless your main involvement is going to be with Switzerland or Belgium rather than France, you had better learn the French system.

PRACTICE

7 Here is a brief description of the layout of a hotel:

L'HÔTEL DES VOYAGEURS

9e étage: chambres 90–97, douches, W.-C.
8e étage: chambres 80–89
7e étage: chambres 70–76, salles de bains, W.-C.
6e étage: chambres 60–69
5e étage: chambres 50–57, douches, W.-C.
4e étage: chambres 40–48
3e étage: chambres 30–36, salles de bains, W.-C.
2e étage: chambres 20–28
1er étage: chambres 10–17, douches, W.-C.
R-de-C: réception, salle à manger, bar, téléphones

Can you answer the following questions about the hotel? To help you commit the words to memory, write them in full rather than just putting the figures.
Example: Où est la chambre vingt-deux?
Au deuxième étage.

a. Où est la chambre soixante-trois?

____

b. Où est la réception?

____

c. Où est la chambre quatre-vingt-neuf?

____

d. Où est la chambre soixante-treize?

____

e. Où sont les toilettes?

____

f. Où est la salle à manger?

____

g. Où sont les chambres quatre-vingt-seize et quatre-vingt-dix-sept?

ANSWERS P. 62

____

8 Your turn to ask questions. You may like to make sure that you know how to say the numbers 57, 64, 71, 85, 90 and 91 before you turn on the recording, where Philippe will prompt you to ask the hotel receptionist the location of each of those rooms in turn. You should begin each request politely with **Pardon, Madame**. Yves will give correct versions of your part after the pauses.

C A N C A L E
LE CONTINENTAL
HC
Hôtel *** Restaurant ***
sur le port
35260 CANCALE
Tél : 02 99 89 60 16
Fax : 02 99 89 69 58

9 Numbers are difficult, so they need lots of practice. Cross out the figures on the bingo card as Yves calls them out in the recording for this exercise. You should be left with one number at the end.

ANSWERS P. 62

52	68	72	79	80
86	90	94	98	100

GRAMMAR AND EXERCISES

Questions

You have already come across the simplest way of asking a question: saying something with a rising intonation, e.g. **Vous pouvez me confirmer par lettre?** In this unit, you have also met **Est-ce que...?**, in the questions

Est-ce que vous pouvez me donner votre nom et votre adresse?
Est-ce que vous avez des chambres pour ce soir?

Est-ce que...? can be put at the start of virtually any sentence to turn it into the kind of question which can be answered by 'yes' or 'no'. For example,

La clé est dans la chambre
The key is in the bedroom
Est-ce que la clé est dans la chambre?
Is the key in the bedroom?

When the word following **Est-ce que** begins with a vowel sound, **Est-ce que** becomes **Est-ce qu'** (in the same way that **je**, **ne** and **me** all run into the next word if it begins with a vowel sound). So one has, for example,

Elle est dans la chambre
She/It is in the bedroom
Est-ce qu'elle est dans la chambre?
Is she/it in the bedroom?

Question words

Est-ce que...? is used to begin only questions that can be answered by 'yes' or 'no'. Other types of questions are introduced by other question words. You have already worked on **Qu'est-ce que...?** (What?). In this unit you have also met **Où?** (Where?) and **Combien?** (How much? How many?). You will be meeting other question words as the course progresses.

Il y a

As you have seen, **il y a** means 'there is' or 'there are':

Il y a une douche au 2e étage
There is a shower on the 2nd floor
Il y a des toilettes au 3e étage
There are toilets on the 3rd floor

If the sentence is said with a questioning intonation, it becomes 'Is there ...?' or 'Are there ...?':

Il y a des toilettes au 3e étage?
Are there toilets on the 3rd floor?

You can also, of course, make it into a question by putting **Est-ce que...?** in front of it:

Est-ce qu'il y a des toilettes au troisième étage?

The verb *vendre*

Vendre (to sell) is the model for a whole group of verbs with infinitives ending in **-re**, e.g. **rendre** (to give up, to give back), **tendre** (to hold out), **pendre** (to hang), **perdre** (to lose), **répondre** (to reply). You should learn it by heart – the recording will show you how it is pronounced:

je vends	**nous vendons**
tu vends	**vous vendez**
il/elle vend	**ils/elles vendent**

Can you remember how the irregular verb **prendre** differs from this pattern in the plural? If not, look back at p. 42.

The verb *faire*

Another essential verb is the verb **faire**, which corresponds to both the English verbs 'to do' and 'to make'. You met it in the phrase **pour faire la réservation.** Like most of the commonest verbs in English and French, **faire** is irregular. Even the pronunciation is not what you might expect, so use the recording to help you learn it:

je fais	**nous faisons**
tu fais	**vous faites**
il/elle fait	**ils/elles font**

10

Can you match up the French sentences with the list of translations below?

a. **Vous pouvez me confirmer par lettre?**
b. **Voulez-vous confirmer votre réservation?**
c. **Est-ce que vous avez une réservation?**
d. **Qu'est-ce que vous voulez comme chambres?**
e. **Combien de chambres voulez-vous?**
f. **Est-ce qu'il y a une douche au deuxième étage?**
g. **Où est la douche?**

i. Where is the shower?
ii. Do you have a reservation?
iii. Can you confirm by letter for me?
iv. Is there a shower on the second floor?
v. Do you want to confirm your reservation?
vi. How many rooms do you want?
vii. What do you want in the way of rooms?

ANSWERS P. 62

11

See if you can fill in the gaps with the correct item from the box.

Où	Combien de	Est-ce que	Est-ce qu'	Qu'est-ce que	Qu'est-ce qu'

a. ____________________ vous voulez comme chambre?

b. ____________________ vous avez une chambre avec salle de bains?

c. C'est pour ____________________ nuits?

d. ____________________ est ma chambre, s'il vous plaît?

e. ____________________ il y a un téléphone dans la chambre?

ANSWERS P. 62

12

Fill in the gaps with the correct parts of the verbs indicated. Remember that **prendre** and its compounds (notably **apprendre** and **comprendre**) follow a different pattern from **vendre** and the other regular verbs which have infinitives ending in **-re**.

a. Est-ce qu'ils ____________________ (vendre) des cartes postales?

b. Qu'est-ce que vous ____________________ (prendre)?

c. J' ____________________ (apprendre) le français.

d. Est-ce que vous ____________________ (vendre) du lait?

e. Ils ____________________ (faire) la réservation.

f. Qu'est-ce que vous ____________________ (faire)?

g. Tu ____________________ (rendre) la clé à la réception.

ANSWERS P. 62

HÔTEL**
Relais de Tréfeuntec
(Près de Sainte Anne La Palud
Au fond de la Baie de Douarnenez)
29550 PLONÉVEZ-PORZAY
☎ 02 98 92 50 03
BAR • GLACES
MER (grandes plages de sable fin)
CAMPAGNE - PÊCHE (mer - rivière)
CHAMBRES TOUT CONFORT
HOTEL

KEY WORDS AND PHRASES

Allo	Hello (on the telephone)
Est-ce qu'il reste encore des places?	Are there any spaces/seats left?
Est-ce que vous avez des chambres pour ce soir?	Do you have any rooms for tonight?
C'est pour	
combien de personnes?	How many people is it for?
combien de jours/nuits?	How many days/nights is it for?
C'est pour	It's for
une personne	one person
deux jours	two days
trois semaines	three weeks
J'ai besoin de …	I need …
J'ai besoin d'une chambre	I need a room
avec salle de bains	with bathroom
avec douche	with shower
avec cabinet de toilette	with washing facilities
avec un grand lit	with a double bed
avec deux lits	with two beds
Bien sûr	Certainly
Où sont les toilettes?	Where are the toilets?
Là, à gauche	There, on the left
Où est (la salle de bains)?	Where is (the bathroom)?
C'est à quel étage?	Which floor is it on?
Au rez-de-chaussée	On the ground floor
Au premier étage	On the first floor
Au deuxième étage	On the second floor
Il y a …	There is, there are …
Il y a des toilettes au troisième étage	There are toilets on the third floor
Pardon/Excusez-moi	Sorry, excuse me
l'homme	the man

The alphabet and the numbers 50–100 are also key language for this unit.

LOGIS
DE FRANCE
CHAMBRES D'ACCUEIL DE ST ELOI
Mr et Mme François JAOUEN
NID VACANCES
29810 BRELES
✆ 02 98 04 35 19

DID YOU KNOW?

Hotels

The prices quoted by French hotels are usually per room rather than per person and will not normally include breakfast. They should be written up on the inside of the bedroom door. Within any one category of hotel (e.g. two-star) you will usually find a better standard of accommodation in the provinces than in Paris, though the price in Paris will be considerably higher.

Among the better annual guides to French hotels are:

- the red *Guide Michelin: France* (covers every town and most large villages in France: French and English editions)
- *Le guide Gault et Millau: France* (fewer addresses: more description)
- *Le guide des hôtels-restaurants Logis de France* (which gives only establishments in the Logis de France federation)
- *Routiers Guide to France* (Relais Routiers: good, inexpensive hotels and restaurants)

All towns and many villages in France have a tourist office, called either **l'office de tourisme** or **le syndicat d'initiative**. They will usually give or send you a free list of accommodation in their locality. The types of accommodation include:

- **Hôtels:** one-star, two-star, three-star, four-star and four-star de luxe.
- **Pensions**: fairly modest hotels where you have to go full board (**en pension complète**) or half-board (**en demi-pension**).
- **Chambres d'hôtes/Chambres chez l'habitant/Nids Vacances** (rooms in private houses offering bed and breakfast)
- **Gîtes** (self-catering houses in the country)
- **Appartements à louer** (flats to let)
- **Auberges de jeunesse** (youth hostels)
- **Campings** (camp-sites)

Camping and caravanning

You will find camp-sites (called **campings**) in nearly every French town. They too have their official rating. More than a third of them are in the top three- or four-star categories and you would be well advised to aim for one of these, as facilities at one- and two-star sites may be minimal. Camp-sites run by local authorities are often good value, so look out for the sign **Camping municipal**. If you intend to camp near the sea in the summer months you should book well in advance or you are likely to meet **complet** signs wherever you go. Crowding is not nearly so bad on inland sites and many of them offer water-sports on lakes and rivers. **Le camping sauvage** (camping on unauthorised land) is frowned on by the authorities.

One easy way to go camping in France – though not the cheapest – is to hire a ready-pitched tent and equipment from one of the many operators now offering this service through the Sunday newspapers. The standard of these companies is generally high. The most comprehensive list of camp-site addresses is to be found in

- the green Michelin paperback *Camping Caravaning France.*

There is also useful information for campers in

- *Traveller in France*, available from the French Government Tourist Office, 178 Piccadilly, London W1J 9AL (and see p.15).

If you are planning a camping holiday in France, it is worth writing to ask what publications are currently available from:

- La Fédération Française de Camping et de Caravaning, 78, rue de Rivoli, 75004 Paris
- La Fédération Nationale d'Hôtellerie de Plein Air, 105, rue Lafayette, 75010 Paris

AND FINALLY...

13 You are at the reception desk of a hotel where you have made an advance booking. You will need an additional key phrase:

▶ **J'ai réservé une chambre** I have booked a room

Initially, the receptionist confuses your booking with someone else's – Philippe will guide you through the muddle. Be warned that you will need to spell your own name during the conversation – Carolle will be saying another surname when she gives the correct versions after the pauses.

ANSWERS

Exercise 2

(a) Yes (The card has **Petit déjeuner** just under the name of the hotel.) **(b)** Yes (**Toutes les chambres avec bain ou douche et W.C.** means 'All rooms with bath or shower and WC'.) **(c)** Yes (**Téléviseur couleur**) **(d)** Yes (**Téléphone direct**) **(e)** No (**Sans restaurant means** 'Without restaurant'.) **(f)** Ascenseur **(g)** Sèche-cheveux (**Saucisson sec** is given as a clue because sec means dry. It is linked to the verb **sécher**, to dry.)

Exercise 5

(b) (d) (f) (g) (i) (k) (n) (o) (r)

Exercise 7

(a) Au sixième étage. **(b)** Au rez-de-chaussée.
(c) Au huitième étage. **(d)** Au septième étage.
(e) Au premier étage, au troisième étage, au cinquième étage, au septième étage et au neuvième étage. (You don't need to repeat the word **étage** each time like this.)
(f) Au rez-de-chaussée. **(g)** Au neuvième étage.

Exercise 9

90

Exercise 10

(a) iii **(b)** v **(c)** ii **(d)** vii **(e)** vi **(f)** iv **(g)** i

Exercise 11

Qu'est-ce que/Est-ce que/combien de/Où ?/Est-ce qu'

Exercise 11

(a) vendent **(b)** prenez **(c)** apprends **(d)** vendez **(e)** font **(f)** faites **(g)** rends

5 DIRECTIONS

What you will learn

- asking for, understanding and giving directions
- understanding directions on the **métro**
- coping with numbers up to 1000
- something about guides to France
- something about the Paris **métro** and the RER

Before you begin

The crucial language for asking and understanding directions is

- **Pour aller à …?** How do you get to …?
- **à gauche** to the left
- **à droite** to the right
- **tout droit** straight on

Quite often, foreign visitors manage to ask the way in France, but not to understand the reply. Listen out for the key words **à gauche**, **à droite** and **tout droit** – don't let them be drowned in the torrent of other words. Another useful strategy is to concentrate on the first instruction you are given: if you set off in the right direction, you can always ask somebody else where to go next!

The greatest single cause of foreigners' getting lost in France must be the similarity between the words **droit** and **droite**. Two clues to help you distinguish them:

- **droit** is rarely used without **tout** – remember 'straight on' as **tout droit** rather than just **droit.**
- neither final **t** in **tout droit** is pronounced, but the **t** in **à droite** is pronounced.

Pronunciation notes

Pronunciation practice in this unit will spotlight the French sound which English speakers find most difficult: the '**u**' which appears in **tu**, **rue** and **musée**. Some people find it helpful to know the mechanics of making the sound: the inside of your mouth should be in the position it has for saying '**i**' (as in **il** or **fille**) while your lips are rounded as they are when you say '**ou**' (as in **vous** and **voulez**). It will feel very artificial at first, but should come eventually with practice.

CONVERSATIONS

Finding where you are on the map

LISTEN FOR...

▶ **un plan de la ville**	a map of the town
au numéro un	at number one
▶ **en face de**	facing
▶ **l'église Saint-Pierre**	St Peter's church
au centre de la ville	in the centre of town

Michel	Bonjour, Madame.
Hôtesse	Bonjour, Monsieur.
Michel	Vous avez un plan de la ville, s'il vous plaît?
Hôtesse	Oui, bien sûr – voilà.
Michel	Oui. Merci. Oui. On est où exactement ici?
Hôtesse	Alors, au numéro 1 sur le plan, en face de l'église Saint-Pierre.
Michel	Ah bon. Au centre de la ville, au fond?
Hôtesse	C'est ça, oui.
Michel	Oui.

▶ **On est où exactement ici?** Where exactly are we here?

au numéro 1 sur le plan at number one on the map.

au centre de la ville, au fond in the centre of the town, in fact. This is often abbreviated to

▶ **au centre-ville.**

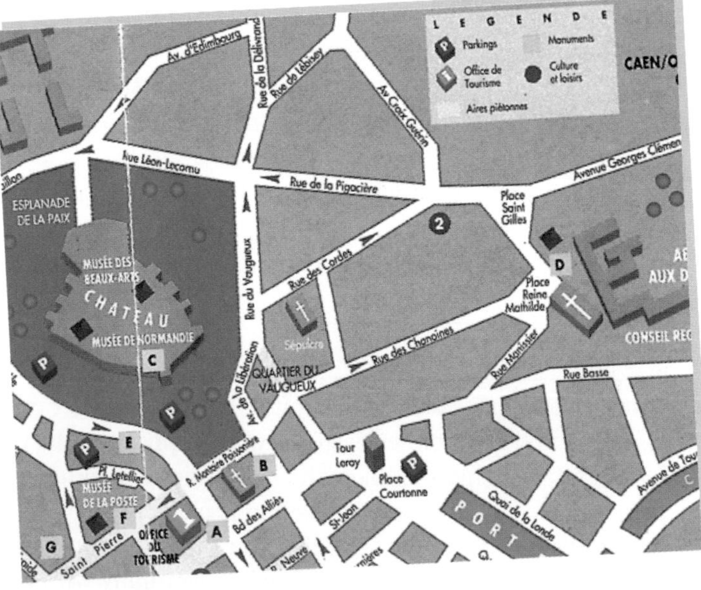

Finding out where the bus-stop is

LISTEN FOR...

l'arrêt de bus	the bus-stop
▶ **l'hôtel de ville**	the town hall
▶ **les horaires**	the times, the timetables

Guy	Est-ce qu'il y a des bus pour Armentières, s'il vous plaît?
Hôtesse	Oui.
Guy	Et où se trouve l'arrêt de bus?
Hôtesse	L'arrêt de bus se trouve derrière l'hôtel de ville.
Guy	Vous avez les horaires?
Hôtesse	Oui – voilà, monsieur.
Guy	Merci.
Hôtesse	Je vous en prie.

Est-ce qu'il y a des bus...? Are there any buses...? For **il y a**, see p. 58.

Où se trouve l'arrêt de bus? Where is the bus-stop situated? (literally where does the bus-stop find itself?) You can equally well use the simpler structure **Où est l'arrêt de bus?**

▶ **derrière l'hôtel de ville** behind the town hall. Another name for **l'hôtel de ville** is

▶ **la mairie. Le maire** is the mayor.

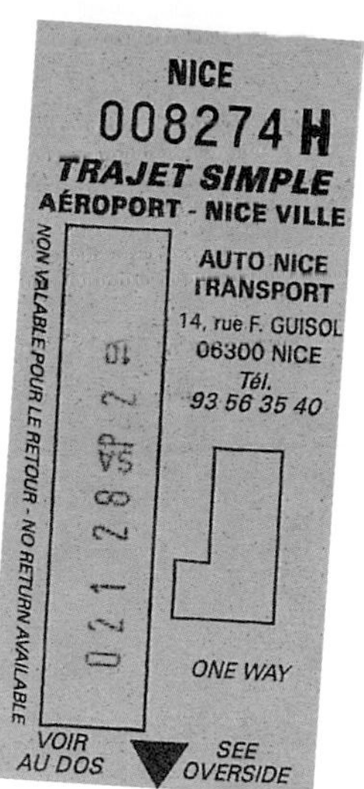

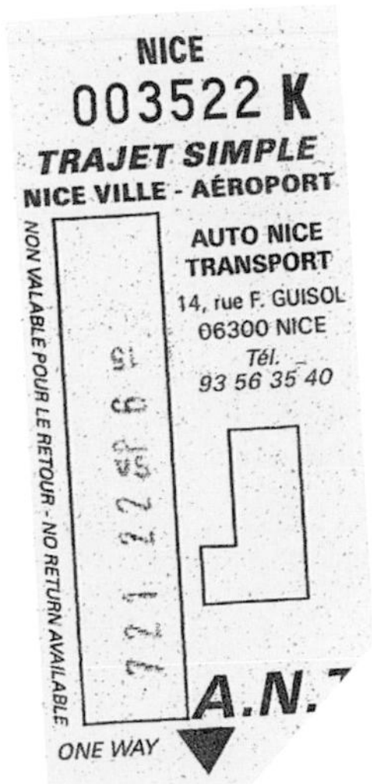

PRACTICE

1

Here is a map of the village of Brélès, near the west coast of Brittany. Study the vocabulary and then turn on the recording for this exercise, where you will hear four short exchanges relating to the map.

la boulangerie	baker's	**la mairie**	town hall
le cimetière	cemetery	**la salle communale**	village hall
† = l'église (f.)	church	**la station-service**	petrol station
l'épicerie (f.)	grocer's	**le tennis**	tennis court
le bar-tabac	bar-cum-tobacconist's	**D27** (etc.) are road numbers	

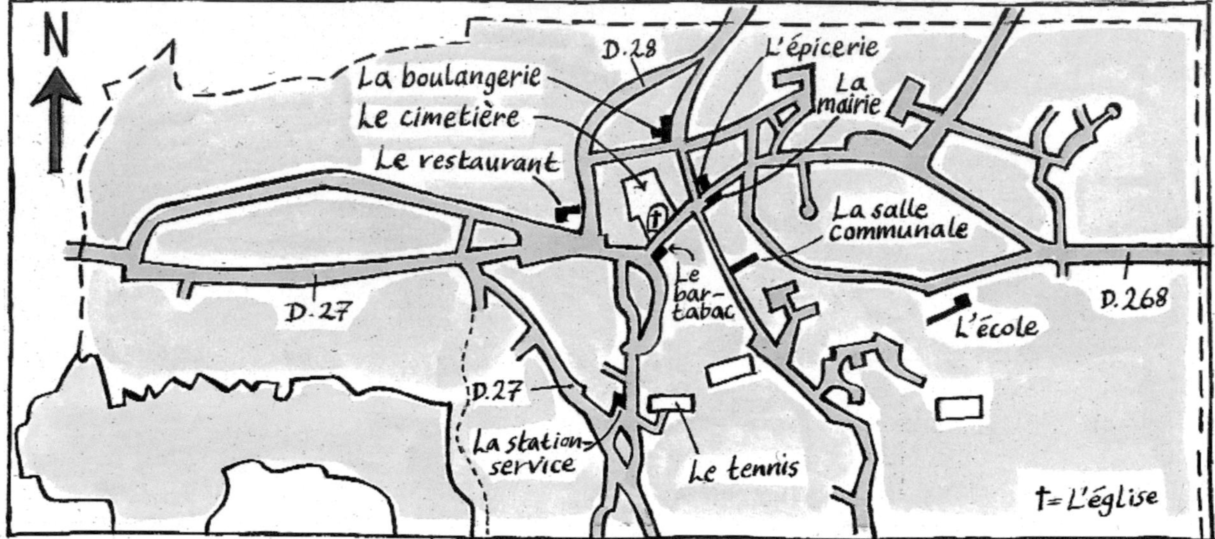

a. Where are the speakers in the first exchange?

b. Where are they in the second one?

c. Where does Yves say the cemetery is?

d. Where does he say the baker's shop is?

ANSWERS P. 78

2

In this exercise, you are in Brélès enquiring about buses to Brest. Philippe will prompt you and Yves will give a correct version after the pauses.

CONVERSATIONS

Directions to the station

LISTEN FOR...

pour aller à ...?	how do I get to ...?
la gare	the station
à pied	on foot
la rue Saint-Jean	St John's Street
le pont	the bridge

Michel Pour aller à la gare?
Hôtesse Oui. Vous voulez aller en voiture ou (en autobus)?
Michel Non, je suis à pied.
Hôtesse Pour aller à pied. Alors, nous sommes ici (*points at map*). Vous prenez la rue Saint-Jean, vous traversez le pont.
Michel Oui.
Hôtesse Et un petit peu après le pont, la troisième rue sur votre gauche.
Michel Merci, Madame.
Hôtesse Et là vous trouverez la gare.

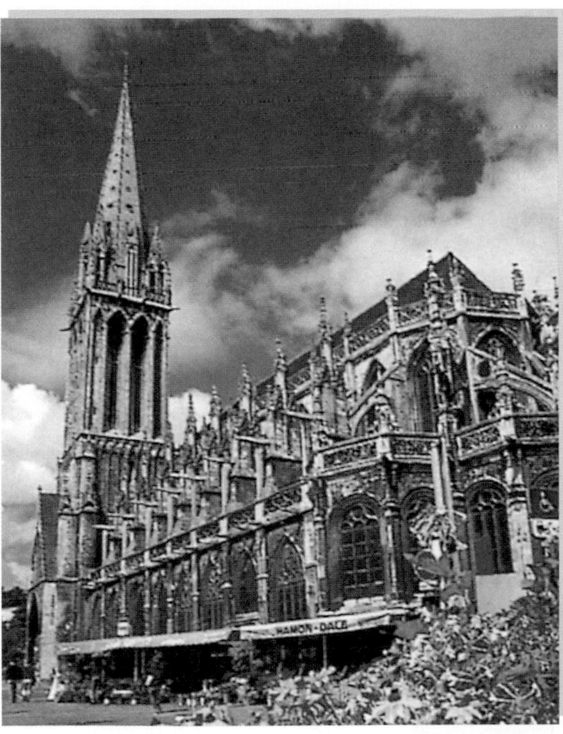

Caen

- **en voiture** by car
- **Pour aller à la gare?** How do I get to the station? (literally For going to the station?)

Vous voulez aller ...? Do you want to go ...?

en autobus by bus. **Bus** is the abbreviation of **autobus.**

- **Vous traversez le pont** You cross the bridge. From the verb **traverser**.
- **un petit peu après le pont** a little bit after the bridge. Note also
- **un petit peu plus loin** a little bit further.
- **sur votre gauche** on your left. This is the same as **sur la gauche** or **à gauche**.

vous trouverez you will find. This is from the future tense of the verb **trouver**. The future tense will be explained in Unit 14.

Directions to the museum

LISTEN FOR...

▶ **au musée**	to the museum
▶ **la pharmacie**	the chemist's
quelques pas	a few steps

MUSEE DES BEAUX-ARTS DE TOURS

Guy	Bonjour, Mademoiselle.
Hôtesse	Bonjour, Monsieur.
Guy	Pour aller au musée, s'il vous plaît?
Hôtesse	Alors, vous traversez la Grand-Place; vous voyez la pharmacie?
Guy	Oui.
Hôtesse	Donc, heu, là où se trouve la pharmacie, c'est la rue du Musée. Vous faites quelques pas et ensuite ... c'est sur votre droite.
Guy	Merci.
Hôtesse	Je vous en prie.

▶ **vous voyez** you see

▶ **ensuite** then

▶ **Pour aller au musée?** How do I get to the museum? This is made up of **Pour aller à** + **le musée. A** + **le** combine to make **au**. (See Grammar, p. 42.)

la Grand-Place the main square. It is a linguistic oddity that certain feminine nouns form compounds with **grand** rather than **grande**. Another example is **la grand-mère**, grandmother.

là où se trouve la pharmacie, c'est la rue du Musée where the chemist's is situated is Museum Street (literally, there where finds itself the pharmacy is Museum Street).

Vous faites quelques pas You go (literally, make) a few steps.

▶ **sur votre droite** on your right. Again, this is the same as **sur la droite** and **à droite**.

▶ **Je vous en prie** You're welcome, Don't mention it (literally, I you of it beg). This is a polite response to **Merci**.

PRACTICE

3

This exercise gives you practice at asking the way, using the key phrase **Pour aller à...?** Remember that **à** + **le** gives **au**, e.g.
Pour aller au centre-ville, s'il vous plaît?
On the recording, Philippe will prompt you in English to ask your way to a number of the places on the map of Brélès. There will be a pause for you to speak and then Yves will give a correct version of your question.

4

On the recording, you will hear two sets of directions. Try to follow them on the map on p. 66. Specifically,

a. Where is the starting-point for the first set of directions (*given by Carolle*)?

____

b. What seems to be the destination?

____

c. Where is the starting-point for the second set of directions (*given by Yves*)?

____

d. What seems to be the destination?

ANSWERS P. 78

____

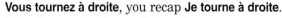

5

When you are given directions, repeating them can be helpful. This exercise gives you practice at it. For example, when Yves says
Vous tournez à droite, you recap **Je tourne à droite.**

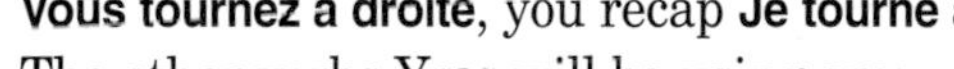

The other verbs Yves will be using are:

faire: vous faites/je fais
prendre: vous prenez/je prends
traverser: vous traversez/je traverse

and the new verb **aller**, which you will be meeting properly in the Grammar section. For now, register its forms **vous allez** and **je vais.**
There are no English prompts on the recording for this exercise, but Carolle will give correct versions of your part after the pauses.

CONVERSATIONS

Going by underground to the Eiffel Tower

LISTEN FOR...

Place-names/underground stations: la Tour Eiffel, Nation, Trocadéro

▶ **le métro** the underground/tube/subway

Bernadette Alors, heu, pour aller à la Tour Eiffel, vous allez prendre le métro, direction Nation. Vous descendez à Trocadéro et c'est à deux cents mètres.

la Tour Eiffel the Eiffel Tower (named after the designer Gustave Eiffel, 1832–1923). Notice the pronunciation.

▶ **Vous allez prendre le métro, direction Nation** You're going to take the underground (on the line going in the) direction (of) Nation.

▶ **vous descendez** you get off (literally, get down). From the verb **descendre**.

▶ **C'est à deux cents mètres** It's two hundred metres (away).

By underground to Notre Dame

LISTEN FOR...

Place-names/underground stations: Notre Dame, l'Étoile, Vincennes, Châtelet, Porte d'Orléans, Cité

Barbara Pour aller à Notre Dame?
Bernadette Pour aller à Notre Dame il faut changer. Tu prends donc à l'Étoile la direction Vincennes et tu changes à Châtelet. Tu reprends la direction Porte d'Orléans, heu, et tu descends à Cité.
Barbara D'accord.

donc so, then

▶ **Il faut changer** You have to change. See Grammar p. 74 for an explanation of **il faut**.

l'Étoile is the site of the Arc de Triomphe. It is called **l'Étoile** because roads radiate out from it like the points of a star. The official name of the metro station there is Charles de Gaulle-Étoile.

Tu changes à Châtelet You change at Châtelet. From the verb **changer**. Note that Bernadette uses **tu** because Barbara is her daughter.

tu reprends you take another (train).

Numbers 100–1000

Cent, cent un, cent deux, cent trois, cent quatre, cent cinq, cent six, cent sept, cent huit, cent neuf, cent dix ... et cetera.
Deux cents, trois cents, quatre cents, cinq cents, six cents, sept septs, huit cents, neuf cents, mille.

100, 101, 102, 103, 104, 105, 106, 107, 108, 109, 110 ... etc.
200, 300, 400, 500, 600, 700, 800, 900, 1000

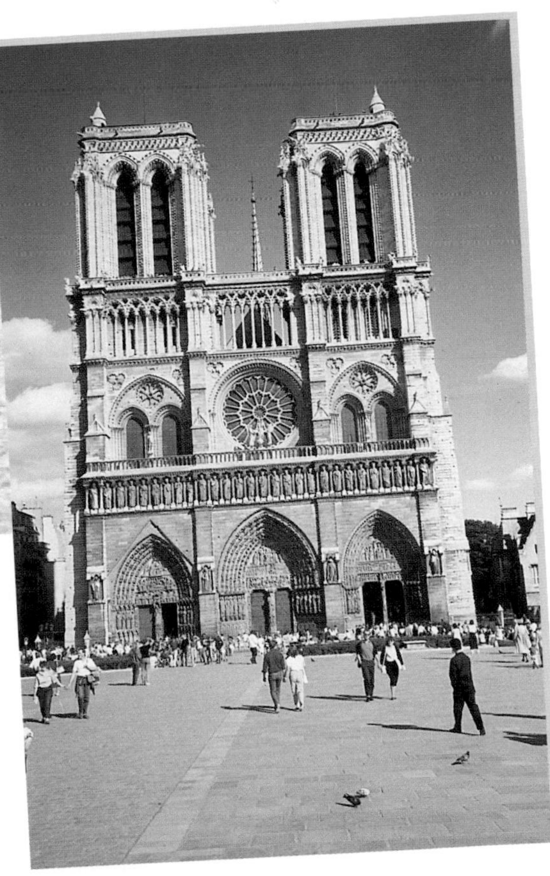

PRACTICE

6 This exercise gives you practice at pronouncing the elusive sound '**u**', which comes in the word **tu**. On the recording, Carolle will repeat some of Bernadette's directions for getting to Notre Dame. Then Yves will say some other sentences from the conversations which include the sound '**u**'. There will be a pause after each group of words for you to repeat them; give particular care to the sound '**u**' when you do so.

7 On the recording for this exercise, you will hear a booking office clerk telling a series of customers how much their tickets cost. Can you write down in figures the prices she gives?

a. ____________________

b. ____________________

c. ____________________

d. ____________________

e. ____________________

f. ____________________

When you have checked your answers, see if you can read aloud the figures you have written down. You can play the recording again if you want to confirm that you have got them right.

ANSWERS P. 78

8 When you finish this unit, you will be a third of the way through the course, so this is a good point at which to do some revision. The crossword will help you recall some of the vocabulary you have met over the last five units. For crossword purposes, you can ignore accents.

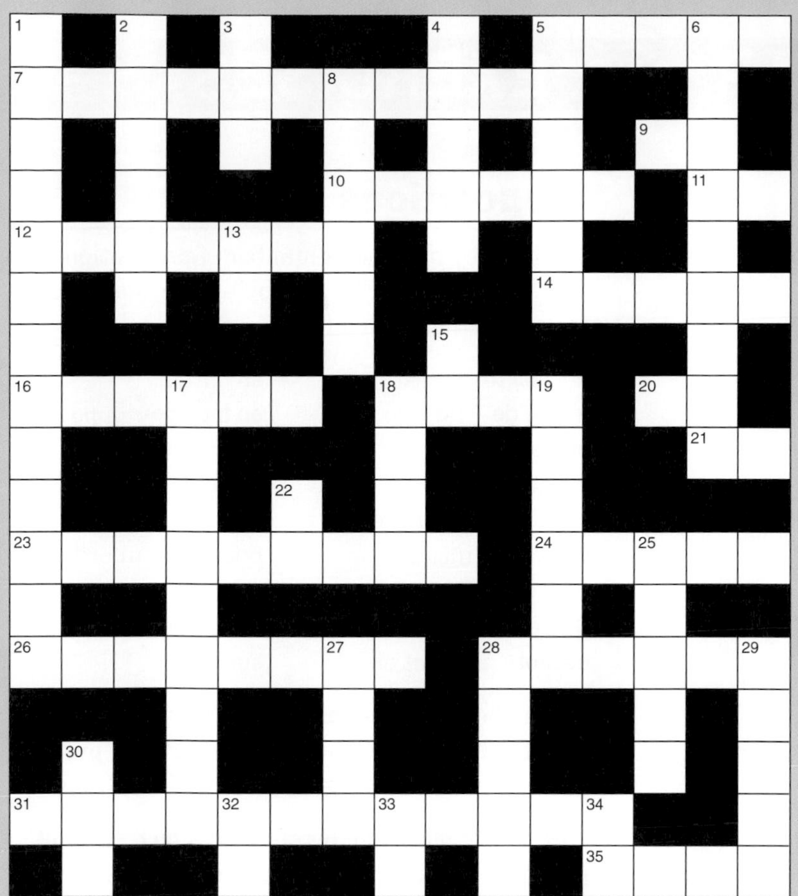

Across

5 To drink (5)
7 Mineral water (3, 8)
9 He (2)
10 Excuse me (6)
11 Is it **le** or **la mairie**? (2)
12 Work (7)
14 Nights (5)
16 Ham (6)
18 In (4)
20 Is it **le** or **la musée**? (2)
21 **La pharmacie ... trouve à droite.** (2)
23 Birth (9)
24 Tobacconist's (5)
26 To book (8)
28 Cold (m.pl.) (6)
31 Town hall (5, 2, 5)
35 Surnames (4)

Down

1 Breakfast (5, 8)
2 Office (6)
3 Bed (3)
4 To do (5)
5 Need (6)
6 Sandwich-filler like pâté (9)
8 Job (6)
13 Year (2)
15 Is it **le** or **la chambre**? (2)
17 Pub-restaurant (9)
18 Then (4)
19 To go out (6)
22 Is it **le** or **la clé**? (2)
25 Bathroom: **salle de ...** (5)
27 To be (4)
28 Daughter (5)
29 Evenings (5)
30 Good (3)
32 Is it **le** or **la cidre**? (2)
33 Goes (2)
34 In (2)

ANSWERS P. 78

GRAMMAR AND EXERCISES

The verb *aller*

You need to know by heart the irregular verb **aller** (to go):

je vais	**nous allons**
tu vas	**vous allez**
il/elle va	**ils/elles vont**

The verb *venir*

The verb **venir** (to come) is, of course, a very useful one in itself. It is also the model for a number of other common verbs, e.g. **revenir** (to come back), **devenir** (to become), **tenir** (to hold), **retenir** (to hold back or retain), **maintenir** (to maintain) and **soutenir** (to hold up).

je viens	**nous venons**
tu viens	**vous venez**
il/elle vient	**ils/elles viennent**

Il faut

In Conversations 3, Bernadette said **Il faut changer**. Depending on context, this could be translated 'I/you/he/she/one/we/they must change' or 'I/you (etc.) have to change' or 'It is necessary to change'. You may find it most helpful to think of **Il faut** as meaning 'It is necessary'. It is followed by an infinitive.

Here are some further examples – you might like to think through the range of possible translations for each of them:

Il faut travailler.
Il faut téléphoner.
Il faut aller à pied.

Il faut is also sometimes used with a noun, e.g.

Il faut un passeport
You need/one needs a passport

Prepositions

You have by now met a number of prepositions (words such as 'at', 'in' and 'by'). Here is a list of them, together with a few new ones:

à at, to	**en** in
à côté de next to	**en face de** opposite
après after	**entre** between
avant before	**jusqu'à** as far as
chez at the house of	**par** by, through
dans in, inside	**pour** for, in order to
de of, from	**près de** near to
derrière behind	**sous** under
devant in front of	**sur** on

Remember that **de + le = du** and **de + les = des.** This applies even when the **de** is part of a phrase like **à côté de**, **en face de** or **près de.** For example,

près de + le restaurant becomes **près du restaurant**
près de + les hôtels becomes **près des hôtels**

9 Tick the correct completion of each sentence:

a. Il faut
☐ allez à pied.
☐ allons à pied.
☐ aller à pied.

b. Tu
☐ prenez le métro.
☐ prend le métro.
☐ prends le métro.

c. Elle
☐ vas à Paris.
☐ va à Paris.
☐ vont à Paris.

d. Il faut
☐ tournez à droite.
☐ tourner à gauche.
☐ allez tout droit.

e. Vous
☐ continuer tout droit.
☐ êtes ici.
☐ faut prendre le métro.

f. Ils ☐ faut aller à l'école.
☐ allons à l'école.
☐ vont à l'école.

ANSWERS P. 78

10

On the basis of the map of Brélès on p. 66, indicate whether each of the statements below is **vrai** (true) or **faux** (false).

a. L'épicerie est en face de la mairie. vrai/faux

b. Il y a un stade à côté du restaurant. vrai/faux

c. Le tennis est près de la station-service. vrai/faux

d. Le cimetière se trouve derrière l'église. vrai/faux

e. L'école est sur la D27. vrai/faux

f. La boulangerie se trouve entre la mairie et la salle communale. vrai/faux

ANSWERS P. 78

11

A gîte-owner has sent this description of the village amenities. Have a go at translating it into English.

Le gîte se trouve dans la rue principale de Saint-Julien. A côté de la maison il y a une épicerie et une boulangerie et en face de la maison il y a un tabac. Derrière le tabac se trouve l'église Saint-Julien. Nous avons une école primaire – elle se trouve près de l'église – et puis devant l'église il y a un bar et un bon petit restaurant.

____

____

____

____

____

____

____

____

12

Now see if you can write out translations for the sentences below:

a. The tennis court is opposite the petrol station.

____

b. The town hall is opposite the grocer's.

____

c. The grocer's is near the baker's.

____

d. The cemetery is next to the church.

____

e. The church is situated between the town hall and the restaurant.

____

____

ANSWERS P. 78

KEY WORDS AND PHRASES

Vous avez un plan de la ville?	Do you have a map of the town?
On est où exactement ici?	Where exactly are we here?
Au centre-ville	In the town centre
En face de	Facing
l'église Saint-Pierre (f.)	St Peter's church
la rue Saint-Jean	St John's Street
Je suis à pied	I'm on foot
Je suis en voiture	I'm in a car
Pour aller à la gare?	How do I get to the station?
Pour aller au musée?	How do I get to the museum?
Vous voyez la pharmacie?	Do you see the chemist's?
Vous allez tout droit	You go straight on
Vous tournez à droite	You turn right
Vous prenez la première rue/route à gauche	You take the first street/road on the left
Vous traversez le pont	You cross the bridge
Un petit peu après le pont	A little bit after the bridge
Un petit peu plus loin	A little bit further
Le musée est à côté de la gare	The museum is next to the station
Merci! – Je vous en prie	Thank you! – You're welcome
L'hôtel de ville (m.)/**la mairie**	The town hall
L'horaire (m.)	Time, timetable
Vous allez prendre le métro, direction Nation	You're going to take the métro, on the Nation line
Vous descendez à Trocadéro	You get off at Trocadero
C'est à deux cents mètres	It's two hundred metres (away)
Il faut changer	You have to change

Numbers 100–1000

DID YOU KNOW?

Pour aller en France

There is an astonishingly large range of guide-books to France, covering every aspect from antique fairs to wild flowers. Here is a selection of some with more general appeal:

Michelin Green Guides

Very thorough guides to practically every place of interest in a particular region, with history, descriptions, plans, maps, itineraries and illustrations.

Cadogan Guides

Well-written guides full of information on the places to go and see, as well as where to eat and stay.

Rough Guides

Quirky and engaging series, giving both basic information on standard places of interest and off-the-beaten-track suggestions for the independent traveller on a budget.

AA Guides

The AA has several ranges: the "Explorer" series, which includes details of hotels and restaurants and a separate map; the "Essential" series of portable practical guides on regions and towns, and the Baedeker's Guides for comprehensive information on the sights and culture.

All of these publications are available from bookshops or by post from the usual mail order booksellers as well as some specialists in guidebooks which can be found on the Internet.

The Paris métro

The Paris **métro** (or **métropolitain**, to give it its full name) is cheap and generally pleasant, though increasing numbers of French women avoid travelling alone on it late at night. There is a flat rate of one ticket for travel in the centre of Paris; it is much more economical to buy your tickets ten at a time. Ask for **un ticket** if you only want one and **un carnet** if you want ten. The same tickets can be used for travel by bus in Paris. You can also buy a weekly ticket (**une carte orange**). Do not be lured into buying from the illegal ticket-touts who prey on unwary foreigners – their prices are generally high and their tickets often invalid.

When you travel on the **métro**, you will find that your line takes its name from the station (**la station**) that is the terminus in that direction. When you travel in the opposite direction, the line has a completely different name. This avoids the London hazard of getting an eastbound train when you want a westbound one. When you change trains, if your next line is not indicated, follow the sign **correspondance** (connections). **Métro** maps are displayed in all underground stations; you can get your own pocket version by asking at the ticket office for **un plan du métro**.

The RER is the network of high-speed underground services connecting the suburbs with the centre of Paris. You can travel on it within the central Paris area for one **métro** ticket, but longer journeys cost more.

AND FINALLY...

13

You are asking your way to l'Auberge de l'Église (literally, the Inn of the Church). Follow Philippe's prompts on the recording. Carolle will give a correct version of your part after each of the pauses.

ANSWERS

Exercise 1

(a) At the grocer's, opposite the town hall. **(b)** At the bar-cum-tobacconist's, opposite the church. **(c)** Behind the church. **(d)** Behind the cemetery and the grocer's.

Exercise 4

(a) The town hall **(b)** The restaurant **(c)** The petrol station **(d)** The baker's

Carolle says:

Bon, alors, nous sommes ici, à la mairie. Vous sortez de la mairie; vous avez l'épicerie en face de vous. Vous tournez à gauche et vous allez tout droit. Vous avez l'église sur votre droite. Au bar, vous prenez à droite la rue de l'Aber Ildut. Vous continuez tout droit et puis c'est sur votre droite.

Yves says:

Pour aller à la boulangerie … alors … Nous sommes ici, à la station-service. Vous sortez de la station-service et vous tournez à gauche. Ensuite vous prenez à droite et vous allez tout droit jusqu'au bar. Au bar, vous tournez à droite. Vous passez devant l'église et vous prenez la première rue à gauche. Vous allez tout droit et puis c'est sur votre gauche.

Exercise 7

(a) 150 € **(b)** 342 € **(c)** 280 € **(d)** 578 € **(e)** 471 € **(f)** 999 €

Exercise 8

1 P		2 B		3 L				4 F		5 B	O	I	6 R	E
7 E	A	U	M	I	N	8 E	R	A	L	E			I	
T		R		T		M		I		S		9 I	L	
I		E				10 P	A	R	D	O	N		11 L	A
12 T	R	A	V	13 A	I	L		E		I			E	
D		U		N		O				14 N	U	I	T	S
E						I		15 L					T	
16 J	A	M	17 B	O	N		18 D	A	N	19 S		20 L	E	
E			R				O			O			21 S	E
U			A		22 L		N			R				
23 N	A	I	S	S	A	N	C	E		24 T	A	25 B	A	C
E			S							I		A		
26 R	E	S	E	R	V	27 E	R		28 F	R	O	I	D	29 S
			R			T			I			N		O
	30 B		I			R			L			S		I
31 H	O	T	E	32 L	D	E	33 V	I	L	L	34 E			R
	N			E			A		E		35 N	O	M	S

Exercise 9

(a) aller à pied **(b)** prends le métro **(c)** va à Paris **(d)** tourner à gauche **(e)** êtes ici **(f)** vont à l'école

Exercise 10

(a) vrai **(b)** faux **(c)** vrai **(d)** vrai **(e)** faux **(f)** faux

Exercise 11

Your translation does not have to be word-for-word the same as this in order to be correct:

The gîte is situated in the main street of Saint-Julien. Next to the house there is a grocer's and a baker's and opposite the house there is a tobacconist's. Behind the tobacconist's is the church of Saint Julien. We have a primary school – it is near the church – and then in front of the church there is a bar and a good little restaurant.

Exercise 12

Again, your translations may not be word-for-word the same as these.

(a) Le tennis est en face de la station-service. **(b)** La mairie est en face de l'épicerie. **(c)** L'épicerie est près de la boulangerie. **(d)** Le cimetière est à côté de l'église. **(e)** L'église se situe entre la mairie et le restaurant.

6 TIME

WHAT YOU WILL LEARN

- telling the time
- the days of the week
- months and dates
- talking about age
- the opening hours of shops
- something about the French weekend and holiday patterns

POISSONNERIE

Horaires d'ouverture

Lundi	fermé	fermé
Mardi	8h45 12h15	fermé
Mercredi	8h45 12h15	fermé
Jeudi	8h45 12h15	fermé
Vendredi	8h45	19h15
Samedi	8h45	19h15
Dimanche	fermé	fermé

BEFORE YOU BEGIN

Being able to ask and understand when things are happening/open/available is essential to the smooth running of a holiday or business trip. Asking the questions is fairly simple:

Quand? When?

and

A quelle heure? At what time?

will cover most eventualities. Understanding and giving the answers requires more practice: you could try saying the time in French when you look at your watch and the day and date when you look at a calendar.

Pronunciation notes

Pronunciation practice in this unit will concentrate on the French '**r**', which sounds something like a gargle! Listen out for it in such phrases as

à quelle heure?	at what time?
à partir de sept heures	from seven o'clock
dans votre chambre	in your room

All of those come in the first recording.

CONVERSATIONS 

 *Finding out about breakfast at the hotel*

Guy	A quelle heure servez-vous le petit déjeuner, s'il vous plaît?
Réceptionniste	Alors, le petit déjeuner est servi à partir de sept heures du matin jusqu'à neuf heures et demie.
Guy	Et on le prend où?
Réceptionniste	Vous pouvez le prendre dans la salle qui se trouve près de la réception ou alors dans votre chambre.
Guy	D'accord.

puis then, next

- **A quelle heure servez-vous ...?** At what time do you serve ...?
  Vous servez means 'you serve'. It comes from the verb **servir**, to serve.

le petit déjeuner est servi breakfast is served. Remember that **le déjeuner** (without the **petit**) is lunch. There is also a verb **déjeuner**, to have lunch.

- **à partir de sept heures du matin** from 7 a.m. (literally, to start from seven hours of the morning).
- **jusqu'à neuf heures et demie** until 9.30 (literally, until nine hours and a half).

on le prend où? where does one have it? (literally, one it takes where?) As well as meaning 'the', **le** can mean 'him' or 'it' (referring to a masculine noun). Similarly, **la** can mean 'her' or 'it' (referring to a feminine noun) and **les** can mean 'them'. In French, pronouns such as 'him', 'her', 'it' or 'them' go in front of the verb.

la salle qui se trouve près de la réception the room which is situated (literally, which finds itself) near reception.

When is the water hot and when is the gate shut at the camp-site?

LISTEN FOR...

- **ferme** (from **fermer**) shuts
- **fermé** shut
- **ouvert** open

Réceptionniste	C'est chaud de six heures à dix heures le matin et ensuite de quatre heures à huit heures le soir.
Marie-Claude	Et le portail – à quelle heure ferme le ...?
Réceptionniste	Alors le portail est ouvert le matin à six heures et fermé à onze heures, sauf le samedi, où il est fermé à ... à minuit.

le portail gate

- **C'est chaud de six heures à dix heures** It's hot from six o'clock to ten o'clock. Marie-Claude has asked when the water is hot.

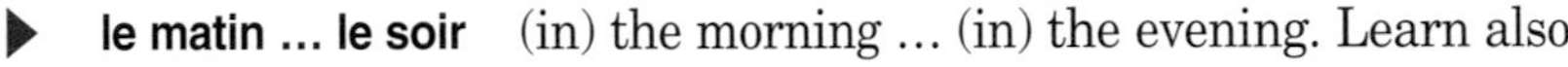

- **le matin ... le soir** (in) the morning ... (in) the evening. Learn also
- **le jour ... la nuit** in the daytime ... at night.

à onze heures meaning 11 o'clock at night.

- **sauf le samedi** except on Saturdays (literally, except the Saturday). 'On Mondays' would be **le lundi**, 'on Tuesdays' **le mardi**, etc. With days of the week, the word 'on' is not translated.

CAMPING-CARAVANING
KER-BEUZ
02.98.26.02.76

• 2 PISCINES
• 2 TENNIS
• MINI-GOLF
• ANIMATIONS de JOURNEE
• ANIMATIONS de SOIREE

CAP FRANCE
CAMPING-CARAVANING ET VILLAGE-VACANCES DE KER-BEUZ
29560 TREGARVAN - Fax 02 98 26 01 20

CAMPING
LA TORCHE
BRETAGNE - FRANCE
Ouvert toute l'année
TOUT CONFORT
BAR - SNACK - JEUX
PISCINE CHAUFFÉE
1 ha d'aire de jeux
LOCATION MOBIL-HOMES
CHALETS
SERVICE CAMPING-CAR
DES VACANCES FAMILIALES

La Torche
29120 PLOMEUR
Tél. 02 98 58 62 82

PRACTICE

Important: you should turn to the Grammar section on p. 90 and study 'Telling the time' before tackling these exercises.

1 In the recording for this exercise, Yves asks Carolle six times over what the time is: **Quelle heure est-il?** Try to note down her replies in figures.

a. ____________________

b. ____________________

c. ____________________

d. ____________________

e. ____________________

ANSWERS P. 94

f. ____________________

2 This time, the recording is a series of answerphone announcements giving the opening times of various amenities. Can you note down what they are?

a. The tourist office ____________________

b. The town hall ____________________

c. The château ____________________

d. The museum ____________________

ANSWERS P. 94

e. The bank ____________________

3 Be prepared to answer Carolle's questions about the opening and closing times of the shop where this photograph was taken. There will be no English prompts as the photograph gives you all the information you need, but Yves will give correct versions of your replies after the pauses. He will use the 12-hour clock (saying e.g. 'two o'clock' rather than 'fourteen hours').

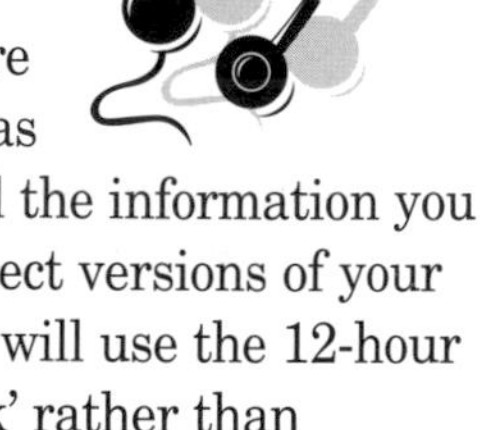

Ils ouvrent is from the verb **ouvrir**, to open, and **ils ferment** is from the verb **fermer**, to shut.

CONVERSATIONS

Train times from La Roche-sur-Yon to Nice

LISTEN FOR...

- **départ** departure
- **arrivée** arrival
- **dormir** to sleep

Employée	Alors départ tous les soirs de La Roche à 18h48 et arrivée à Nice à 8h37.
Robert	18h48, ça fait 6h48.
Employée	C'est ça. Sept heures moins le quart.
Robert	Sept heures moins le quart. Oui, merci. Et on arrive à Nice à quelle heure?
Employée	A 8h37.
Robert	Ah, c'est bien – le matin, oui. Ça fait une bonne nuit dans le train pour dormir.

- **tous les soirs** every evening (literally, all the evenings). Learn also
- **tous les jours** every day.

de La Roche from La Roche(-sur-Yon).

Ça fait That makes, that is.

- **on arrive à Nice** one arrives in Nice. From the verb **arriver**. **On** is used much more frequently in French than 'one' in English.

Ça fait une bonne nuit dans le train pour dormir That gives you a good night's sleep in the train (lit. That makes a good night in the train for to sleep).

The school week

LISTEN FOR...

- **lundi** Monday
- **mardi** Tuesday
- **mercredi** Wednesday
- **jeudi** Thursday
- **vendredi** Friday
- **samedi** Saturday
- **dimanche** Sunday

Isabelle Alors, heu, les écoliers français travaillent le lundi, le mardi, le jeudi et le vendredi toute la journée. En général on commence à huit heures et demie le matin et on termine le soir vers quatre heures et demie, cinq heures, quelquefois plus tard. Et le mercredi matin on travaille et l'après-midi est libre. Les écoliers travaillent aussi le samedi matin. Donc en général les gens partent en week-end le samedi à midi et ils reviennent le dimanche soir.

l'écolier (m.) schoolchild

▶ **en général** in general

▶ **vers** (*here*) around

▶ **l'après-midi** (m. or f.) afternoon

libre free

▶ **toute la journée** all day long. The normal word for 'day' is **le jour**: **les jours de la semaine** the days of the week. **La journée** puts more emphasis on how you are spending the day. This is a fairly subtle distinction, so don't worry about it at this stage. Note that 'a journey' is **un voyage** in French.

▶ **on commence … on termine** they begin … they finish (literally, one begins … one finishes). From the verbs **commencer** and **terminer**.

quelquefois plus tard sometimes later. Comparatives (like late–later, big–bigger) will be covered on p. 120.

▶ **les gens partent** people leave, from the verb **partir**. Note also

▶ **A quelle heure part l'autobus?** At what time does the bus leave?

▶ **Le train part à six heures** The train leaves at six o'clock.

en week-end for the weekend.

ils reviennent le dimanche soir they come back again on Sunday evenings. **Reviennent** is from the verb **revenir**, to come back again, which is made up of **venir** (which you studied on p. 74) and **re-**, which is often tacked on to the front of verbs to mean 'again'.

PRACTICE

Which of these statements are true and which false?

a. Vingt et une heures trente, ça fait neuf heures et demie. vrai/faux

b. Dix-neuf heures quinze, ça fait sept heures et quart. vrai/faux

c. Dix-huit heures quarante-cinq, ça fait six heures moins le quart. vrai/faux

d. Vingt-deux heures cinquante-cinq, ça fait onze heures moins cinq. vrai/faux

e. Quatorze heures quinze, ça fait trois heures moins le quart. vrai/faux

f. Vingt-trois heures quarante, ça fait minuit moins vingt. vrai/faux

5

Here is the timetable for trains from Limoges to Poitiers:

circuler, used of trains, means 'to run'.
lun, **ven** and **dim** are short for **lundi**, **vendredi** and **dimanche**.
fêtes are public holidays.

Limoges ▶ Poitiers		312km
Départ Les trains circulent	**Arrivée** ↓	↓
• les lun	05.21	07.29
• tous les jours sauf les dim et fêtes	06.30	08.34
• tous les jours	13.09	15.19
• les ven, dim et fêtes	16.08	18.10
• tous les jours	17.18	19.30
• les ven, dim et fêtes	18.32	20.40

a. Est-ce qu'il y a un départ à six heures et demie le samedi matin? oui/non

b. Est-ce que le train de seize heures huit circule le samedi? oui/non

c. A quelle heure est-ce que le train de treize heures neuf arrive à Poitiers?

____

d. A quelle heure est le premier départ de la journée le jeudi?

____

e. Si on prend le train de dix-huit heures trente-deux, à quelle heure est-ce qu'on arrive à Poitiers? ______________________________

ANSWERS P. 94

6

Carolle and Yves need to have a half-hour meeting tomorrow, but Carolle's diary is already pretty full. Listen to their conversation on the recording, and see if you can fill in the times of her **rendez-vous** (appointments) with:

l'attaché culturel ______________________________

le directeur de l'école ______________________________

Madeleine ______________________________

le directeur du Théâtre de Versailles ______________________________

le coiffeur ______________________________

ANSWERS P. 94

At what time do Carolle and Yves finally agree to meet? ______________________________

7

Now you are trying to arrange a meeting with Carolle, but it is quite difficult to find a time when you are both free. On the recording, Philippe will prompt you and Yves will back you up.

Remember the phrases **je ne peux pas** (I can't) and **je ne suis pas libre** (I'm not free), which you met in Unit 2.

CONVERSATIONS 

 School holidays

LISTEN FOR MOST OF...

▶ **janvier**	January	▶ **juillet**	July
▶ **février**	February	▶ **août**	August
▶ **mars**	March	▶ **septembre**	September
▶ **avril**	April	▶ **octobre**	October
▶ **mai**	May	▶ **novembre**	November
▶ **juin**	June	▶ **décembre**	December

Françoise Heu, fin octobre, heu, début novembre, il y a les … les vacances de la Toussaint qui durent une semaine. Heu, il y a des vacances, heu, de Noël qui sont en général du 21 décembre jusqu'au 4 janvier. Il y a les vacances de février qui durent une semaine. Il y a aussi les vacances de Pâques qui durent deux semaines pleines, qui sont, heu, vers les mois de mars/avril et les grandes vacances qui durent deux mois et demi, du 30 juin jusqu'au 15 septembre.

▶ **durent** (from **durer**)	last
pleines (f.pl.)	full
▶ **le mois**	month

fin octobre, début novembre (at the) end of October, beginning of November. The months of the year do not require a capital letter in French.

la Toussaint All Saints'. 1 November is a traditional bank holiday, when literally millions of French people make a point of putting flowers on the graves of their loved ones.

▶ **Noël** Christmas. 'At Christmas' is **à Noël.**

▶ **du 21 décembre jusqu'au 4 janvier** from 21 December until 4 January.

▶ **Pâques** Easter. 'At Easter' is **à Pâques.**

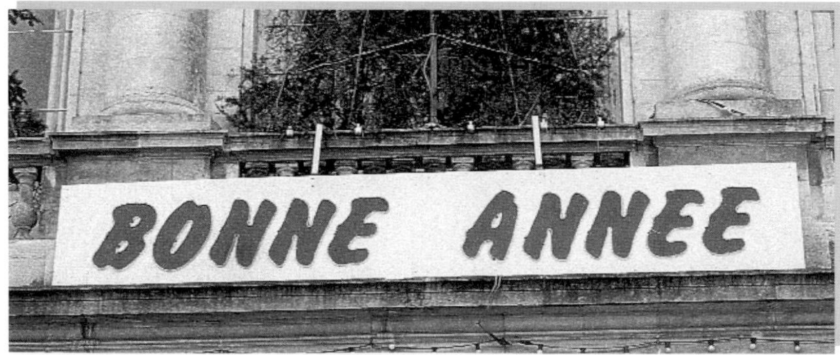

Happy New Year

les grandes vacances is the usual term for the long summer holiday. The word **vacances** is always used in the plural.

The summer holidays

LISTEN FOR...

▶ **la fête nationale**	national holiday
▶ **il faut éviter**	it is necessary to avoid
on peut pas rouler	one can't drive/move
▶ **sur la côte**	on the coast

Isabelle Heu, les Français aiment bien prendre leurs vacances, heu, vers le 14 juillet, la fête nationale et il y a un jour de départ en vacances en France – c'est le 1er (premier) août. Là, il faut éviter les routes parce que vraiment on peut pas ... on peut pas rouler. Et après le 15 août, heu, c'est assez calme sur la côte. Heu, c'est l'idéal pour les ... pour les Anglais pour venir chez nous.

▶ **aiment bien** like. From **aimer bien.**

▶ **le 14 juillet, la fête nationale** 14 July, the national holiday – which is not known as Bastille day in French as it is in English.

un jour de départ en vacances one day for going off on holiday. An amazing number of French people set off on holiday on 1 August (see Did you know?).

▶ **il faut éviter les routes** you should keep off the roads (literally, it is necessary to avoid the roads). See p. 74 if you want to refresh your memory on **il faut.**

vraiment ... on peut pas rouler really you can't move (because the roads are so congested). Although the grammatically correct way of forming a negative is to put **ne** in front of the verb and **pas** after it, in speech people very often leave out the **ne**.

▶ **assez calme** fairly quiet.

l'idéal (*here*) the ideal time.

How old are you?

Nadine	Tu as quel âge?
Pierre-Yves	...
Nadine	Quel âge tu as?
Pierre-Yves	...
Nadine	Quel âge as-tu?
Pierre-Yves	Deux!
Nadine	Deux ans.
Pierre-Yves	Deux ans.

▶ **Tu as quel âge?/Quel âge tu as?/Quel âge as-tu?** How old are you? You must use the verb **avoir**, not **être**, for age, e.g.

▶ **Quel âge avez-vous? J'ai soixante ans.** How old are you? I am sixty. (Literally, What age do you have? I have sixty years.)

PRACTICE

Important: you should turn to the Grammar section on p. 91 and learn how dates are expressed before you go on to these exercises.

8 Here is part of a tourist brochure about a château. Towards the end of it, you will find its opening times.

Accueil:
Château de Kerjean
Horaires:
- Juillet et août: tous les jours 10h-19h
- Juin, septembre: tous les jours sauf le mardi 10h-12h, 14h-18h
- Octobre, mai: tous les jours sauf le mardi 14h-18h
- Novembre à mars: mercredi et dimanche, 14h-18h
- Avril: tous les jours sauf mardi et samedi, 14h-17h, dimanche 14h-18h

a. Is the château open on Monday afternoons in January?
yes/no

b. Is it open on Saturday afternoons in April?
yes/no

c. Is it open on Tuesday afternoons in May?
yes/no

d. Is it open on Sunday mornings in June?
yes/no

e. Is it open on Tuesday mornings in August?
yes/no

Answers p. 94

9 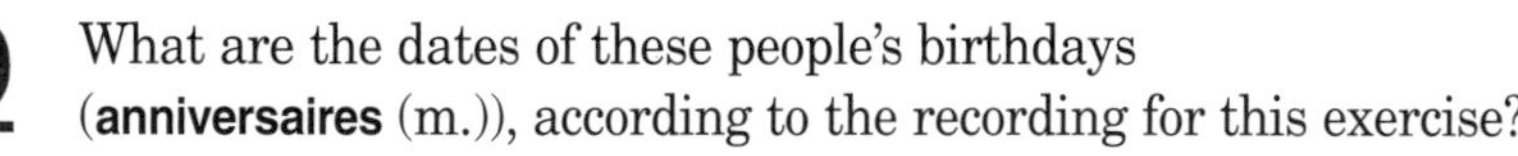

What are the dates of these people's birthdays (**anniversaires** (m.)), according to the recording for this exercise?

Georges:	☐ 23 April	or	☐ 27 April ?
Patrick:	☐ 15 June	or	☐ 25 June ?
Jeanne-Marie:	☐ 1 July	or	☐ 21 July ?
Claude:	☐ 3 August	or	☐ 13 August ?
Lisette:	☐ 2 September	or	☐ 12 September ?

Answers p. 94

CENTRE D'INFORMATION SUR L'HABITAT

DUNKERQUE
1, rue de Beaumont
☎ **03.28.63.23.40**

HEURES D'OUVERTURE :

Tous les jours
de 9 h 00 à 12 h 30
et de 13 h 30 à 17 h 00

Samedi
de 9 h 00 à 12 h 00 *sur rendez-vous*

10 The following photographs show the opening hours of the **agence postale** (a kind of sub-sub-post office) and the **mairie** in the village of Plourin in Brittany.

OUVERTURE
DU LUNDI AU VENDREDI
9H00 À 12H00
LE SAMEDI
9H00 À 11H30

On the recording, Yves will ask you questions about those opening hours. Pause the recording while you find the information in the photographs, give your answer aloud and then listen to Carolle giving her version. Carolle will be using the 12-hour system (e.g. she will be saying **Quatre heures** rather than **Seize heures** and **Neuf heures et demie** rather than **Neuf heures trente**).

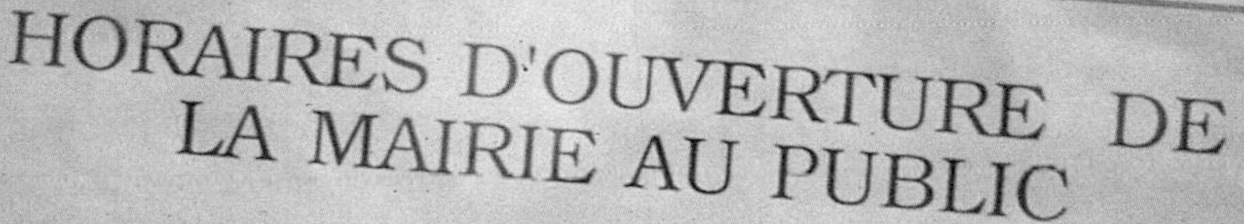

HORAIRES D'OUVERTURE DE
LA MAIRIE AU PUBLIC
o Du Lundi au Vendredi
de 9 h à 12 h et de 14 h à 16 h
o Le Samedi de 9 h 30 à 11 h 30

11 You are checking in at a camp-site with your large family. The man on the desk wants to know everyone's age. Tell him! (Philippe and Carolle will help you.)

Remember that in French you use the verb **avoir** to talk about age, e.g.

J'ai trente ans I am thirty
Elle a quarante ans She is forty

GRAMMAR AND EXERCISES

Telling the time

Telling the time in French is fairly straightforward. Study these examples with their literal translations:

Quelle heure est-il? What time is it?

5.00 **Il est cinq heures**
It is 5 hours

5.05 **Il est cinq heures cinq**
It is 5 hours 5

5.10 **Il est cinq heures dix**
It is 5 hours 10

5.15 **Il est cinq heures et quart**
It is 5 hours and quarter

5.20 **Il est cinq heures vingt**
It is 5 hours 20

5.25 **Il est cinq heures vingt-cinq**
It is 5 hours 25

5.30 **Il est cinq heures et demie**
It is 5 hours and half

5.35 **Il est six heures moins vingt-cinq**
It is 6 hours minus 25

5.40 **Il est six heures moins vingt**
It is 6 hours minus 20

5.45 **Il est six heures moins le quart**
It is 6 hours minus the quarter

5.50 **Il est six heures moins dix**
It is 6 hours minus 10

5.55 **Il est six heures moins cinq**
It is 6 hours minus 5

6.00 **Il est six heures**
It is 6 hours

So

- 'quarter past' is **et quart**
- 'half past' is **et demie**
- for minutes 'to' the hour, use **moins**
- 'a quarter to' is **moins le quart**

If it is unclear whether you are talking about a.m. or p.m., you can specify:

Il est neuf heures du matin
It is nine o'clock in the morning

Il est trois heures de l'après-midi
It is three o'clock in the afternoon

Il est dix heures du soir
It is ten o'clock in the evening

Il est midi	It is midday (12 noon)
Il est minuit	It is midnight

A quelle heure ...?	At what time ...?
A neuf heures	At nine o'clock
A dix heures et demie	At half past ten
A midi	At noon
A minuit	At midnight

'From ... to ...' is either **de ... à ...** or **à partir de ... jusqu'à ...**:

De six heures et demie à minuit	From half past six till midnight
A partir de six heures et demie jusqu'à minuit	From half past six till midnight

The 24-hour clock

In English we tend to use the 24-hour clock for such things as timetables (e.g. we say 'eighteen thirty' instead of 'half past six in the evening'). The same happens in French, only more so: theatre times, for example, are generally expressed as **vingt heures** or **vingt heures trente** rather than **huit heures** or **huit heures et demie.** (The word **heures** is never omitted.) Here are some examples from a railway timetable:

Le train part à ... The train departs at ...
dix-huit heures quinze 18.15
dix-neuf heures vingt-neuf 19.29
vingt heures trente 20.30
vingt-et-une heures trente-sept 21.37
vingt-deux heures quarante-cinq 22.45

Dates

As you heard in Conversations 3, **le vingt-et-un décembre** is 21 December – and it is literally 'the twenty-one December', not 'the twenty-first'. Similarly, **le quatre janvier** (literally, the four January) is used where in English we say 'the fourth'. The only one that does not follow this pattern is the first of the month, which is **le premier février**, **le premier mars**, etc.

When the day of the week is given with a date, the usual word order is, for example, **le lundi trente juin** or **le vendredi premier juillet**.

12 Write out in full the times shown on these watches. Assume that 12 o'clock is noon and that all the other times are a.m.

a.  *Il est* ______________________

b.  ______________________

c. ______________________

d.  ______________________

e.  ______________________

f. 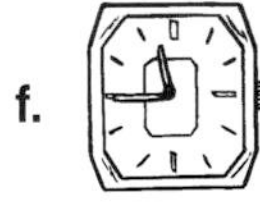 ______________________

g.  ______________________

ANSWERS P. 94

13 Give these dates in French, writing them out in full for practice:

a. Saturday the fourth of July.

____

b. Thursday the twenty-third of August.

____

c. Tuesday the twenty-first of February.

____

d. Wednesday the eighteenth of December.

____

e. Sunday the first of March.

____

f. Friday the thirty-first of January.

____

ANSWERS P. 94

KEY WORDS AND PHRASES

A quelle heure servez-vous le petit déjeuner?	At what time do you serve breakfast?
De sept heures du matin à neuf heures et demie	From 7 a.m. till 9.30
A partir de sept heures du matin jusqu'à neuf heures et demie	From 7 a.m. till 9.30
Quand?	When?
lundi	Monday
mardi	Tuesday
mercredi	Wednesday
jeudi	Thursday
vendredi	Friday
samedi	Saturday
dimanche	Sunday
le lundi (etc.)	on Mondays (etc.)
C'est ouvert/fermé	It is open/shut
de six heures à dix heures	from six o'clock to ten o'clock
le matin	(in) the morning
le soir	(in) the evening
le jour	(in) the day(-time)
la nuit	(at) night
tous les soirs	every evening
tous les jours	every day
sauf le samedi	except on Saturdays
Il ferme vers onze heures en général	It shuts around eleven o'clock in general
le départ	departure
l'arrivée (f.)	arrival
Le train part à une heure	The train leaves at one o'clock
On arrive à Nice à quelle heure?	One arrives in Nice at what time?
la date	the date
le mois	the month
le 1er janvier	1 January
février	February
mars	March
avril	April
mai	May
juin	June
le 14 juillet (**la fête nationale**)	14th July (the national holiday)
août	August
septembre	September
octobre	October
novembre	November
décembre	December
fin octobre	(at the) end of October
début novembre	(at the) beginning of November
à Noël	at Christmas
à Pâques	at Easter
Du 21 mars au 4 mai/Du 21 mars jusqu'au 4 mai	From 21 March until 4 May
Quel âge as-tu?/Quel âge avez-vous?	How old are you?
J'ai soixante ans	I am sixty

Plus telling the time

DID YOU KNOW?

Opening times of shops

French shops usually stay open into the evening. Large stores in the big towns stay open at midday; small shops traditionally close for two or three hours, though there is a general trend away from these long lunch-breaks. Many shops are shut for all or part of Monday or Wednesday; rather than an early-closing day it tends to be a late-opening day.

The baker's (**la boulangerie**) often opens as early as 7.30 a.m. and does not close until 7–8 p.m. The baker's and the cake-shop (**la pâtisserie**) usually open also on Sunday mornings. French people generally shop for bread every day or even twice a day in order to have it as fresh as possible.

The French weekend

The geographical area of France is more than twice that of the UK and three times that of New England. The size of the population (56,700,000) is similar to that of the UK and four and a half times that of New England. In other words, France is overall less crowded than the UK and more crowded than New England. People in French cities tend to live in fairly cramped rented flats (**appartements**) and escape to the country at weekends. If they have any spare money, they will often buy a house in the country or by the seaside. They then go off to this **résidence secondaire** at every opportunity. This is what Isabelle means when she says '**En général les gens partent en week-end** …'.

The French on holiday

If you are going on holiday in France in the summer, you should try to avoid travelling on 1, 14, 15 and 31 July and on 1, 15 and 31 August as these are the traditional dates for what the French call the July and August 'migrations': the trains are very crowded and traffic jams build up. This occurs because many factories shut down completely for the month of July or the month of August, so that large numbers of people with exactly the same holiday period want to make the most of it. This custom is now being changed and staggered holidays are on the increase. The public holidays on 14 July and 15 August are also landmarks in the holiday calendar; the period between them is when resorts are at their most crowded and, particularly on the south coast, at their most expensive. Bank holidays in France are as follows:

New Year's Day **le jour de l'an**
Easter Monday **le lundi de Pâques**
Labour Day **le premier mai**
VE Day (8 May) **le huit mai**
Ascension Day (in May) **l'Ascension**
Whit Monday (in May or June) **le lundi de la Pentecôte**
Bastille Day (14 July) **la Fête Nationale**
Assumption Day (15 August) **l'Assomption**
All Saints' Day (1 November) **la Toussaint**
Remembrance Day **le onze novembre**
Christmas Day (25 December) **Noël**

AND FINALLY...

14 Listen first to Carolle asking Yves a series of questions about himself, his family and his routine. She will then ask you the same questions. There will be pauses for you to answer, but no correct versions are given because the answers depend on you.

s.a.r.l. **CASSE-AUTO**
Rue Joseph Coste (Ancienne Raffinerie) **59500 Courchelettes**
Tél. : 03 27 88 10 02
VENTES ET ACHATS
Pièces détachées automobiles occasions
Siège Social : 225, rue Lepinoy - 59230 St-Amand - **Tél. : 03 27 27 81 99**
A votre service de 10 h à 12h - de 14h à 18h (fermé lundi matin)

VISITES

Beffroi : visite le dimanche et jours fériés, à 10h, 11h 15h, 16h et 17h.
Tous les jours en juillet et en août, à 10h, 11h, 14h, 15h, 16h et 17h.

Visites guidées de la ville : de mai à octobre, tous les dimanches (sauf dimanche de Gayant) à 15h30. Plusieurs thèmes. Rendez-vous au Beffroi.

(Durée : 2 heures)

Pour les groupes : toute l'année sur demande.

ANSWERS

Exercise 1
(a) 1.30 **(b)** 12 noon **(c)** 4.35 **(d)** 3.15 **(e)** 11.40 p.m. **(f)** 10.10

Exercise 2
(a) 10.00–12.00 and 14.30–18.00 **(b)** 9.00–12.00 and 15.00–18.00 **(c)** 10.30–19.00 **(d)** 10.00–12.30 and 14.00–18.30 **(e)** 8.15–12.00 and 13.30–15.45

Exercise 4
(a) vrai **(b)** vrai **(c)** faux **(d)** vrai **(e)** faux **(f)** vrai

Exercise 5
(a) Oui (It is every day except Sundays and holidays.)
(b) Non (It runs only on Fridays, Sundays and holidays.)
(c) A quinze heures dix-neuf **(d)** A six heures trente
(e) A vingt heures quarante

Exercise 6
l'attaché culturel: 9.15 a.m./le directeur de l'école: 11.45 a.m./Madeleine: 1.00 p.m./le directeur du Théâtre de Versailles: 3.30 p.m./le coiffeur: 6.00 p.m./Carolle and Yves finally agree to meet at 5 p.m.

Exercise 8
(a) no **(b)** no **(c)** no **(d)** yes **(e)** yes

Exercise 9
23 April/15 June/1 July/13 August/12 September

Exercise 12
(a) Il est six heures et demie/Il est six heures trente
(b) Il est sept heures vingt **(c)** Il est une heure et quart/Il est une heure quinze **(d)** Il est deux heures dix **(e)** Il est midi/Il est douze heures **(f)** Il est midi moins le quart/Il est onze heures quarante-cinq **(g)** Il est quatre heures moins dix/Il est trois heures cinquante

Exercise 13
(a) le samedi quatre juillet **(b)** le jeudi vingt-trois août
(c) le mardi vingt-et-un février **(d)** le mercredi dix-huit décembre **(e)** le dimanche premier mars **(f)** Le vendredi trente-et-un janvier.

7 SHOPPING FOR FOOD

S.A.
ERNEST
TRAITEUR
COCKTAILS - LUNCHS
ERNEST
CANNES
52, RUE MEYNADIER-2, RUE LOUIS-BLANC

WHAT YOU WILL LEARN

- basic shopping language
- asking for advice in shops
- improved comprehension of numbers and prices
- the names of shops in France
- something about the French post office
- metric weights and measures

BEFORE YOU BEGIN

Shopping is a major area of language use, so the next two units will be devoted to different aspects of it. The single most useful expression you will be meeting in them is **Je voudrais** (I'd like), which you can use in all sorts of contexts, e.g.

Je voudrais quatre oranges
I'd like four oranges

Je voudrais téléphoner aux États-Unis
I'd like to telephone (to) the United States

Pronunciation notes

This unit will give further attention to the sound '**r**', since it is one that people generally find difficult. Exercise 1 will pick up examples from Conversations 1, including **je voudrais**, **croissants**, **ordinaires** and **beurre**.

CONVERSATIONS 1

Buying bread

Simone Heu, je voudrais une baguette.
Boulangère Oui, Madame.
Simone Et cinq croissants.
Boulangère Cinq croissants – ordinaires ou beurre?
Simone Heu, ordinaires.
Boulangère Ordinaires.

la boulangère baker (woman). A male baker is **un boulanger** and a baker's shop is **une boulangerie.**

▶ **je voudrais une baguette** I'd like a French stick. There are several different kinds of French bread – **une baguette** is a medium-sized stick, **une ficelle** (literally, a string) is thinner, **un gros pain** is a large round loaf and **un petit pain** is a bread roll. Bakers are usually willing to sell you half a French stick: **une demi-baguette.**

ordinaires ou beurre? ordinary or (made with) butter? (**Un vin ordinaire** is ordinary wine as opposed to vintage.) **Ordinaires** ends in an **-s** because it is a plural adjective referring to **croissants. Beurre** does not end in an **-s** because it is not an adjective – it is short for 'made with butter'.

Buying fruit juice on special offer

LISTEN FOR...

des promotions	special offers
dix pour cent	ten per cent
▶ **les jus de fruits**	fruit juices

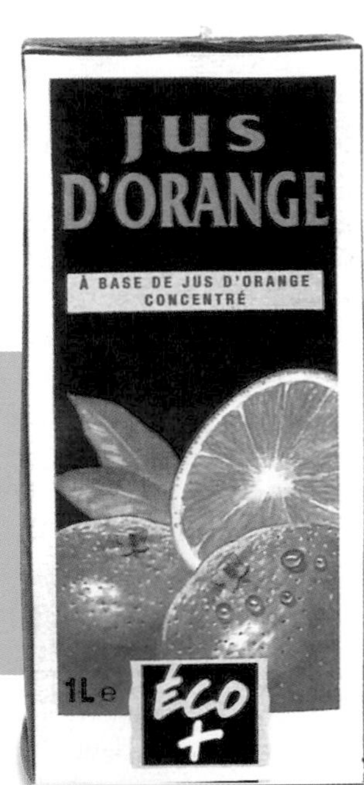

Vendeuse J'ai des promotions en ce moment. Vous avez dix pour cent sur les vins, heu, et les jus de fruits.
Simone Vous avez, heu, jus d'orange?
Vendeuse Jus d'orange, oui.
Simone Oui. Un jus d'orange et un jus de ...
Vendeuse Pamplemousse, ananas ...
Simone Heu, ananas.

▶ **le jus d'orange** orange juice
▶ **le pamplemousse** grapefruit

J'ai des promotions en ce moment I have some special offers at the moment (literally, at this moment). For **ce**, see Grammar p. 120.

- **Vous avez dix pour cent sur les vins** You have 10 per cent off wines (literally, on wines!).
- **ananas** pineapple. The final **-s** can be pronounced or not, as you prefer. Other fruit juices include **le jus de pomme** (apple juice), **le jus de tomate** (tomato juice).

PRACTICE

1 Repeat after Carolle the words from Conversations 1 which include that tricky sound **r**.

2 Listen to Carolle shopping in a village store. Here is a gapped transcript of the conversation she has with the shopkeeper: can you fill in the missing words and phrases?

Yves	S'il vous plaît, Madame?
Carolle	Bonjour, Monsieur. ______________________ quatre croissants et ______________________, s'il vous plaît.
Yves	Voilà, Madame.
Carolle	Et puis, ______________________ vous avez comme jus de fruits?
Yves	Pamplemousse, ______________________, orange, ______________________ et tomate.
Carolle	Alors, ______________________ pamplemousse et un jus de tomate, s'il vous plaît.
Yves	Voilà, Madame.

ANSWERS P. 108

3 Your shopping list keeps growing as Yves thinks of more items to add to it. Each time, pause the recording and repeat the list from the beginning, adding the new item he mentions at the end.

e.g. You start with **Une baguette.**
Yves will say **Et quatre croissants.**
You say **Une baguette et quatre croissants.**
To be sure you have got it right, Carolle will say **Une baguette et quatre croissants.**
Then Yves adds the next item and you recap the list from the beginning.

CONVERSATIONS

Shopping for eggs and dairy produce

LISTEN FOR...

- **quatre yaourts** four yoghurts
- **Boursin** the name of a cheese
- **six œufs** six eggs
- **petits suisses** cream cheeses

Guy Bonjour, Monsieur.
Commerçant Bonjour, Monsieur.
Guy Monsieur, je voudrais quatre yaourts nature, s'il vous plaît …
Commerçant Oui, Monsieur … Voici.
Guy Merci. Mettez-moi un Boursin …
Commerçant Oui … Voilà.
Guy Six œufs …
Commerçant Voilà, Monsieur.
Guy Et … quatre petits suisses aussi.
Commerçant Quatre petits suisses … Voilà, Monsieur.
Guy Merci.
Commerçant Ce sera tout, Monsieur?
Guy Oui, Monsieur.
Commerçant Oui …

quatre yaourts nature four natural/plain yoghurts. Even though the word **yaourts** is plural, it is a quirk of French grammar that **nature** (which is really a noun) never takes an **-s** when it is used as an adjective.

▶ **Voici** Here they are. You can also say, for example, **Voici les yaourts** (Here are the yoghurts) or **Voici le fromage** (Here is the cheese).

Mettez-moi Give me (literally Put me), which sounds abrupt in English but is perfectly polite in French.

▶ **Voilà** There it is. As with **Voici**, you can also say **Voilà les yaourts** or **Voilà le fromage**.

▶ **six œufs** six eggs. Notice that the **f** is not pronounced in the plural, whereas it is pronounced in **un œuf**.

petits suisses cream cheeses (often eaten with sugar). **Suisse** actually means Swiss and **la Suisse** is Switzerland.

Ce sera tout? Will that be all? You would do better to learn the simpler

- **C'est tout?** Is that all? and **C'est tout** That's all.

Buying fruit and vegetables

LISTEN FOR...

un sac de pommes de terre	a bag of potatoes
une salade	a lettuce
une livre de tomates	a pound of tomatoes
un kilo de pommes	a kilo of apples

Alain Vous pouvez me mettre un sac de pommes de terre, Monsieur, s'il vous plaît.
Commerçant Oui, Monsieur. Voici: 2,07€, s'il vous plaît.
Alain Merci. Je vais prendre une salade.
Commerçant Oui, Monsieur. 0,63€.
Alain Et puis, une livre de tomates, s'il vous plaît.
Commerçant Oui, 565 grammes, Monsieur.
Alain C'est bien. Vous laissez.
Commerçant C'est bien? 1,57€.
Alain Et puis, un kilo de pommes.
Commerçant Oui, Monsieur. Des, des pommes golden, des pommes rouges, des pommes granny?
Alain Mettez-moi les golden, s'il vous plaît.
Commerçant Les golden? 2,39€.
Alain Merci. Ça sera tout.

Vous pouvez me mettre un sac de pommes de terre You can put me a bag of potatoes.

- **une pomme** is an apple
- **une pomme de terre** (literally, an apple of earth) is a potato.
- **une salade** (*here*) a lettuce, though the word means 'salad' in phrases like **une salade de tomates** or **une salade de fruits**.
- **une livre de tomates** a pound of tomatoes. This is understood as a metric pound, i.e. 500 g, which is slightly more than an imperial pound.

Vous laissez. That's fine (literally, You leave): he does not mind having 565 grammes instead of 500.

des pommes golden ... des pommes granny Golden Delicious, Granny Smith's. Names used as adjectives do not take an **-s** in the plural.

PRACTICE

4 Here is Thierry's shopping list. Listen to the recording and see if you can write down the prices he is charged.

4 yaourts aux fruits
____
4 petits suisses
____
12 œufs
____
Un camembert
____
250 grammes de beurre
____

ANSWERS P. 108

5 Here's your shopping list for fruit and vegetables. Prepare the vocabulary (including genders) by looking at the list following the Key words and phrases on p. 106. Then turn on the recording, where Yves will play the greengrocer. Ask him for each of the items in turn, in the order in which they appear on the list. Each time, there will be a pause for you to speak, and then Yves will repeat the item as he hands it to you. Remember to use courtesy phrases like **je voudrais** and **s'il vous plaît, Monsieur**.

1 bag of potatoes
1 kilo of carrots
1 kilo of apples
1 lettuce
1 pound of tomatoes
1 pound of strawberries

CONVERSATION 

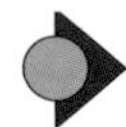

Shopping for wine

LISTEN FOR ...

- **du vin rouge** red wine
- **champagne brut** dry champagne

Alain Je voudrais du vin rouge, s'il vous plaît, pour servir avec le fromage.
Commerçante Oui, Monsieur. On a du côtes-du-roussillon, on a du bordeaux, du bourgogne, on a du côtes-du-rhône.
Alain Qu'est-ce qui serait le mieux avec le fromage?
Commerçante Un bon côtes-du-rhône?
Alain Bon, ben, je vais le prendre, s'il vous plaît.
Commerçante Voilà, Monsieur. 2,15€, s'il vous plaît.
Alain Qu'est-ce que vous avez comme champagne brut, Madame, s'il vous plaît?
Commerçante Comme champagne brut, nous avons du, du champagne de la maison Écuyer, du champagne de la maison Amarande ...
Alain Heu, je vais prendre le champagne Écuyer, s'il vous plaît.
Commerçante Oui, Monsieur. Voilà. 16,15€, s'il vous plaît, Monsieur.
Alain Merci.

- **du vin rouge pour servir avec le fromage** red wine to serve with cheese. 'White wine to serve with fish' would be
- **du vin blanc pour servir avec le poisson.**
- **On a ...** We have (literally, One has). He lists suitable wines; **du bourgogne** is burgundy. Although it seems odd to write a place-name without a capital letter, it is correct to do so when it is being used as the name of a wine.
- **Qu'est-ce qui serait le mieux avec le fromage?** Which would be the best with cheese? This is complicated to unpick grammatically – you are better just learning the whole expression **Qu'est-ce qui serait le mieux**?
- **Je vais le prendre** I'll take it (literally, I am going it to take).
- **champagne brut** dry champagne. **Brut** is used of champagne and **sec** of dry still wine. A sweet wine is
- **un vin doux.**

la maison means 'firm' as well as being the normal word for 'house'.

Champagne can be

extra brut	extremely dry
brut	dry
extra sec	dry to medium-dry
sec*	in effect, medium-sweet
demi-sec	sweet
doux	intensely sweet

* Note this confusing use of **sec**, which means 'dry' when applied to anything other than a sparkling wine!

PRACTICE

6 

On the recording, Magalie is shopping for wine for a big dinner-party and asking the wine-merchant for advice on what to serve with each course. The menu and the wine-merchant's suggestions are shown below. Can you catch which wines Magalie chooses and write down their prices per bottle?

			Price per bottle
Pâté	☐	mâcon blanc	
	☐	graves	
	☐	chablis	
Coq au vin	☐	gevrey-chambertin	
	☐	beaune	
	☐	côte-de-nuits villages	
Fromage	☐	châteauneuf-du-pape	
	☐	vacqueyras	
	☐	cahors	
Sorbet au citron		?	
Mousse au chocolat		?	

ANSWERS P. 108

1992
ROSÉ DU PRACAMIN
CÔTES DE PROVENCE
APPELLATION CÔTES DE PROVENCE CONTRÔLÉE
MIS EN BOUTEILLE A LA PROPRIETE
Sélection Rallye
PRODUCE OF FRANCE
Bergerac
Appellation Bergerac Contrôlée
1988
Union de Viticulteurs de la Dordogne
48.000 BOUTEILLES
e75cl
Mis en bouteilles par les producteurs réunis
GIGONDAS
APPELLATION GIGONDAS CONTRÔLÉE
13,5 % vol
MIS EN BOUTEILLE PAR LES CAVES DU PRÉ BEAUCAIRE FRANCE
75 cl

7

Here are advertising blurbs for four drinks. Read them through three times and then see if you can answer the questions below. The questions should actually help you understand some of the vocabulary you don't know.

Martini rosso, un goût unique, apprécié dans le monde entier. A consommer nature, sur glace ou en cocktail avec du gin, de la vodka ou allongé de tonic.

Gigondas: débouchez ce vin une heure avant de servir. Buvez-le à la température ambiante (17–18°). Il convient particulièrement aux rôtis, gigots, viandes rouges, fromages.

Muscadet de-sèvre-et-maine: ce vin blanc sec est un des plus populaires du Val de Loire. Fruité, c'est l'accompagnement idéal de tous les produits de la mer, mais aussi des hors d'œuvre et de la charcuterie.

Le savoir-faire de Laurent-Perrier permet de conserver tous les arômes primaires du raisin: un champagne reconnu pour sa finesse, son équilibre et sa régularité.

Can you find in the texts the French versions of the phrases below? Writing them out will help you commit the vocabulary to memory.

a. appreciated throughout the world (lit. in the entire world)

____

b. to be drunk on its own (*Clue*: as nature intended!)

____

c. open this wine an hour before serving

____

d. it goes particularly well with roasts (lit. it suits …)

____

e. it is the ideal accompaniment of all sea produce

____

f. a champagne renowned for its delicacy, its balance and its consistency

____

____

ANSWERS P. 108

8

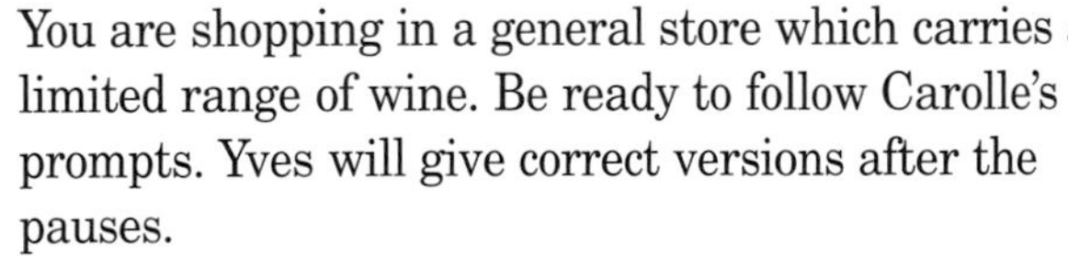

You are shopping in a general store which carries a limited range of wine. Be ready to follow Carolle's prompts. Yves will give correct versions after the pauses.

GRAMMAR AND EXERCISES

Je voudrais

Je voudrais (I'd like) is a very useful expression. It can be followed by a noun:

Je voudrais une baguette
I'd like a French stick
Je voudrais du vin rouge
I'd like some red wine

or by an infinitive:

Je voudrais manger des escargots
I'd like to eat snails

Adjectives

Adjectives describe nouns (e.g. big, green, wonderful). In French they also 'agree' with nouns; that is, they have a feminine ending if the noun is feminine and a plural ending if it is plural. As a general rule, they add an **-e** in the feminine and an **-s** in the plural, on the model:

	singular	*plural*
masculine	**petit**	**petits**
feminine	**petite**	**petites**

- Adding an **-e** often changes the pronunciation. For example, the final **t** is pronounced in **petite** whereas it is silent in **petit**. However, there are also many adjectives where the pronunciation remains the same, e.g. **noir/noire** (black), **mûr/mûre** (ripe), **seul/seule** (alone), **sucré/sucrée** (sweet).
- Adjectives which already end in an **-e** in the masculine stay the same in the feminine, e.g.

  Il est jeune/Elle est jeune
  He is young/She is young

  However, as you have seen with **sucré(e),** an adjective ending in **-é** does take an extra **-e** in the feminine.
- Adjectives which end in **-er** in the masculine end in **-ère** in the feminine, e.g. **premier/première** (first) and **cher/chère** (dear – in both senses of the word).
- Adjectives which end in **-x** in the masculine end in **-se** in the feminine, e.g. **heureux/heureuse** (happy) and **délicieux/délicieuse** (delicious).
- Adjectives which end in **-eau** in the masculine end in **-elle** in the feminine, e.g. **beau/belle** (handsome/beautiful) and **nouveau/nouvelle** (new).
- When the masculine ends in **-as**, **-os**, **-el**, **-en**, **-il** or **-on**, the feminine is formed by doubling the last consonant and adding an **-e**:

gras/grasse	greasy, plump
gros/grosse	fat, large (voluminous)
visuel/visuelle	visual
ancien/ancienne	ancient/former
gentil/gentille	nice, kind
bon/bonne	good

- To form the plural, add an **-s**. You add it to the masculine form if the noun is masculine and to the feminine form if it is feminine. (Have another look at the table with **petit**, near the top of this section.) If the word already ends in an **-s** or an **-x**, it stays the same in the plural, e.g.

Il est anglais/Ils sont anglais
He is English/They are English
Le plat est délicieux/Les plats sont délicieux
The dish is delicious/The dishes are delicious

Most adjectives follow the noun in French, e.g. **du vin blanc** (white wine), **un journal anglais** (an English newspaper), but some of the most common ones precede it, e.g. **un petit sac** (a small bag), **une grosse boîte** (a large box/tin), **un bon vin** (a good wine), **une grande bouteille** (a big bottle).

There was a lot in that Grammar section and you're not likely to be able to learn it all in one go. Read it slowly and carefully at least three times before you go on any further. The exercises will help to fix some of the forms in your mind. Thereafter, as with so many aspects of language learning, it is a question of exposure and practice until the right forms come instinctively.

9 Which of the options in the right-hand column is a possible completion of the sentence begun on the left?

a.	Je voudrais	**i.**	des pommes rouges.
		ii.	mettez-moi des pommes rouges.
b.	Je voudrais	**i.**	de carottes.
		ii.	un kilo de carottes.
c.	Je voudrais	**i.**	téléphone au Canada.
		ii.	téléphoner au Canada.
d.	Je voudrais	**i.**	parlez français.
		ii.	parler français.
e.	Je voudrais	**i.**	partir en France.
		ii.	pars en France.

ANSWERS P. 108

10 A young woman has written to a dating agency describing her ideal man:

Il est jeune (25–30 ans); il est grand, il est beau, il n'est pas gros. Il est assez intelligent et il est très gentil. Et, bien sûr, il est célibataire!

How would an identically minded man describe his ideal woman?

Elle est ______________________________

____

____

____

____

____

ANSWER P. 108

11 Here is a conversation at the greengrocer's. Can you write in the gaps the correct forms of the adjectives in the box?

mûr bon gros petit anglais français délicieux petit

Cliente	Vos tomates sont [good] ______________________?
Commerçante	Ah, elles sont [delicious] ______________________, Madame.
Cliente	Elles sont [French] ______________________?
Commerçante	Non, elles sont [English] ______________________
Cliente	Bon. Vous pouvez m'en mettre un kilo, s'il vous plaît.
Commerçante	…Voilà, Madame.
Cliente	Et puis je voudrais deux avocats [ripe] ______________________ C'est pour manger ce soir.
Commerçante	Vous voulez des [small] ______________________ ou des ['fat'] ______________________?
Cliente	Des [small] ______________________, s'il vous plaît.
Commerçante	Voilà. C'est tout?
Cliente	Oui, c'est tout. Merci, Madame.

ANSWERS P. 108

KEY WORDS AND PHRASES

Je voudrais	I'd like
une baguette	a French stick
et cinq croissants	and five croissants
Vous avez	You have
dix pour cent	ten per cent
sur les vins	off wines
le jus de fruit	fruit juice
le jus d'orange	orange juice
le pamplemousse	grapefruit
l'ananas (m.)	pineapple
Voici le fromage/les yaourts	Here is/are the cheese/the yoghurts
Voilà l'œuf/les œufs	There is/are the egg/eggs
Je vais le prendre	I'll take it
Je voudrais du vin blanc/	I'd like some white wine/
du vin rouge	some red wine
pour servir avec le fromage	to serve with cheese
Qu'est-ce qui serait le mieux	What would be best
avec le fromage?	with cheese?
On a du champagne brut	We have dry champagne
du vin sec	dry wine
Mettez-moi	Put me
un kilo de pommes (f.)	a kilo of apples
un sac de pommes de terre	a bag of potatoes
une livre de tomates (f.)	a pound of tomatoes
la salade	lettuce
la salade de fruits	fruit salad
C'est tout	That's all

D'autres fruits et légumes / Other fruit and vegetables

l'orange (f.)	orange
la poire	pear
la banane	banana
la prune	plum
la pêche	peach
la nectarine	nectarine
la framboise	raspberry
la fraise	strawberry
le raisin	grape
le melon	melon
l'avocat (m.)	avocado
la carotte	carrot
le petit pois (pl. **les petits pois**)	pea
le chou	cabbage
le chou-fleur	cauliflower
le champignon	mushroom
le haricot vert	green bean

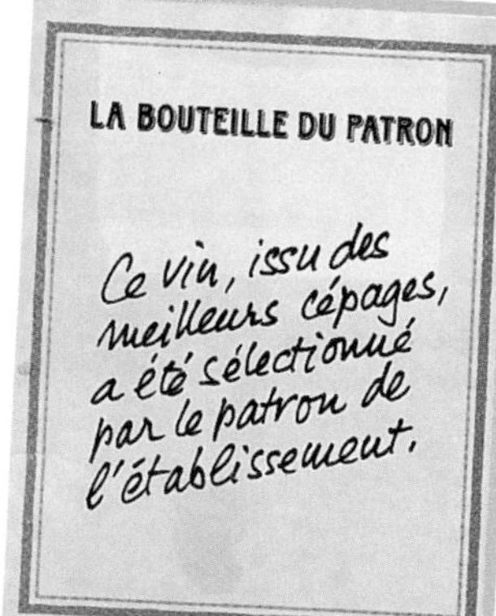

LA BOUTEILLE DU PATRON
Ce vin, issu des meilleurs cépages, a été sélectionné par le patron de l'établissement.

(The majority of words beginning with '**h**' are treated as though they began with a vowel, so that **le** and **la** become **l'** in front of them, e.g. **l'homme, l'heure. Le haricot** is one of a substantial minority which are treated as beginning with a consonant, even though the '**h**' is not actually sounded.)

8 MORE ABOUT SHOPPING

WHAT YOU WILL LEARN

- shopping for household goods
- shopping at the chemist's: explaining your ailments
- buying clothes: getting the right size
- equivalent sizes of clothes
- the names of colours

BEFORE YOU BEGIN

Faire les courses generally means 'to go shopping', but **une course** has a wider meaning something like 'errand' or 'job'; for example, it is **une course** when, in Conversations 1, Simone goes into the hairdresser's to book an appointment. (The word **course** literally means 'run' – it is something you 'run around' doing.)

This unit marks the halfway point of the course. It is an odd fact that, rather than finding this a matter for self-congratulation, people often find it a low spot in their language-learning motivation. There seems to be so much left to do and they don't feel that they are making as much progress as they were to start with: indeed, they keep forgetting the words that they learned earlier on in the course. If it is affecting you like that, take a deep breath and remember

- It is quite normal to react like this – it does not mean that you are no good at language learning.
- In the early stages of learning a language, you make rapid, linear progress because everything is new. After that, the process is more subtle because you are having to manipulate words you have already met (and may have forgotten) along with new vocabulary in more complicated structures. The progress you are making is not so obvious.
- The prescription: when you have finished this unit, dedicate the next few hours of your language-learning time to reviewing the first half of the course. You can then boost your morale by reminding yourself that, only a few units ago, you were learning to say '**Bonjour**'!

Pronunciation notes

In Exercise 7, you will practise the pronunciation of a range of sounds as you repeat the names of colours after one of the speakers on the recording.

CONVERSATIONS

Buying a stamp for England

LISTEN FOR...

- **des timbres** stamps

Alain	Est-ce que vous avez des timbres, s'il vous plaît?
Réceptionniste	Oui, Monsieur, j'ai des timbres.
Alain	Je voudrais un timbre pour l'Angleterre.
Réceptionniste	Un timbre pour l'Angleterre – à 0,46€?
Alain	Je crois, oui.
Réceptionniste	D'accord.
Alain	Merci.
Réceptionniste	Merci bien.

- **Est-ce que vous avez des timbres?** Do you have stamps? (He is asking the hotel receptionist.)

- **Un timbre pour l'Angleterre – à 0,46€?** A stamp for England – at 46 euro cents? Use **à** when giving the price of things, e.g. **une bouteille de vin à 3 euros** a bottle of wine at 3 euros.

Making a hair appointment

LISTEN FOR...

- **un rendez-vous** an appointment
- **shampooing-mise en plis** shampoo and set

Simone	Je voudrais un rendez-vous pour shampooing-mise en plis …
Coiffeuse	Oui …
Simone	… heu, vendredi après-midi si possible.
Coiffeuse	Vendredi après-midi. A quelle heure?
Simone	Heu, vers deux heures ou trois heures …
Coiffeuse	Oui, deux heures. C'est pour une mise en plis?
Simone	Oui.
Coiffeuse	Mise en plis-coupe ou …
Simone	Non, mise en plis simplement.
Coiffeuse	Mise en plis.
Simone	Shampooing et mise en plis.
Coiffeuse	Bon. Deux heures, alors, vendredi.
Simone	D'accord.
Coiffeuse	Voilà.

- **la coupe** cut
  simplement simply, only
- **un rendez-vous** an appointment. Used for any kind of appointment, not just at the hairdresser's, e.g.
  Je voudrais prendre (un) rendez-vous avec Monsieur X.
  I'd like to make an appointment with Mr X.
  J'ai (un) rendez-vous avec Madame Y. I have an appointment with Mrs Y. In both cases, the **un** is optional.

shampooing (note the pronunciation) shampoo.

- **Du shampooing** is also what you ask for when buying shampoo.
- **une mise en plis** a set. You may also need
- **un brushing** a blow-dry
- **si possible** if possible.

PRACTICE

1 On the recording for this exercise, Carolle is buying lots of stamps. Fill in the grid below with the number of each kind that she buys.

	Pour lettre	Pour carte postale
Pour la France		
Pour l'Angleterre		
Pour l'Allemagne		
Pour les États-Unis		
Pour le Canada		

ANSWERS P. 124

2 Listen to Yves making an appointment to see his dentist, Madame Lagneau.

a. When would he originally have liked the appointment?

____

b. What time, day and date do they eventually agree on?

____

ANSWERS P. 124

3 Now you make an appointment for a haircut: **pour une coupe**. Philippe will prompt you on the recording and Carolle give correct answers after the pauses.

CONVERSATIONS

Shopping for cleaning products

LISTEN FOR...

lessive	washing powder
laver à la main	to wash by hand
en machine	in a machine
la vaisselle	the washing up
Sopalin	kitchen towels

Alain	Qu'est-ce que vous avez comme lessive, Monsieur, s'il vous plaît?
Commerçant	Pour laver à la main ou pour laver en machine, Monsieur?
Alain	Pour la machine.
Commerçant	Pour la machine, nous avons du Bonux, du Persil et de l'Omo.
Alain	Mettez-moi un paquet de Persil, s'il vous plaît.
Commerçant	Un paquet de Persil? Voilà, Monsieur. 13,02€, s'il vous plaît.
Alain	Merci. Je voudrais du produit pour la vaisselle.
Commerçant	Oui. Nous avons du Soleil citron et du Paic citron.
Alain	Soleil citron.
Commerçant	Oui. Voilà, Monsieur. 1,89€.
Alain	Et mettez-moi deux rouleaux de Sopalin.
Commerçant	Voilà, Monsieur. 1,20€.

- **lessive** (f.) (*here*) washing powder. It also means 'washing' – either the process or the dirty clothes themselves. Note the expression
- **faire la lessive** to do the washing. Another useful word is
- **le savon** soap.

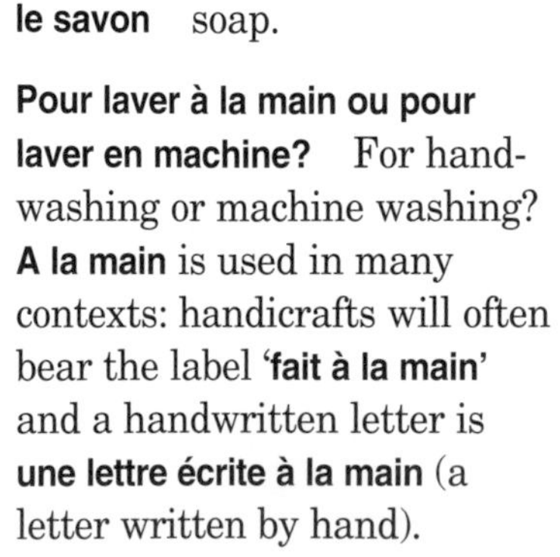

- **Pour laver à la main ou pour laver en machine?** For hand-washing or machine washing? **A la main** is used in many contexts: handicrafts will often bear the label **'fait à la main'** and a handwritten letter is **une lettre écrite à la main** (a letter written by hand).

- **du produit pour la vaisselle** washing-up liquid (literally, product for the washing up). The word **produit** is a useful one to know as it is used much more than 'product'. **La vaisselle** means either the process of washing up or the actual crockery (clean or dirty!). Note also
- **faire la vaisselle** to do the washing up, and
- **faire le ménage** to do the housework.

du Soleil citron et du Paic citron brand names of washing-up liquids, both of them lemon-scented (**citron**).

- **deux rouleaux de Sopalin** two rolls of kitchen towels. Sopalin is a trade name, but it is the word that people generally use for kitchen rolls, regardless of their make. The other piece of vocabulary that you should know in this area is
- **le papier hygiénique** toilet paper. You might ask for (**deux**) **rouleaux de papier hygiénique**.

Shopping at the chemist's

LISTEN FOR...

le mal de tête	headache
des comprimés	tablets
la diarrhée	diarrhoea
des mouchoirs en papier	paper hankies

Alain	Bonjour, Madame.
Pharmacien	Bonjour, Monsieur.
Alain	Vous avez quelque chose contre le mal de tête, s'il vous plaît?
Pharmacien	Oui, je peux vous proposer des comprimés d'aspirine.
Alain	Ah non. Non, non, je ne peux pas prendre d'aspirine.
Pharmacien	Bien. Alors, on a du paracétamol – ça existe en sachets, en comprimés ou en suppositoires.
Alain	Mettez-moi les comprimés, s'il vous plaît.
Pharmacien	Oui. Voilà. Ça fait 1,59€. Est-ce qu'il vous fallait autre chose, Monsieur?
Alain	Oui. J'ai la diarrhée depuis deux/trois jours.
Pharmacien	Oui, alors, dans ce cas-là, je peux vous donner des comprimés renfermant des levures et du charbon – et cela marche très bien.
Alain	D'accord.
Pharmacien	Voilà. Donc, 4,32€.
Alain	Merci.
Pharmacien	Autre chose, Monsieur?
Alain	Oui, des mouchoirs en papier, s'il vous plaît.
Pharmacien	Voilà. 1,24€, s'il vous plaît ... Autre chose, Monsieur?
Alain	Non, c'est tout, Madame, merci.

le paracétamol paracetamol

- **donner** to give

- **Vous avez quelque chose contre le mal de tête?** Do you have something for headaches? (literally, You have something against the pain of head?) You should also learn
- **j'ai mal** I have a pain
- **j'ai ...** I have ...

mal à la tête	a headache
mal au dos	backache
mal à la gorge	a sore throat
mal à l'oreille	earache
mal aux dents	toothache
mal au ventre	tummy-ache

The trick one is

- **j'ai mal au cœur.** As **cœur** means 'heart', you would expect this to have something to do with angina, but it actually means 'I feel sick'.

je peux vous proposer des comprimés d'aspirine I can offer you aspirin tablets.

- **je ne peux pas prendre d'aspirine** I can't take aspirin.

- **ça existe en sachets, en comprimés ou en suppositoires** that exists in sachets (i.e. powder form), in tablet form or in suppository form. The French make far more use than we do of suppositories – so be careful what you swallow!

Est-ce qu'il vous fallait autre chose? Did you need anything else? **Il fallait** is the imperfect (past) tense of **il faut** (it is necessary). You do not need to use it yourself yet.

- **J'ai la diarrhée depuis deux/trois jours** I have had diarrhoea for two or three days (literally, I have diarrhoea since two/three days. See p. 22 for the **depuis** construction.)

dans ce cas-là in that case (literally, in that case there).

renfermant des levures et du charbon containing yeast and charcoal.

- **cela marche très bien** it works very well. You can use this expression in all sorts of contexts.
- **des mouchoirs en papier** paper handkerchiefs. As with **Sopalin**, you will often hear these called **des Kleenex**.

PRACTICE

Here is a list of some of the shops in the village of Le Grand-Bornand.

AU GRAND-BORNAND VILLAGE

BOUCHERIE - CHARCUTERIES
Charc. Traiteur Le Palais Savoyard ... 04 50 02 24 71
Perrillat Martial ... 04 50 02 20 62

BOULANGERIES - PATISSERIES
Bétemps ... 04 50 02 20 03
Vulliet ... 04 50 02 20 71

BOUTIQUES VETEMENTS
Clin d'Oeil ... 04 50 02 20 25
Kiki H ... 04 50 02 34 30
Snow in ... 04 50 02 37 23

CHAUSSURES - PEAUX
Perrillat J-Claude ... 04 50 02 20 25

CLES MINUTES
"Trouvailles" ... 04 50 02 24 98

COIFFURE
Andrée Coiffure ... 04 50 02 21 50
Tif-Tif Coiffure (unisexe) ... 04 50 02 38 10

DECORATION - CADEAUX
Fleurine ... 04 50 02 34 88
Passionnément ... 04 50 02 25 62

ELECTRO-MENAGER
Télé Recour ... 04 50 02 21 09

GARAGES
Alparavis ... 04 50 02 21 09
Missillier (Station BP) ... 04 50 02 20 01

HORLOGERIE - BIJOUTERIE
SUIZE C. ... 04 50 02 20 01

LAVERIE AUTOMATIQUE
Le Delta ... 04 50 02 26 25

LOCATION DE TELEVISIONS
Perrillat Photos ... 04 50 02 26 49
Télé Recour ... 04 50 02 21 09

MAGASINS DE SPORTS
Antonin Sports ... 04 50 02 20 54
La Randonnée ... 04 50 02 21 62
Ski 3 ... 04 50 02 35 61
Sport Alp ... 04 50 02 26 26
Sport Neige ... 04 50 02 33 79

PHOTO
Perrillat Photo ... 04 50 02 20 49
Studio "Images" (Loto) ... 04 50 02 71 56

PRESSE
Perrillat-Collomb R ... 04 50 02 20 28
"Trouvailles" (Loto) ... 04 50 02 24 98

SOUVENIR - CADEAUX CARTERIE - LIBRAIRIE
Perrillat Photo ... 04 50 02 20 49
"Trouvailles" ... 04 50 02 24 98
Librairie-Carterie (pl de l'église) ... 04 50 02 36 18

SUPERMARCHE
Superm. Bastard 8 à Huit ... 04 50 02 20 10

TABAC
Perrillat-Collomb Régis ... 04 50 02 20 28

Can you find the French words for:

a. Sports shops

b. Hairdressing

c. Laundrette

d. Card shop–bookshop

e. Electrical household equipment

f. Television rental

ANSWERS P. 124

5 You are shopping for toilet paper, paper towels, washing-up liquid and soap powder. Follow Philippe's prompts on the recording. Carolle will give a correct version after the pauses.

6 Carolle's children are both under the weather. On the recording, she tells the pharmacist **Mes enfants sont malades** (My children are ill). She goes on to explain what is wrong with each of them. Just as **J'ai mal** means 'I have a pain', **Il a mal** and **Elle a mal** mean 'He has a pain' and 'She has a pain'. See if you can note down the children's ages and symptoms.

Daughter ____

Son ____

New word: **pastilles**, the meaning of which is not hard to guess when you see it written down. The final **-lles** is pronounced '-y' (roughly as in 'yacht').

ANSWERS P. 124

CONVERSATION

Buying a sweater

LISTEN FOR...

▶ **un pull**	a sweater (pullover)
▶ **taille**	(*here*) size
▶ **marine**	navy
▶ **trop petit**	too small
▶ **essayer**	to try (on)
▶ **bleu**	blue
▶ **plus grand**	bigger
▶ **trop grand**	too big
▶ **je préfère**	I prefer

Juliette Bonjour, Madame. J'aurais voulu un ... un pull, s'il vous plaît.
Vendeuse Qu'est-ce que vous faites comme taille?
Juliette 40 ... 40/42, enfin, ça dépend de ... de la coupe.
Vendeuse Oui. Alors, j'ai plusieurs modèles, heu, comme ça, marine avec une encolure blanche ...
Juliette Oui. Ça, ça va être trop petit pour moi.
Vendeuse On a ça, en blanc avec des grosses côtes.
Juliette Hm hm. C'est le pull de tennis, ça?
Vendeuse Oui.
Juliette D'accord. Je vais essayer.
Vendeuse Oui.

A minute later:

Juliette Je crois que c'est la bonne taille, oui ... je peux essayer le bleu?
Vendeuse Oui.
Juliette Oui?

A minute later:

Juliette Non, je crois que le ... le bleu est plus grand, hein? Il est trop grand, là.
Vendeuse Il est plus grand que le blanc, hein?
Juliette Oui, oui. Oui, c'est trop grand. Je crois que je préfère le blanc. Il vaut combien?
Vendeuse 36 euros.
Juliette Je peux vous régler par chèque?
Vendeuse Oui, bien sûr.
Juliette D'accord.

le modèle style
l'encolure (f.) neck (of a garment)
▶ **blanche** (f.) white
▶ **en blanc** in white

j'aurais voulu is a more tentative version of **je voudrais.**

Qu'est-ce que vous faites comme taille? What size are you? (literally, What do you make in the way of size?) See p. 123 for clothes sizes.

▶ **enfin, ça dépend de la coupe** well, that depends on the cut.

Ça, ça va être trop petit pour moi That one's going to be too small for me. Learn the simpler

▶ **Ça, c'est trop petit pour moi** That one's too small for me. (The extra **ça** at the beginning adds some emphasis to 'that one', but you can just say **C'est trop petit pour moi.**)

avec des grosses côtes with wide ribbing (the pattern in which it is knitted).

▶ **Je vais essayer** I'm going to try (it on). Learn also

▶ **Je peux essayer?** May I try it on?

▶ **la bonne taille** the right size.

▶ **plus grand** bigger (literally, more big).

▶ **trop grand** too big.

▶ **Il est plus grand que le blanc** It is bigger than the white (one).

▶ **je préfère** I prefer. From the verb **préférer.**

Il vaut combien? How much is it? (literally, It is worth how much?)

Je peux vous régler par chèque? Can I pay you by cheque?

PRACTICE

7

Here are the names of the commonest colours. Where the feminine form is written differently, the additional ending is given in brackets. The list is read out on the recording both as a pronunciation exercise and to help you learn the colour names by heart. There are only three colours in the list where the feminine form is actually pronounced differently. They are **blanche**, **verte** and **violette.** As an **aide-mémoire**, Carolle will say just those three forms, while Yves reads the rest of the list.

Les couleurs	Colours
noir(e)	black
blanc(he)	white
marron	brown
rouge	red
orange	orange
jaune	yellow
vert(e)	green
bleu(e)	blue
bleu marine	navy blue

violet(te)	violet
rose	pink
beige	beige
crème	cream
foncé e.g. **bleu foncé**	dark/dark blue
clair e.g. **bleu clair**	light/light blue

8

Imagine that this photograph (a stained glass window of St Louis, patron saint of France) is to be used as the basis for a painting-by-numbers kit. Can you write in the French names for each of the colours marked?

a. ______________

b. ______________

c. ______________

d. ______________

e. ______________

f. ______________

ANSWERS P. 124

g. ______________

9

You are shopping for a jacket: **une veste**. You will hear the shop assistant on the recording ask

Je peux vous aider? Can I help you?

In your reply, you will need to use the new verb **chercher** (to look for):

Je cherche une veste. I'm looking for a jacket.

GRAMMAR AND EXERCISES

Trop grand/plus grand

Make sure you have got clear in your mind the difference between
trop grand too big, and
plus grand bigger
To say that one thing is bigger/smaller, etc. than something else, use **plus ... que**:
Le bleu est plus grand que le blanc
The blue is bigger than the white
Le blanc est plus cher que le bleu
The white is more expensive than the blue

Ce, cet, cette, ces

Ce, cet, cette and **ces** all mean 'this' or 'that'.

- **Ce** is used with most masculine singular nouns, e.g. **ce pull** (this sweater), **ce médicament** (this medicine).
- **Cet** is used before a masculine singular noun which begins with a vowel sound: **cet enfant** (this child), **cet homme** (this man), **cet hôtel** (this hotel). Remember that most words beginning with an **h** are counted as beginning with a vowel sound.
- **Cette** (which sounds the same as **cet**) is used before any feminine singular noun, e.g. **cette pharmacie** (this chemist's shop), **cette aspirine** (this aspirin).
- **Ces** is the plural, i.e. 'these' or 'those', whether the noun is masculine or feminine: **ces mouchoirs** (these handkerchiefs), **ces dames** (these ladies).

The verb *pouvoir*

Je peux can be translated 'I can', 'I may' or 'I am able'. It is followed by an infinitive, e.g. **Je peux vous aider?** (Can I help you?)

je peux	**nous pouvons**
tu peux	**vous pouvez**
il/elle peut	**ils/elles peuvent**

To translate 'Can I...?' or 'May I...?', you can say either **Est-ce que je peux...?** or **Puis-je...?**

The verb *savoir*

The verb **savoir** means to know (a fact) or to know how to (do something). Examples: **Je sais que vous aimez les vins secs** (I know that you like dry wines), **Elle sait choisir les vins** (She knows how to choose wines). It follows a very similar pattern to **pouvoir**:

je sais	**nous savons**
tu sais	**vous savez**
il/elle sait	**ils/elles savent**

The verb *connaître*

Connaître is the other verb 'to know', used of knowing a person or a place, e.g. **Je connais votre père** (I know your father), **Je connais Marseille** (I know Marseilles).

je connais	**nous connaissons**
tu connais	**vous connaissez**
il/elle connaît	**ils/elles connaissent**

10 Can you pair up these half-sentences appropriately?

New words: **La chaussette** (sock) and **la chemise** (shirt).

a. C'est trop grand	i. trop petite pour moi
b. Le pull blanc est plus grand	ii. trop petites
c. Ces chaussettes sont	iii. que la blanche
d. Cette chemise est	iv. que le noir
e. Le pull jaune est plus	v. petit que le vert
f. La chemise rose est plus grande	vi. pour moi

ANSWERS P. 124

11

Put **ce**, **cet**, **cette** or **ces**, as appropriate, in each of the gaps below. The genders are all given, but remember that **ces** is used in the plural whether the word is masculine or feminine.

a. ______________ chemise (f.)

b. ______________ comprimé (m.)

c. ______________ chaussettes (f.)

d. ______________ veste (f.)

e. ______________ mal de tête (m.)

f. ______________ taille (f.)

g. ______________ mouchoir (m.)

h. ______________ produits (m.)

i. ______________ nom (m.)

j. ______________ adresse (f.)

k. ______________ hôtel (m.)

l. ______________ ascenseur (m.)

ANSWERS P. 124

12

Fill in the gaps with the correct words from the box. Be warned that not all the words will be needed!

partons	**partir**	**peuvent**	**aidez**	**aider**
peut	**peux**	**pouvez**	**pouvoir**	

a. ______________ -vous me mettre sept roses rouges, s'il vous plaît?

b. Ils ne ______________ pas venir ce soir.

c. Vous pouvez m' ______________ ?

d. Je ne ______________ pas venir au cinéma samedi.

e. Nous pouvons ______________ en vacances le 5 juillet.

f. Alain ne ______________ pas prendre d'aspirine.

ANSWERS P. 124

13

Fill in the appropriate parts of **savoir** or **connaître**:

a. *Georges* Quelle heure est-il?

Jean Je ne ______________ pas.

b. *Annie* Est-ce que tu ______________ ma sœur?

Jeanne Oui, bien sûr, je ______________ ta sœur et tes parents.

c. *Julien* Est-ce que ton frère ______________ mes parents?

Jean Je ne ______________ pas, mais je ______________ qu'il ______________ ta sœur.

d. *Isabelle* Mes parents ne ______________ pas que je suis ici. Est-ce que je peux téléphoner à la maison?

Pierre Bien sûr. Tu ______________ où le téléphone se trouve.

e. *Henri* Est-ce que vous ______________ Paris?

Patricia Oui, bien sûr, nous ______________ très bien Paris depuis vingt ans.

ANSWERS P. 124

KEY WORDS AND PHRASES

un timbre à 0,46€	a stamp at 46 euro cents
Qu'est-ce que vous avez comme lessive?	What have you got in the way of washing powder?
faire la lessive	to do the washing
pour laver à la main ou pour laver en machine?	for hand-washing or machine washing?
faire la vaisselle	to do the washing up
Je voudrais	I'd like
du produit pour la vaisselle	washing-up liquid
deux rouleaux de Sopalin	two rolls of kitchen towels
du papier hygiénique	some toilet paper
du savon	some soap
du shampooing	some shampoo
Vous avez quelque chose contre le mal de tête?	Have you got something for headaches?
J'ai mal	I have a pain
J'ai ...	I have ...
mal à la tête	a headache
mal au dos	backache
mal à la gorge	a sore throat
mal à l'oreille	earache
mal aux dents	toothache
J'ai mal au cœur	I feel sick
Je ne peux pas prendre d'aspirine	I can't take aspirin
Ça existe en sachets, en comprimés ou en suppositoires	It exists in sachets, in tablet form or in suppository form
J'ai la diarrhée depuis deux/trois jours	I have (had) diarrhoea for two or three days
Cela marche très bien	It works very well
des mouchoirs en papier (m.)	paper handkerchiefs
Je voudrais un rendez-vous	I'd like an appointment
Vendredi après-midi si possible	Friday afternoon if possible
le shampooing	shampoo
la coupe	cut
la mise en plis	set
le brushing	blow-dry
Le pull marine est trop petit pour moi	The navy sweater is too small for me
Je peux essayer le blanc?	May I try on the white (one)?
Il est plus grand que le bleu	It is bigger than the blue (one)
Je vais essayer le vert	I'm going to try the green (one)
C'est trop grand	It's too big
Je préfère le blanc	I prefer the white (one)
C'est la bonne taille	It's the right size

The names of colours (pp. 118–119) are also key language for this unit.

DID YOU KNOW?

The chemist's

The word **pharmacie** is usually displayed prominently outside a chemist's shop, often along with a green cross. The pharmacist (**le pharmacien**) will be able to advise you on minor ailments. A French **pharmacie** normally sells medicines and medicated beauty products only. For films and development you have to go to a photographic shop, usually called simply **photo**. For perfumes and cosmetics you should go to a **parfumerie** or a department store (**un grand magasin**). Of course, a hypermarket (**un hypermarché**) will also sell films and cosmetics.

Post offices

Post offices (**bureaux de poste**) are open from 8 a.m. to 7 p.m. on weekdays and 8 a.m. to 12 noon on Saturdays. In small towns and villages, they usually close at lunch-time. Letter-boxes are yellow in France and Switzerland and red in Belgium. At the post office, use the slot marked **étranger** (abroad) for your mail home.

Clothes

Here are the names of a range of garments. Unless you have an exceptionally good memory, you are not likely to retain them all now, but you can refer back to this page when you need them.

VETEMENTS	**CLOTHES**
la chaussure	shoe
la chaussette	sock
le bas	stocking
le collant	pair of tights
le pantalon	pair of trousers
le jean	pair of jeans
le short	pair of shorts
le slip	pair of pants
la jupe	skirt
le jupon	petticoat
le soutien-gorge	bra
la chemise	(man's) shirt
le chemisier	(woman's) shirt
la robe	dress
le foulard	scarf
la cravate	tie
la ceinture	belt
la veste	jacket
le manteau	coat
l'imperméable (m.)	raincoat

Here are some approximately equivalent sizes for clothes:

Men's clothes									
GB/US	36	38	40	42	44	46	48 04 50		
France	46	48 04 50		52	54	56	58	60	
Men's shirts									
GB/US	14	14½	15	15½	16	16½	17		
France	36	37	38	39	40	41	42		
Women's clothes									
GB	8	10	12	14	16	18	20	22	24
US	6	8	10	12	14	16	18	20	22
France	36	38	40	42	44	46	48 04 50		52
Measurements									
Inches	32	34	36	38	40	42	44	46	48
Centimetres	80	85	90	95	100	105	110	115	120

AND FINALLY...

14 You are shopping at the chemist's. Follow Philippe's prompts on the recording. Carolle will give correct versions after the pauses.

ANSWERS

EXERCISE 1

	Pour lettre	Pour carte postale
Pour la France	2	8
Pour l'Angleterre	5	
Pour l'Allemagne		2
Pour les États-Unis	3	
Pour le Canada		1

EXERCISE 2

(a) Tuesday morning **(b)** 15.45, Thursday 21 August

EXERCISE 4

(a) Magasins de sports **(b)** Coiffure **(c)** Laverie automatique **(d)** Carterie-Librairie **(e)** Électro-ménager **(f)** Location de télévisions

EXERCISE 6

Carolle's daughter is six. She has a sore throat and a headache.
The son is eight. He has diarrhoea and feels sick.

EXERCISE 8

(a) noir **(b)** marron **(c)** jaune **(d)** rouge **(e)** blanc **(f)** bleu **(g)** vert

EXERCISE 10

(a) vi **(b)** iv **(c)** ii (**chaussettes** are plural, so **petites** has to end in an **-s**) **(d)** i **(e)** v **(f)** iii

EXERCISE 11

(a) cette chemise **(b)** ce comprimé **(c)** ces chaussettes **(d)** cette veste **(e)** ce mal de tête **(f)** cette taille **(g)** ce mouchoir **(h)** ces produits **(i)** ce nom **(j)** cette adresse **(k)** cet hôtel (because **hôtel** begins with a vowel sound) **(l)** cet ascenseur

EXERCISE 12

(a) pouvez **(b)** peuvent **(c)** aider (**aider** and **aidez** sound exactly the same, but **aider** is the spelling of the infinitive, and **Vous pouvez** has to be followed by an infinitive.) **(d)** peux **(e)** partir **(f)** peut

EXERCISE 13

(Remember that parts of **savoir** are used when it is a question of knowing a fact or knowing how to do something, but parts of **connaître** when 'knowing' means being acquainted with a person or a place.)

(a) sais **(b)** connais/connais **(c)** connaît/sais/sais/connaît **(d)** savent/sais **(e)** connaissez/connaissons

9 MAKING TRAVEL ARRANGEMENTS

WHAT YOU WILL LEARN

- asking for and understanding travel information
- buying rail and air tickets
- booking seats, couchettes and sleepers
- hiring a car
- understanding train timetables and travel brochures
- something about rail travel in France

BEFORE YOU BEGIN

Working through this unit should make you competent to sort out your own travel arrangements in French. It will also build up your confidence at tackling written texts where you don't understand every word. In most cases, when you are reading the kind of texts that appear in this unit – tourist brochures and car-hire information – you are reading for a purpose: to find out how much things cost and what is included in the price, for example. To do that, you don't necessarily have to understand every bit of the text. What you do need is the will not to be frightened off by the words you don't know. A very good tip is to read things through three times before you reach for the dictionary. Try it – you will be surprised how much more you understand the third time through.

Pronunciation notes

Exercise 1 of this unit will give you practice at pronouncing two of the nasal vowels:

- the one usually written **on** (sometimes **om**), which appears in such words as
  avons, **ont**, **réservation** and **nom**, and
- the one written **en** or **an**, which you have met in words such as **enfant** and **prendre**.

CONVERSATIONS

Buying a train ticket to Soulac

LISTEN FOR...

▶ **un aller** a single

Robert	Alors, pour moi un aller Soulac pour demain.
Employé	Souillac?
Robert	Soulac. Soulac en Gironde.
Employé	(*looking up the fare*) Soulac ... Soulac.
Robert	Il y a bien une gare.
Employé	Soulac-sur-Mer?
Robert	Oui – c'est ça.
Employé	Pas de réduction, Monsieur?
Robert	Pas de réduction, mais avec une réservation. On peut prendre une réservation jusqu'à Bordeaux?
Employé	Oui.

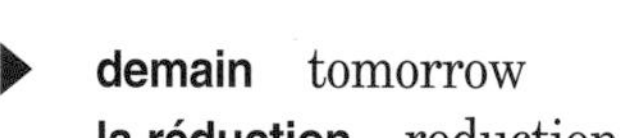

▶ **demain** tomorrow
la réduction reduction
▶ **la réservation** reservation

▶ **un aller Soulac** a single (to) Soulac. In full, this would be
▶ **un aller simple pour Soulac.** A return ticket is
▶ **un aller et retour** (a there and back ticket).

Souillac? He mishears the name.

Gironde the **département** around Bordeaux.

Il y a bien une gare There *is* a station.

Soulac-sur-Mer? Soulac-on-Sea?

Pas de réduction? No reduction? Many French people have a right to reduced fares on account of disability or military service or because they have a rail card.

On peut prendre une réservation jusqu'à Bordeaux? Can one take a reservation as far as Bordeaux (where he will change trains)? The reservation is for **une place assise** (literally, a seated place). On some longer journeys – and on ferries – it may also be possible to book **un siège inclinable** (a reclining seat).

Booking a couchette

LISTEN FOR...

▶ **billet**	ticket
▶ **couchette**	couchette!
supérieure, inférieure	upper, lower
▶ **en haut**	at the top
▶ **compartiments**	compartments
▶ **non-fumeurs**	no smoking

Sauf le dimanche !!

Robert Je prends le train demain soir pour Nice.
Employé Je peux vous faire votre billet et votre réservation couchette en même temps.
Robert Oh, mais c'est très bien.
Employé Une couchette de deuxième classe?
Robert Oui, oui, oui, en deuxième classe.
Employé Bien. Supérieure, inférieure – vous avez une préférence?
Robert Ah – je préfère être en haut.
Employé Vous préférez être en haut. Bien.
Robert Bien. Dans les couchettes, ce sont des compartiments non-fumeurs, j'espère?
Employé Toujours non-fumeurs.
Robert Ah, c'est très bien.

- **la préférence** preference
- **j'espère** (from **espérer**) I hope
- **toujours** (*here*) always

Je peux vous faire votre billet et votre réservation couchette en même temps
I can do your ticket and your couchette reservation for you at the same time. You are more likely to need to be able to ask

- **Pouvez-vous faire les billets et les réservations en même temps?**

- **en deuxième classe** in second class. 'In first class' is
- **en première classe.**

- **Supérieure, inférieure** upper, lower. The adjectives are feminine (they end with an '**-e**') because they refer to **une couchette**.

- **en haut** on the top. Notice the pronunciation. 'On the bottom' is
- **en bas** (The '**s**' is not pronounced.)

ce sont they are – the plural of **c'est** (it is).

PRACTICE

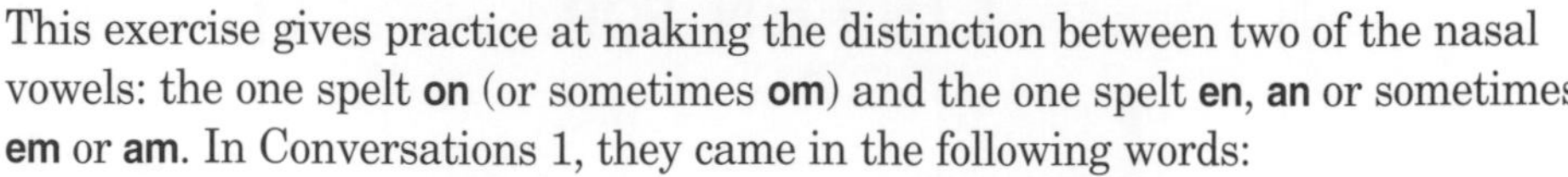

1

This exercise gives practice at making the distinction between two of the nasal vowels: the one spelt **on** (or sometimes **om**) and the one spelt **en**, **an** or sometimes **em** or **am**. In Conversations 1, they came in the following words:

on/om	***en/an*** (*also spelt* **em/am**)
Gir*on*de	**pr*en*dre**
réservati*on*	**t*em*ps**
s*on*t	**préfér*en*ce**
n*on*-fumeurs	***en* haut**

On the recording for this exercise, Yves and Carolle read this list through twice. Just listen to them the first time, concentrating on the difference between these two sounds. Then, when they start the list again, repeat the words after them.

2

ANSWERS P. 140

On the recording, Magalie is booking a train ticket.

a. Is she booking a single or a return? ________

b. On which day will she be travelling? ________

c. Is she entitled to a reduction? ________

d. Will she be travelling first or second class? ________

e. Does she ask for a smoking or a non-smoking compartment? ________

f. Where will she have to change trains? ________

3

Now you try booking a single to Saint-Omer. Philippe will prompt you and Yves will give correct versions after the pauses on the recording.

CONVERSATIONS

 *Finding out travel options*

LISTEN FOR...

▶ **possibilités**	possibilities, options
▶ **l'avion**	aeroplane
▶ **au départ de Lille**	departing from Lille

Alain	Madame, je voudrais me rendre à Marseille. Qu'est-ce qu'il y a comme possibilités?
Agent de voyages	Vous avez donc deux possibilités: le train ou l'avion. Oui alors, au départ de Lille, par avion, vous avez un tarif aller simple à 152 euros. Par le train, aller simple Lille–Marseille, seconde classe, 75 euros.
Alain	D'accord … Je préfère prendre le train de nuit.
Agent de voyages	Oui. Vous avez deux possibilités: la couchette, à 14 euros ...
Alain	Oui
Agent de voyages	... ou le wagon-lit, à 65 euros.
Alain	Heu, ben, je vais prendre un wagon-lit.
Agent de voyages	Parfait.

▶ **parfait** perfect

je voudrais me rendre à Marseille I'd like to go to Marseilles (literally, to get myself to). You can just as well use the simpler

▶ **je voudrais aller à Marseille.**
'Marseilles' ends in an 's' in English but not in French.

▶ **Agent de voyages** travel agent, who works in

▶ **une agence de voyages** a travel agency.

▶ **Qu'est-ce qu'il y a comme possibilités?** What options are there? (literally, What are there in the way of possibilities?)

▶ **par avion** by plane. It is also, of course, what you write on the envelope of an airmail letter.

vous avez un tarif aller simple you have a single fare.

seconde classe is the same as **deuxième classe.**

▶ **Je préfère prendre le train de nuit** I prefer to take the night train.

Hiring a car

LISTEN FOR...

- **louer une voiture** to hire a car
- **kilométrage illimité** unlimited 'mileage'

Alain	Je voudrais louer une voiture au départ de la gare de Marseille.
Agent de voyages	Oui. Quel type de voiture?
Alain	Oh, un petit modèle.
Agent de voyages	Oui, et pour combien de temps?
Alain	Une semaine.
Agent de voyages	Nous avons donc un tarif à 510 euros, kilométrage illimité.
Alain	C'est parfait.
Agent de voyages	Bien – je vous fais la réservation. (*Picks up phone*)

- **Je voudrais louer une voiture** I'd like to hire a car. Learn also
- **louer un vélo** to hire a bicycle, and
- **la location** hire.
- **Une voiture de location** is a hired car.

PRACTICE

4 On p. 131 is a sample SNCF timetable. There are plenty of words you won't know, but see if you can work out the following information for a friend's trip from Paris-Gare-de-Lyon to Milano Centrale:

a. Will the 20.12 run on Sunday 30 August?

____

b. If your friend takes the 20.12, at what time should he reach Milano Centrale?

____

c. At which other Milan station will he have to change?

____

d. Does one have to pay a supplement to travel on this train?

____

e. Does it have both first and second class carriages?

____

f. What categories of sleeping accommodation are available on it?

____

ANSWERS P. 140

EXEMPLE FICTIF

Paris – Milan						T.A.A.		821km
(Paris – Gare-de-Lyon – Milano-Centrale)								954 km via Turin
Les trains circulent	Départ ↓	Arrivée ↓	Changement		Nº	Type	Places	Services offerts
• tous les jours	10.47	20.45			941	TGV	R1.2	EA
			Aix-les-B.	13.49/14.04	417		R1.2	
			Torino-P-N	17.20/19.10	663	★	1.2	
• du 19 juin au 29 août 03: tous les jours	15.05	23.00			849	TGV	R1.2	★
			Lyon-Part-D	17.05/17.14	218	★	R1.2	
• Jusqu'au 5 juil. 03: les sam; PB • du 8 juil. au 30 août 03: les mar et sam; • les 6, 13 et 20 sept 03	19.25	06.27	MG		1325		R	T2 Sp
• tous les jours	20.09	04.53	MG		227		R	
• du 26 juin au 6 sept 03: tous les jours	20.12	05.11	ML		1127		R1.2	T2 Sp
• tous les jours	20.56	08.52	MG		211		R1.2	
			Torino-P-N	06.10/07.20	649•(1)		★	1.2

(1) Train étranger.

MG Milano-Porta Garibaldi
ML Milano-Lambrate
PB Paris-Bercy

649 MANIN

Gares de correspondance avec les heures d'arrivée et de départ

Type de train

- TGV Resa TGV. Réservation obligatoire
- IC Intercités
- EC EuroCity
- • Train dénommé (se reporter en bas du tableau de la relation)
- ★ Train à supplément
- # Train à supplément modulé

Type de places

- 1.2 Places assises de 1re et 2e classes
- 1 Places assises de 1re classe
- 2 Places assises de 2e classe
- R Réservation recommandée

Services offerts

- EA Resa Euraffaires. Réservation obligatoire en 1re classe
- Places semi-allongées «Cabine 8»
- Sièges à dossier inclinable
- Couchettes
- T 3 Voiture-lit Touriste 3 (3 lits, 2e classe)
- T 2 Voiture-lit Touriste 2 (1 ou 2 lits, 2e classe)
- D Voiture-lit Double (2 lits, 1re classe)
- Sp Voiture-lit Spécial (1 lit, 1re classe)
- S Voiture-lit Single (1 lit, 1re classe)
- Voiture-lit toutes places
- Voiture restaurant
- Libre-service Gril-Express
- Repas à la place
- Bar
- Vente ambulante
- Train famille
- Facilité pour personnes à mobilité réduite
- Train acheminant gratuitement les vélos en bagages à main

5 You are in a travel agency in Paris enquiring about how to get to Copenhagen (**Copenhague**). Follow Philippe's prompts on the recording, reusing as much of the language from the conversations as you can. Carolle will give a correct version of each of your lines after you have had a chance to speak. To help you:

- 'How long does it take?' is **Ça prend combien de temps?**

Here is a tariff for car-hire on Jersey and Guernsey.

VOUS VOULEZ CONDUIRE A L'ANGLAISE

Pour tous vos séjours à Jersey ou Guernsey, nous pouvons vous proposer des locations de voitures.

Mais attention:

- *N'oubliez pas votre permis de conduire*
- *Age minimum: 20 ans*
- *Age maximum: 80 ans*
- *Permis de conduire de plus d'un an*
- *Conduisez à gauche*

TARIF par jour (Ce tarif comprend: kilométrage illimité et assurance)

	Du 15.03 au 23.04	Du 24.04 au 01.10	Du 02.10 au 15.11
Catégorie A Journée suppl.	33,00 24,00	37,00 27,00	35,00 25,00
Catégorie B Journée suppl.	35,00 27,00	39,00 31,00	37,00 29,00
Catégorie G Mini-bus Journée suppl.	63,00 53,00	69,00 59,00	69,00 59,00

In the recording for this exercise, Carolle is booking a car for her holiday there. Using both the recording and the printed information, see if you can note down:

a. which category of car Carolle books __________

b. for how many days she wants it __________

c. what the starting date will be __________

d. what the total price will be __________

e. the French word for 'insurance' __________

f. for how long you have to have held a driving licence (**un permis de conduire**) __________

ANSWERS P. 140

CONVERSATIONS

Tickets, platform numbers and train times

LISTEN FOR...

Nantes	place-name
▶ **quel quai?**	which platform?
revenir	to come back

Marie-Pierre	Un aller Nantes, s'il vous plaît.
Employé	Oui, voilà; vingt-quatre, s'il vous plaît.
Marie-Pierre	C'est sur quel quai?
Employé	Alors, quai numéro 2, 12h21.
Marie-Pierre	Est-ce que vous pouvez me dire les horaires pour revenir de Nantes ce soir?
Employé	Ce soir, alors vous avez un départ à 17h34.
Marie-Pierre	Oui. Merci.

vingt-quatre **euros** is understood

▶ **quel quai?** which platform? She might equally well have asked

▶ **quelle voie?** which track? Like other adjectives, **quel** (which ...?, what ...?) has different endings for

	singular	*plural*
the masculine:	**quel**	**quels**
the feminine:	**quelle**	**quelles**

but the good news is that they all sound exactly the same!

▶ **Est-ce que vous pouvez me dire les horaires pour revenir de Nantes ce soir?**
Can you tell me the times for coming back from Nantes this evening?

Booking a plane ticket to New York

LISTEN FOR...

souhaitez-vous?	do you wish?
un minimum de séjour	a minimum stay

Alain	Madame, je voudrais me rendre à New York.
Agent de voyages	Oui, Monsieur. A quelle date souhaitez-vous partir?
Alain	Heu, je prendrai l'avion le 8 mars pour rentrer le 15 mars.
Agent	Oui, donc le 8, 9, 10, 11, 12, 13, 14, 15 ... C'est parfait: nous avons un tarif avec un minimum de séjour de sept jours sur place à 536 euros aller et retour.
Alain	Bon, ben, faites-moi un Paris–New York, s'il vous plaît.
Agent	D'accord, Monsieur.

souhaitez-vous partir? do you wish to leave? From the verb **souhaiter**.

je prendrai I shall take. We shall be covering the future tense later in the course.

▶ **rentrer** come back. The word often has an implication of homecoming.

le 8, 9, 10, 11, 12, 13, 14, 15 She is counting the number of days, to see if he is eligible for a special fare.

un minimum de séjour de sept jours sur place a minimum (of) stay of seven days there.

▶ **faites-moi** do (for) me.

PRACTICE

7

ANSWERS P. 140

The station announcement for Marie-Pierre's train would have been something like **Départ à destination de Nantes: 12h21, quai numéro 2.** Listen to the series of station announcements on the recording for this exercise and pick out the time and platform of the trains to:

	time	and	platform
a. Toulouse	____________		____________
b. Nantes	____________		____________
c. Angoulême	____________		____________
d. Poitiers	____________		____________
e. Clermont-Ferrand	____________		____________
f. Paris-Austerlitz	____________		____________

8 You are booking a flight to Edinburgh (**Édimbourg**). Follow Philippe's prompts on the recording. Carolle will back you up.

9 The unit has so far covered trains, hire-cars and planes … boats must be next! Below is a brochure from the company **Les Vedettes de Bréhat**. Their boats (**vedettes**) ply between the north coast of Brittany and the island of Bréhat, ten minutes out to sea. They also offer inland cruises (**croisières**) up the River Trieux. Read the brochure through three times – and don't let yourself be fazed by the words you don't know. Then see if you can answer the following questions:

a. How many seats are there on each of the boats? ______________

b. How many decks are there?

(Clue: The French refer to decks as 'bridges'.) ______________

c. What is the horsepower of the engine?

(Clue: 'Horses' are **Chevaux**.) ______________

d. How long does the river cruise last?

____

e. What did local poets so often sing about?

____

f. In which century was the Château de la Roche-Jagu built?______________

g. Up to what age can a child get a reduction on the cruise? ______________

ANSWERS P. 140

CONFORT ET SÉCURITÉ

Prenez place à bord de l'une des nouvelles **VEDETTES DE BRÉHAT** de 200 places pour un voyage confortable en toute sécurité.
Vous choisirez le pont couvert ou le pont supérieur panoramique.
Nos vedettes sont équipées de sièges autocar, de toilettes et d'une sonorisation.
Propulsées par des moteurs de 500 CV, elles possèdent les équipements les plus modernes en terme de navigation et sont pilotées par des équipages expérimentés.

LES CROISIÈRES

Remontée du Trieux

Embarquez pour une splendide croisière de 4 heures au départ de la Pointe de l'Arcouest puis sur les eaux calmes de la rivière du Trieux.
Vous découvrirez ainsi confortablement certains des plus fameux sites magiques de Bretagne si souvent chantés par les poètes locaux.
De splendides lieux chargés d'histoire, comme le pont de Lézardrieux (construit en 1840) ou le château de la Roche-Jagu (15e siècle) vous offriront leurs plus beaux secrets, depuis la rivière. Un souvenir inoubliable!

Départ: Pointe de l'Arcouest - Réservation : Tél. 02.96.55.79.50

Prière de retirer les billets 30 minutes avant le départ.
Tarifs : Adultes : 17€ - Enfants (4-11 ans) : 12€.

GRAMMAR AND EXERCISES

Vous et nous

You are used to **vous** being used as the subject of a sentence, e.g.

Vous avez les horaires?
Do you have the times/timetables?

You also use **vous** in sentences such as:

Je peux vous faire votre réservation
I can make your reservation for you
Je vous comprends
I understand you
Je vous invite
I am inviting you
Elle vous parle
She is speaking to you
Il vous donne le billet
He gives the ticket to you

Notice that in all these cases, **vous** comes before the relevant verb.

Nous works in exactly the same way. Examples:

Nous avons les horaires
We have the times/timetables
Elle nous comprend
She understands us
Vous nous invitez?
Are you inviting us?
Elle nous parle
She is speaking to us
Il nous donne les billets
He gives the tickets to us

Votre, vos; notre, nos

Votre is the word for 'your' when it refers to one item belonging to a person (or persons) whom you call **vous**, e.g. **votre train, votre père**.

Vos is used for 'your' when the other person has more than one of the items, e.g. **vos places, vos parents**.

The words for 'our' are very similar. **Notre** is used if there is only one item, as in **notre hôtel** or **notre mère. Nos** is used when there is more than one item, as in **nos couchettes** or **nos enfants**.

Me et te

'I' is **je**, but 'me' or 'to me' is **me** (in most contexts). Examples:

Elle me comprend
She understands me
Tu m'invites?
Are you inviting me?
Il m'aime
He loves me
Il me donne le billet
He gives the ticket to me

Notice that **me** comes before the verb and that it abbreviates to **m'** before a vowel sound.

In the same way, **tu** is used as the subject of the verb, but **te** or **t'** is used in contexts like:

Je te comprends
I understand you
Je t'aime
I love you
Je te téléphone lundi
I('ll) phone you on Monday
Qu'est-ce qu'ils te donnent?
What do they give you?

The verbs *dire* (to say, to tell) and *partir* (to leave)

Here are two more slightly irregular verbs to learn:

je dis	**nous disons**
tu dis	**vous dites**
il/elle dit	**ils/elles disent**

je pars	**nous partons**
tu pars	**vous partez**
il/elle part	**ils/elles partent**

Note: **on dit**, literally 'one says', is used in French where English has 'they say',

On dit que l'amour est aveugle.
They say that love is blind.

10 Cross out the incorrect option in each of the following:

- **a.** Est-ce que votre/vos parents peuvent venir avec vous?
- **b.** Voici votre/vos place, Monsieur.
- **c.** Est-ce que vous avez votre/vos billets?
- **d.** Votre/vos train part à 21h46.
- **e.** Notre/nos parents habitent en Australie.
- **f.** Notre/nos fils est ingénieur.
- **g.** Nous allons en Australie pour voir notre/nos petits-enfants.
- **h.** Ah! Voici notre/nos places.

ANSWERS P. 140

11 Rewrite these jumbled sentences with the words in the correct order:

a. He understands us.
nous comprend il

____

b. They love you.
vous ils aiment

____

c. She is giving us the times.
horaires nous elle donne les

____

d. He is making the reservation for us.
réservation fait nous il la

____

e. She loves me.
m' elle aime

____

f. He telephones me every day.
tous me il les téléphone jours

____

g. I am giving you my address.
adresse te je donne mon

____

h. They invite you to the house.
t' à invitent maison ils la

____

ANSWERS P. 140

12 Can you fill in the gaps to translate these sentences into French? Take it that 'your' is being used to someone addressed as **vous**.

a. Your train leaves at nine o'clock.
________ **train** ________ **à neuf heures.**

b. Our children are leaving tomorrow.
________ **enfants** ________ **demain.**

c. We are leaving on Sunday with our daughter.
Nous ____________ **dimanche avec** ____________ **fille.**

d. He says yes.
Il ________ **oui.**

e. What do you say?
Qu'est-ce que vous ________ **?**

f. They say you are leaving this evening.
On ________ **que vous** ________ **ce soir.**

ANSWERS P. 140

KEY WORDS AND PHRASES

la gare	station
le billet	ticket
un aller (simple)	a single
un aller et retour	a return
avec une réservation	with a reservation
pour demain	for tomorrow
en première/deuxième classe	in first/second class
C'est quel quai?	Which platform is it?
C'est quelle voie?	Which track is it?
Est-ce que vous pouvez me dire les horaires?	Can you tell me the times?
Pouvez-vous faire les billets et les réservations en même temps?	Can you do the tickets and the reservations at the same time?
la voiture/le wagon	carriage
le compartiment non-fumeurs	no-smoking compartment
la couchette	couchette
supérieure/en haut	upper/at the top
inférieure/en bas	lower/at the bottom
Vous avez une préférence?	Do you have a preference?
J'espère (from **espérer**)	I hope
toujours	always
Je voudrais aller à Marseille	I'd like to go to Marseilles
Qu'est-ce qu'il y a comme possibilités?	What options are there?
Je préfère prendre	I prefer to take
le train de nuit	the night train
l'avion	the plane
au départ de Lille	ex Lille
Je préfère voyager	I prefer to travel
par avion	by plane
un agent de voyages	a travel agent
une agence de voyages	a travel agency
Je voudrais louer	I'd like to hire
une voiture	a car
un vélo	a bicycle
une voiture de location	a hired car
kilométrage illimité	unlimited 'mileage'
l'assurance (f.)	(*here*) insurance
parfait	perfect
rentrer	return, come home
Faites-moi un Paris–New York s'il vous plaît	Do me a Paris–New York please

DID YOU KNOW?

Rail travel in France

La gare SNCF is the railway station, not to be confused with **la gare routière**, the bus station. The French railway network is the most extensive in western Europe. The main lines are served by high-speed trains: **TGVs** (**trains à grande vitesse**) and **Corails**, both of which are comfortable and punctual, but often crowded, so reserving a seat is advisable – indeed, seat reservations are compulsory on **TGVs**. You also have to pay a supplement to travel on **TGVs** and on certain other high-speed trains. You are fined if you board one of these trains without having done so. On popular routes in the summer months trains can be fully booked some time in advance, so that the only way of reaching your destination can be to board the train illegally (i.e. without a reservation) and then pay a fine for the privilege of standing in the corridor for several hours.

Even though you have paid for your ticket, it is not valid (**en règle**) until you have had it punched (**composté**) by one of the machines (orange-red pillars) at the entrance to the platform. You should also note that children have to pay adult fares from the age of twelve in France.

If you plan to travel around much by rail, it's worth looking out for the various discount fares available from SNCF (see details below), particularly if travelling with one or more others. You can buy a timetable for the whole of the French network (**Indicateur horaires**) in the first station bookshop you see in France and there are, of course, numerous brochures and pocket timetables available.

Useful addresses for rail travel

Rail Europe, Rail Europe House, 34 Tower View, Kings Hill, West Malling, Kent ME19 4ED. Tel. 08705 848848 or Rail Europe, Travel Centre, 179 Piccadilly, London W1J 9BA. Website: www.raileurope.co.uk

The SNCF office number is 020 7647 4949. Website: www.sncf.com.

Eurostar Enquiries: Eurostar House, Waterloo Station, London SE1 7LT Tel. 0870 160 6600. Reservations: Kent House, Station Road, Ashford TN23 1AP. Tel. (call centre) 0870 518 6186. Website www.eurostar.com

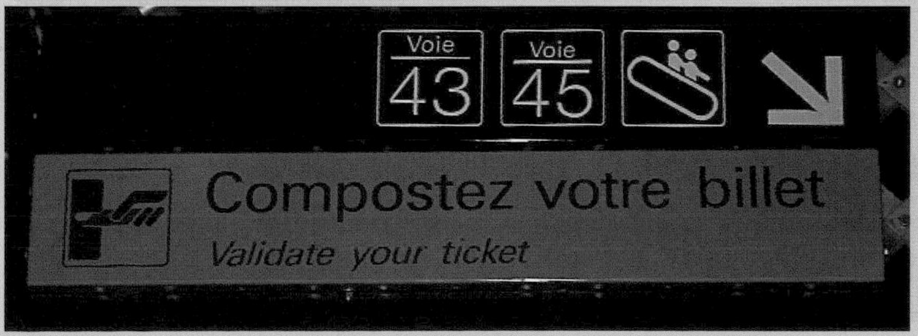

AND FINALLY...

13 You are in Strasbourg and want to travel on an overnight train to Nice. Follow Nicolas' prompts on the recording to find out the information you need and make your booking. Correct answers will be given after the pauses, but remember that there is often more than one way to say things. For example, the first thing you will need to ask is 'How much is a single to Nice, please?' It does not matter whether you say **C'est combien, un aller Nice, s'il vous plaît?** or **C'est combien, un aller simple pour Nice, s'il vous plaît?**

One final new expression:
Pas de problème! No problem!

ANSWERS

Exercise 2

(a) a return **(b)** Thursday **(c)** no **(d)** second **(e)** non-smoking **(f)** Bordeaux

Exercise 4

(a) yes (It runs every day between 26 June and 6 September.) **(b)** 05.11 **(c)** Milano-Lambrate **(d)** no (**Trains à supplément** are indicated by a star.) **(e)** yes (It has 1.2 in the column headed **Places**.) **(f)** **spécial** (1st class sleeper with one bed) and **T2** (2nd class sleeper with one or two beds).

Exercise 6

(a) category B **(b)** 2 **(c)** 28 July **(d)** 70 euros (€39 for the first day + €31 for the extra day) **(e)** **assurance** **(f)** more than a year

Exercise 7

(a) Toulouse: 16.55, Platform 2 **(b)** Nantes: 17.05, Platform 3 **(c)** Angoulême: 17.08, Platform 1 **(d)** Poitiers: 17.18, Platform 5 **(e)** Clermont-Ferrand: 17.25, Platform 7 **(f)** Paris-Austerlitz: 17.38, Platform 4

Exercise 9

(a) 200 **(b)** 2 **(c)** 500 (CV stands for **chevaux**.) **(d)** 4 hours **(e)** the magical sites of Brittany **(f)** 15th **(g)** 11

Exercise 10

The correct forms are: **(a) vos** (because **parents** has an **'s'** on the end and is therefore plural) **(b) votre** **(c) vos** **(d) votre** **(e) nos** **(f) notre** (The word **fils** is spelt the same in the singular and the plural, but the verb **est** is singular – as is the noun **ingénieur**) **(g) nos** **(h) nos**

Exercise 11

(a) Il nous comprend. **(b)** Ils vous aiment. **(c)** Elle nous donne les horaires. **(d)** Il nous fait la réservation. **(e)** Elle m'aime. **(f)** Il me téléphone tous les jours. **(g)** Je te donne mon adresse. **(h)** Ils t'invitent à la maison.

Exercise 12

(a) Votre train part à neuf heures. **(b)** Nos enfants partent demain. **(c)** Nous partons dimanche avec notre fille. **(d)** Il dit oui. **(e)** Qu'est-ce que vous dites? **(f)** On dit que vous partez ce soir.

10 FOOD AND DRINK

WHAT YOU WILL LEARN

- booking a table
- asking what dishes are
- ordering a meal
- paying the bill
- something about French eating habits

BEFORE YOU BEGIN

The French take eating and drinking very seriously and like to talk about them. One of the results of this is that the language of food and drink is highly developed and can be quite difficult for foreigners to understand. It is useful to learn general terms like 'meat', 'fish' and 'vegetable', so that when you are trying to find out what something is you can ask, for example:

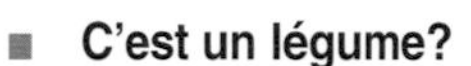

- **C'est un légume?** Is it a vegetable?
- **C'est une boisson?** Is it a drink?
- **C'est du poisson?** Is it fish?
- **C'est de la viande?** Is it meat?
- **C'est quelle viande?** What meat is it?

And, of course, don't forget the catch-all

- **Qu'est-ce que c'est?** What is it?

Pronunciation notes

Intonation is the music of a language, or, more prosaically, the way the pitch of the voice goes up and down in the course of a sentence. It goes up more often in French than it does in English, and the musical range between the high and the low notes is rather greater. Exercise 3 will give you an opportunity to imitate the intonation of some French speakers.

There will also be more work on vowel sounds in Exercise 6. Remember that French vowels have the same sound from beginning to end.

CONVERSATION 

 ## Booking a table

LISTEN FOR...

- **réserver une table** to book a table

Guy	Bonjour, Madame.
Serveuse	Bonjour, Monsieur.
Guy	Est-ce que je peux réserver une table pour ce soir?
Serveuse	Oui – à quel nom?
Guy	Au nom de Fontaine.
Serveuse	Vous pensez arriver vers quelle heure?
Guy	Vers sept heures, sept heures et demie?
Serveuse	D'accord. Pour combien de personnes, s'il vous plaît?
Guy	Pour deux personnes.
Serveuse	D'accord. C'est noté. A ce soir!

- **Au nom de** In the name of.

  Vous pensez arriver vers quelle heure? Around what time are you thinking of arriving?

- **A ce soir!** Till this evening! Note also
- **A demain!** Till tomorrow!
- **A la semaine prochaine!** Till next week! and
- **A la prochaine!** Till our next (meeting)!

PAINS A LA LIGNE
Autogrill - Gares de Lille
1, Place de la Gare - 59800 Lille
Tel : 03.20.06.15.50 - Fax : 03.20.06.10.40
RCS MARSEILLE 313 455 800 - NAF 553 A

DelphineM

SALADE	3.90
JUS D'ORANGE 33	2.10
DOUBLE EXPRESSO	2.10
TOTAL Euro	**8.10**

	HT	TVA	TTC
TVA 19.6%	6.77	1.33	8.10

REGLEM.EURO 8.10

LUNDI ... 00046/1

restaurant kermarec
Rue Saint-Yves - 29290 ST RENAN
☎ 02 98 84 23 47

Spécialisé dans l'accueil des groupes - Important parking à 50 mètres

PRACTICE

1 On the recording for this exercise, you will hear a woman telephoning to make a booking at a restaurant. See if you can you note down

a. which of the restaurants it is:

- ☐ L'Hôtel-Restaurant de la Poste
- ☐ L'Auberge de Monplaisir
- ☐ L'Auberge Bellevue

b. the day and date for which the booking is made ____________________

c. the time for which it is made ____________________

d. the number of people in her party ____________________

ANSWERS P. 154

e. the client's name (which she will spell) ____________________

2 Now you telephone the same restaurant to make the same booking. There are no English prompts on the recording this time; in the first pause, you should say

Bonjour, Monsieur. Est-ce que je peux réserver une table?

Thereafter, reply to the restaurateur's questions using as your prompts the answers you wrote in the last exercise. You will find it helpful to practise saying the date and spelling the customer's name before you turn on the recording. Carolle will give correct versions of your lines after the pauses.

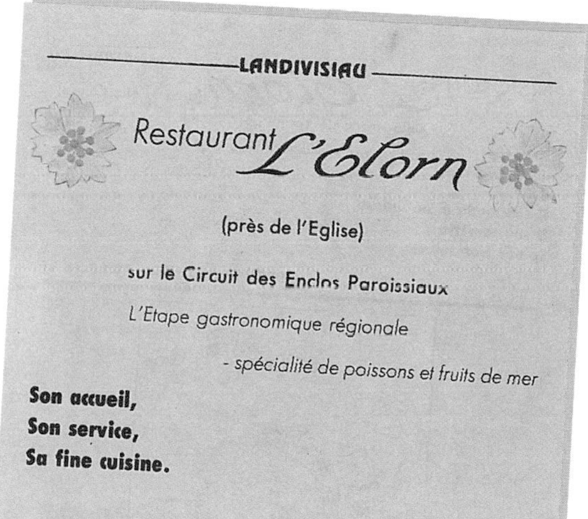

LANDIVISIAU
Restaurant L'Elorn
(près de l'Eglise)
sur le Circuit des Enclos Paroissiaux
L'Etape gastronomique régionale
- spécialité de poissons et fruits de mer
Son accueil,
Son service,
Sa fine cuisine.

« Le Petit Bedon »
Restaurant
3, rue Gouin de Beauchêne
35400 Saint-Malo

BAR - RESTAURANT
"Le Saint-Yves"
Repas Ouvriers - Banquets
KIG-HA-FARZ le Mercredi
SALLE V R P
24, rue Général-de-Gaulle
29260 PLOUDANIEL - TÉL. 02 98 83 61 97
Spécialités du Sud-Ouest
IMP. J.-A. PROVOST LESNEVEN

CONVERSATIONS 

Deciding what to eat in a bistro

LISTEN FOR...

▶ **des croque-madame** toasted ham and cheese sandwiches with an egg on top

Bernadette	Qu'est-ce que tu voudrais manger?
Barbara	Qu'est-ce qu'il y a?
Bernadette	Ils ont des croque-monsieur, sans doute des sandwichs au jambon, heu, saucisson, rillettes, fromage … Ils ont également des tartes maison, des omelettes …
Barbara	Est-ce qu'il y a aussi des croque-madame?
Bernadette	Alors des croque-madame avec un œuf, c'est cela?
Barbara	Oui, c'est ça.
Bernadette	Eh bien, je ne sais pas s'ils ont des croque-madame. On demandera – on verra bien.
Barbara	Parce que s'il y en a, je veux bien essayer.
Bernadette	(Un croque-dame.)
Barbara	S'il n'y en a pas, je prends un croque-monsieur.
Bernadette	Entendu.

sans doute doubtless, certainly

▶ **l'omelette** (f.) omelette

▶ **bistro** (also spelt **bistrot**) a café or bar which serves some food.

des tartes maison home-made tarts.

des croque-madame are **croque-monsieur** with an egg on top. As was mentioned in Unit 3, these two words do not add an **-s** in the plural.

c'est cela? is that right? You have already met the abbreviated form of this: **C'est ça?**

s'ils ont if they have. Before another **-i**, **si** (if) becomes **s'** (as it does in **s'il vous plaît**).

On demandera – on verra bien We'll ask – we'll see. The future tense will be covered later in the course.

▶ **s'il y en a** if there are any of them. This is made up of
si (if) + **il y a** (there are) + **en** (of them).

There is more explanation in the Grammar section on p. 150.

- **Je veux bien essayer** I'd like to try. **Je veux** (I want) is, on its own, rather rude, but the **bien** modifies it to something with the impact of 'I'd like'. If you are offered food or drink,
- **Je veux bien** is a polite way to accept.

s'il n'y en a pas if there aren't any of them. Like many people, Barbara swallows some of her syllables, so what she says sounds more like **s'y en a pas.**

Ordering a light lunch

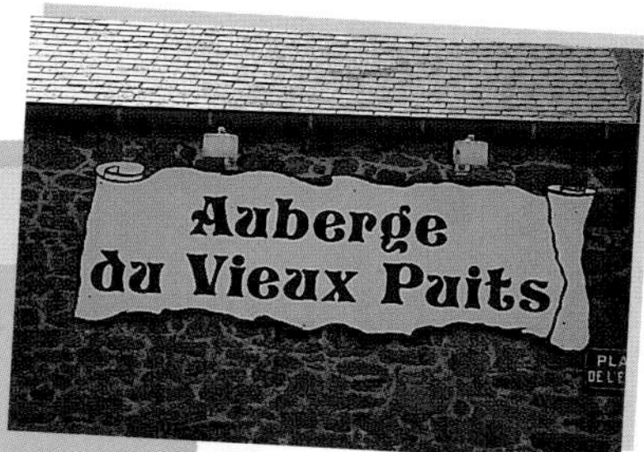

LISTEN FOR...

la salade brivoise	the name of a dish
▶ **des filets d'oie fumée**	fillets of smoked goose
▶ **un œuf poché**	a poached egg
▶ **comme plat du jour**	as dish of the day
du bœuf gros sel	beef cooked in coarse-crystal salt

Guy	Qu'est-ce que c'est que la salade brivoise, s'il vous plaît?
Serveuse	Ce sont des filets d'oie fumée, des croutons, de la salade et un œuf poché.
Jeanne	Tiens! je vais prendre ça.
Guy	Et qu'est-ce que vous avez comme plat du jour?
Serveuse	Il y a du bœuf gros sel.
Guy	Ben, je vais prendre un bœuf gros sel.
Serveuse	D'accord. Donc une salade brivoise et un bœuf gros sel.

la salade brivoise The waitress gives the composition of the salad in her reply. Even French people need to ask for explanations of items on menus.

- **qu'est-ce que vous avez comme plat du jour?** what have you got as dish of the day?

LA MAISON DE LA MER

DÉGUSTATION DE FRUITS DE MER

29830 PORTSALL - Tél. 02 98 48 69 77

PORTSALL Port traditionnel où les pêcheurs pratiquent toujours la pêche à la ligne et débarquent tous les jours du poisson frais mais aussi des fruits de mer

- A 20 minutes de Brest
- Au bord des plages
- Dans une salle panoramique avec vue sur port

Au dessus des PÊCHERIES PORTSALLAISES, "LA MAISON DE LA MER", vraie table de la mer, vous propose ses poissons et ses fruits de mer fraîchement débarqués

OCEANOCOLOR - 98 05 46 21

PRACTICE

3 The conversation 'Ordering a light lunch' is re-created in the studio, this time with gaps for you to repeat the lines after the speakers. Take particular care to imitate their intonation.

4 Listen to Yves ordering snacks for the family. Try to note down (in English or French) the items he orders.

ANSWERS P. 154

5 You are ordering in a bistro. You'll find that the dish of the day is **des spaghettis à la bolognaise**, which you can doubtless understand when you see it written down! You will need to use the structures

Est-ce que vous avez...? and
Qu'est-ce que vous avez comme...?

On the recording, Philippe will prompt you and Yves will give correct versions after the pauses.

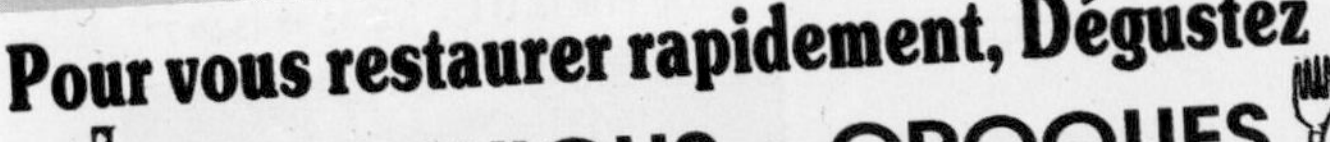

CONVERSATIONS

Ordering dinner

LISTEN FOR...

▶ **une assiette de saumon**	a plate of salmon
▶ **une côte d'agneau grillée**	a grilled lamb chop
une rillettes d'oie	a potted goose-meat
un jambon de Pragues	a Prague ham
▶ **le vin de la maison**	the house wine

Alain Alors, heu, une assiette de saumon et une côte d'agneau grillée, c'est bien ça?
Juliette C'est ça.
Alain Et pour moi, un menu à 18 euros: heu, une rillettes d'oie, un jambon de Prague braisé au champagne.
Serveuse Et comme boisson?
Alain Oh, on va prendre le, le vin de la maison?
Serveuse Oui, ou il y a la réserve Pomme d'Or – c'est du côtes du rhône.
Alain Très bien. Heu, est-ce que vous pourriez mettre aussi une bouteille d'eau minérale, s'il vous plaît?
Serveuse Oui, vous voulez de la vittel ou de l'évian?
Alain De l'évian, c'est parfait.
Serveuse D'accord.

▶ **une côte d'agneau grillée** a grilled lamb chop. **Grillée** is in the feminine (it has an extra **e** on the end) because it refers to **une côte**.

c'est bien ça? that is right, isn't it?

▶ **un menu à 18 euros** a set menu at 18 euros. **Un menu** is a set menu. The 'à la carte menu' is not **le menu** but
▶ **la carte.**

une rillettes d'oie one (portion of) goose rillettes.

braisé au champagne braised in champagne.

Et comme boisson? What would you like to drink? (literally And in the way of drink?)

la réserve Pomme d'Or the Pomme d'Or reserve. La Pomme d'Or (the Golden Apple) is the name of the restaurant. Their **réserve** will be rather better than their basic house wine.

vittel ... évian are, of course, varieties of mineral water. Both are feminine because **eau** (water) is feminine.
One of the few rules about gender in French is that all nouns ending in **-eau** are masculine ... except for **l'eau** and **la peau** (skin).

Getting the bill

Alain	Vous pouvez nous apporter l'addition, s'il vous plaît?
Serveuse	Oui. *(The waitress fetches the bill)*
Alain	Est-ce que le service est compris?
Serveuse	Oui, Monsieur, le service est compris.
Alain	Je peux vous payer avec ma carte de crédit?
Serveuse	Oui, bien sûr.

- **Vous pouvez nous apporter l'addition?** Can you bring us the bill? You can just say **L'addition, s'il vous plaît.**
- **Est-ce que le service est compris?** Is service included? Service usually is included. If it is not, you will generally see on the menu either **service en sus** (service extra) or the letters **s.n.c.**, which stand for **service non compris** (service not included). Better news on the menu is **boissons comprises** (drinks included).
- **Je peux vous payer avec ma carte de crédit?** Can I pay you with my credit card? Other methods of payment would be **avec un traveller's** (with a traveller's cheque) or **en espèces** (in cash).

PRACTICE

6 First, study this menu:

le plateau *(here)* platter (usually, tray)
les fruits de mer (m.) seafood
le poisson fish
le canard duck
le gigot d'agneau roast leg of lamb

On the recording for this exercise, Carolle will read out the menu. Repeat after her, paying particular attention to your pronunciation of vowel sounds.

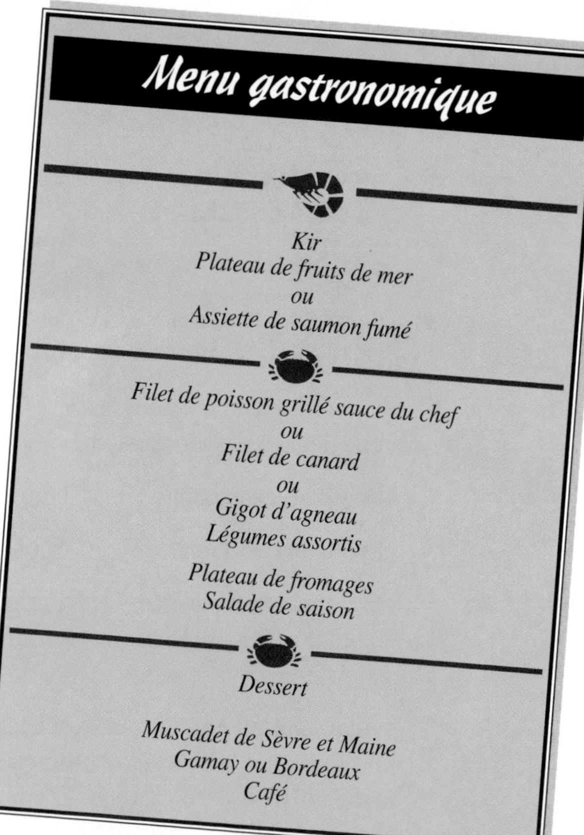

Menu gastronomique

Kir
Plateau de fruits de mer
ou
Assiette de saumon fumé

Filet de poisson grillé sauce du chef
ou
Filet de canard
ou
Gigot d'agneau
Légumes assortis

Plateau de fromages
Salade de saison

Dessert

Muscadet de Sèvre et Maine
Gamay ou Bordeaux
Café

7 You are ordering from the menu printed in Exercise 6. Follow Philippe's prompts on the recording. Carolle will confirm that you have said the right thing after each of the pauses.

8 Here are advertisements for some restaurants.

RESTAURANTS

Hôtel de la Plage
vous propose SA NOUVELLE CARTE.
Menus à 17,25€, 28€. Grand menu gastronomique et menu dégustation à 51,75€. Plateau de fruits de mer à emporter sur commande.
Informations, réservations : 02.98.27.61.90

• **BREST, centre-ville : RESTAURANT LE FEVRE,** spécialiste des produits de mer, vous propose son menu marin à 19,30€. Formule le midi à 10,35€. Menu à partir de 14,90€. Ouvert midi et soir + le dimanche midi. 1, rue Jean-Barbet, tél. 02.98.46.07.70.

HOTEL RESTAURANT**
DU HORS-MURS - CARANTEC
informe son aimable clientèle que son restaurant est ouvert tous les jours
Menus: 14,90€, 20,15€, 27,20€
42€+ carte

02.98.67.00.52

• **BREST : LE MICRO,** tous les dimanches et jour fériés à midi, menu à 25,40€ (apéritif, vin et café compris), buffet d'entrées à volonté avec fruits de mer, plats chauds au choix, fromage, buffet de desserts. Tél. 02.98.02.32.83.

AUBERGE SAINT-PHILIPPE
HOTEL RESTAURANT**
Entre ville et plage
• Chambres*** (en attente de classement) à partir de 47,35€
• Repas du terroir à partir de 16€
Tél. 02.98.79.61.18

• **BREST : RESTAURANT "LE CHATEAU ROUGE",** plage du Château Bleu. Spécialités de la mer, viandes. Nombreux menus + carte. Tél. 02.98.28.36.72. Repas de groupe, baptême, etc. (Fermé lundi en saison).

• **CAMARET : HOTEL D'ANGLETERRE**.** Sur le port, salle panoramique au 1e étage (nouveau décor). Menus 16,65€, 22,45€, 28,90€. Menu dégustation 51,75€ (avec $\frac{1}{2}$ homard grillé). 02.98.27.93.06.

• **LESNEVEN : HOTEL-RESTAURANT LES VACANCES.** Banquets, mariages, repas de groupe, menus : 10,85€, 15,60€, 21,00€, 28,90€. Paella le vendredi sur réservation. Tél. 02 98 25 40 57.

a. Which one has good views from the first floor? ______

b. Which ones are keen to cater for groups? ______

c. Which is the only one to specify that drinks are included in the price of the set menu? ______

d. Which one specifically mentions Sunday lunch? ______

e. Which one will do a take-away seafood platter on request? ______

f. Which one is closed on Mondays during the season? ______

ANSWERS P. 154

GRAMMAR AND EXERCISES

En

En can mean 'of it', 'of them', 'some of it', 'any of it', 'some of them' or 'any of them'. In English, we can say things like 'I have five'. In French, you have to say the equivalent of 'I have five of them':

Vous avez combien d'enfants?
    How many children do you have?
J'en ai cinq.
    I have five (of them).

More examples:

Est-ce que vous buvez du whisky?
    Do you drink whisky?
Oui, j'en bois quelquefois.
    Yes, I drink some (of it) sometimes.
Est-ce que vous prenez de l'aspirine?
    Do you take aspirin?
Je n'en prends pas souvent.
    I don't often take any (of it).

En comes before the verb in all sentences except a positive command like **Prenez-en!** (Take some!) or **Goûtez-en!** (Taste some!).

You met **en** in Conversations 2 in the discussion about **croque-madame**:

Parce que s'il y en a, je veux bien essayer. S'il n'y en a pas, je prends un croque-monsieur.

In the expression **il y a** (there is, there are) the verb is **a** (from **avoir**). That is why the **en** comes immediately before it.

Le, la, l', les

Le, **la**, **l'** and **les** don't just mean 'the'. **Le** is used for 'him' or 'it' (referring to a masculine noun); **la** is used for 'her' or 'it' (referring to a feminine noun); **le** and **la** both abbreviate to **l'** before a vowel sound; **les** is used for 'them' (whatever the gender). When **le**, **la**, **l'** and **les** are used in this way they are called direct object pronouns. (There is more explanation in the Grammar summary on p. 239.)

Like **en**, **le**, **la**, **l'** and **les** all go immediately before the verb. Here are some examples:

Je le comprends.	I understand him/it.
Je la comprends.	I understand her/it.
Je les comprends.	I understand them.
Je l'aime.	I love him/her/it.

The verbs *voir* (to see) and *finir* (to finish)

voir	**je vois**	**nous voyons**
	tu vois	**vous voyez**
	il/elle voit	**ils/elles voient**

- **Vois**, **voit** and **voient** all sound exactly the same. **Revoir** (to see again) follows the same pattern as **voir**.

finir	**je finis**	**nous finissons**
	tu finis	**vous finissez**
	il/elle finit	**ils/elles finissent**

- **Finis** and **finit** sound the same, but **finissent** is different because the **-ss-** is pronounced. **Finir** is the model for a good number of verbs, including:

choisir (to choose)	**réussir** (to succeed)
maigrir (to grow thin)	**grossir** (to grow fat)
grandir (to grow taller)	**vieillir** (to grow old)

9

The words of the replies to each of these questions are jumbled up. Can you write them out in the correct order?

a. Tu as combien de frères?
deux en j' ai

____

b. Ta sœur a combien d'enfants?
trois a en elle

____

c. Est-ce que vous prenez du sucre?
quelquefois prends en j'

____

d. Est-ce que vous buvez du cognac?
souvent bois n' je en pas

____

e. Tu veux un croque-madame?
a en s' y il

____

ANSWERS P. 154

10

Can you complete the answers to these questions following the model:

Est-ce que tu aimes Marie?
Oui, je l'aime.

a. Est-ce que tu comprends le français?

Oui, ______________________________

b. Est-ce que tu prends la voiture?

Oui, ______________________________

c. Est-ce que tu manges les escargots?

Oui, ______________________________

d. Est-ce que tu vois mon mari?

Oui, ______________________________

e. Est-ce que tu invites Monsieur Dupont?

Oui, ______________________________

ANSWERS P. 154

11

Fill in the gaps with the correct form of the verb given in brackets:

a. Nous [voir] __________________ très souvent notre fille.

b. Jean-Luc a des problèmes à l'école. Ses parents [voir] __________________ son professeur ce soir.

c. Le plombier et l'électricien [finir] __________________ demain.

d. Oh! nous [vieillir] __________________

e. Comment tu fais? Toi, tu [maigrir] __________________ et moi, je [grossir] __________________ !

f. Qu'est-ce que vous [choisir] __________________ ?

ANSWERS P. 154

KEY WORDS AND PHRASES

réserver une table	to book a table
au nom de	in the name of
Pour combien de personnes?	For how many people?
le numéro de téléphone	telephone number
A ce soir!	Till this evening!
A demain!	Till tomorrow!
A la semaine prochaine!	Till next week!
A la prochaine!	Till our next (meeting)
le menu	set menu
la carte	'à la carte menu'
l'omelette (f.)	omelette
C'est un légume?	Is it a vegetable?
C'est du poisson?	Is it fish?
C'est de la viande?	Is it meat?
C'est quelle viande?	What meat is it?
Est-ce que le service est compris?	Is service included?
Je veux bien	Yes please
Qu'est-ce que vous avez comme plat du jour?	What have you got as dish of the day?
une assiette de saumon	a plate of salmon
une côte d'agneau grillée	a grilled lamb chop
un œuf poché	a poached egg
le vin de la maison	the house wine
L'addition, s'il vous plaît	The bill, please
Je peux vous payer avec ma carte de crédit?	Can I pay you with my credit card?

Additional vocabulary for carnivores: You can hear this pronounced on the recording.

la viande	meat
le bœuf	beef
bleu	blue (i.e. very rare)
saignant	rare
à point	medium
bien cuit	well done
le bifteck	beefsteak
le veau	veal
le porc	pork
l'agneau	lamb
le poulet	chicken
la dinde	turkey
l'andouille (f.)	sausage
le cheval	horsemeat (sorry, but it is eaten in France!)
le ragoût	casserole
rôti	roast
grillé	grilled
frit	fried
bouilli	boiled
à la vapeur	steamed
à la cocotte	casseroled

And if you're not a carnivore, you'll need

Je suis végétarien/végétarienne	I am a vegetarian

DID YOU KNOW?

Table manners

There are differences in table manners between France and Britain or America. In France, it is considered slovenly to have one or both of your hands on your lap during a meal: hands which are not being used to eat with should be kept on the table. Well-brought-up French people respect food and the preparation that has gone into it and will savour each mouthful before starting to cut up the next one. It is also respect for good food which makes French people find it perfectly acceptable to mop up any sauce left on their plates with a piece of bread.

French eating habits

After a light breakfast, most French people have a substantial meal at midday, so the standard lunch-break is from noon to 2 p.m. to give them time to enjoy a big meal. There is, however, a move towards shorter lunch-breaks and a main meal in the evening. Indeed, the French are increasingly having their lunch in snack-bars, self-service restaurants and McDonald's. A main meal, whether at home or in a restaurant, has more courses in France than in Britain. After the main course, salad is often served to freshen the palate before the cheese, which is served before the pudding, if the meal includes both. On a menu, look to see whether it is **fromage et dessert** or **fromage ou dessert**.

'Proper meals' are usually better value for money than snacks in France, particularly if you order from a fixed-price menu rather than à la carte, but if you want a snack or quick meal, look out for these signs:

Pizzéria (Pizza house), **Snack** (Snack-bar), **Self** (Self-service restaurant), or, of course, **Crêperie**, **Brasserie** or **Fast food.**

As regards alcohol, the British and the French have interesting cultural stereotypes about each other. The British think of the French as heavy drinkers. It is true that their per capita consumption of alcohol (particularly wine) is relatively high, but there is less drunkenness and drink-related hooliganism in France than in Britain. The French often think of the British as drunkards, because of the way so many British visitors to France fall on cheap plonk and drink more than they can hold.

Consumption of alcohol follows a different pattern in France. Drinking wine with meals is very much part of the culture, going out to spend an evening drinking much less so. Meals may be preceded by apéritifs: American and British visitors are often surprised to find that port (**le porto**) is drunk as an apéritif rather than as a **digestif** in France. Because the word **alcool** is, rather misleadingly, usually applied only to spirits, campaigns to persuade French people to drink less alcohol have found it necessary, in recent years, to point out that wine and beer contain alcohol too.

AND FINALLY...

12

On the menu is a dish called **Salade de chèvre chaud**. You have looked up **chèvre** and found that it means 'goat' but are not convinced that it really means 'hot goat salad'! You are also puzzled by **Saint-pierre au cidre**, which must surely mean something other than 'Saint Peter in cider'! Follow Philippe's lead as you question the not-very-bright waiter about them. Carolle will give correct versions of your lines after the pauses.

When you have completed this unit, you will have covered the language necessary for coping with all the basic tourist situations. **Félicitations!** From now on, we shall be going into the kind of language that you will need as you make friends with French people: telling them about yourself, your likes and dislikes, your background and your plans for the future – and, of course, understanding them when they tell you about themselves and their lives.

Gérard et Bernadette Van De Sype
Terrasse Panoramique - Parking clients
Ste Anne La Palud ☎ 02 98 92 54 10

Niché dans un oasis de cyprès, directement sur la plage, le restaurant "Les Dunes" vous propose sa carte gastronomique, riche en fruits de mer et poissons, ainsi que plusieurs menus. Après la baignade ou la randonnée, une carte brasserie vous attend.

OUVERT DE PÂQUES A FIN SEPTEMBRE
Fermeture hebdomadaire Dimanche soir et Lundi
Juillet et Août : ouvert tous les jours.

A découvrir : Homard de l'atlantique, pêché dans notre vivier,

ANSWERS

EXERCISE 1

(a) L'Hôtel-Restaurant de la Poste **(b)** Tuesday 16 September **(c)** 8.30 p.m. **(d)** 6 **(e)** Lamy

EXERCISE 4

A cheese sandwich/Un sandwich au fromage
A toasted cheese and ham sandwich/Un croque-monsieur
Two strawberry tarts/Deux tartes aux fraises
A large bottle of fizzy mineral water/Une grande bouteille d'eau minérale gazeuse

EXERCISE 8

(a) Hôtel d'Angleterre **(b)** Restaurant 'Le Château Rouge' and Hôtel-Restaurant Les Vacances **(c)** Le Micro
(d) Restaurant 'Le Fèvre' **(e)** Hôtel de la Plage
(f) Restaurant 'Le Château Rouge'

EXERCISE 9

(a) J'en ai deux **(b)** Elle en a trois. **(c)** J'en prends quelquefois. **(d)** Je n'en bois pas souvent. **(e)** S'il y en a.

EXERCISE 10

(a) Oui, je le comprends. **(b)** Oui, je la prends.
(c) Oui, je les mange. **(d)** Oui, je le vois. **(e)** Oui, je l'invite.

EXERCISE 11

(a) voyons **(b)** voient **(c)** finissent **(d)** vieillissons
(e) maigris/grossis **(f)** choisissez

11 LIKES AND DISLIKES

What you will learn

- understanding and expressing likes and dislikes
- more vocabulary to do with food
- understanding descriptions of towns and villages
- describing your own town or village
- saying what you do and do not like about it
- something about the towns and villages mentioned in the conversations

Before you begin

As soon as you get on friendly terms with a French person, you will find yourself wanting to express likes and dislikes. The unit approaches this topic in two ways:

- In Conversations 1 and 2, various people say what food and drink they like and dislike. Most of them use the verb **aimer** (to like/love).
- In Conversations 3, the participants talk about the towns and villages where they live or where they go on holiday. They express what they like or don't like about them chiefly through the adjectives they use to describe them. The most commonly used one is **agréable** (nice, pleasant).

Pronunciation notes

The unit will concentrate on the vowel '**ou**' (as in **vous**) – and the distinction between it and the vowel '**u**' (as in **tu**).

CONVERSATIONS 

LISTEN FOR...

la gelée jelly
le riz rice

Anything except jelly!

Martin Dans la nourriture française j'aime tout; dans la nourriture anglaise, à peu près tout, sauf la gelée.

Wines

Lisette Je déteste les vins doux – ils me font mal. Je préfère les vins secs.

Rice, potatoes and fruit

Fabienne J'aime, heu, beaucoup le riz, les pommes de terre, les fruits rouges: les fraises, les framboises, les cerises. Heu, je n'aime pas beaucoup les bananes et les oranges – les fruits que l'on mange l'hiver.

- **la cerise** cherry
- **détester** to detest/hate
- **la nourriture française** French food. He might equally well have said
- **la cuisine française** French cooking. Note that **la cuisine** also means 'kitchen'.
- **à peu près tout** almost everything. **A peu près** also means 'approximately'.
- **ils me font mal** they make me ill (literally, they to me do harm). If you want to say that one thing makes you ill, the verb **faire** must be in the singular, e.g. **Le cognac me fait mal** (Cognac makes me ill).
- **les fruits que l'on mange l'hiver** the fruit that one eats in the winter. Notice that it is **les fruits** where English uses 'fruit' as a plural. People sometimes say **que l'on** instead of **qu'on** simply because it is thought to sound better. It does not matter which you say.
- **l'hiver** winter, used here for 'in winter'. The other seasons are **le printemps** (spring), **l'été** (m.) (summer) and **l'automne** (m.) (autumn).

PRACTICE

1 Here is a list of most of the foodstuffs mentioned in Conversations 1. Without looking back at the transcript, play the conversations again and put a ✔ by the items which the speakers like and a ✘ by the ones which they dislike.

Martin	☐	la nourriture française
	☐	la nourriture anglaise
	☐	la gelée
Lisette	☐	les vins doux
	☐	les vins secs
Fabienne	☐	le riz
	☐	les pommes de terre
	☐	les framboises
	☐	les cerises
	☐	les bananes
	☐	les oranges

Lisette

ANSWERS P. 170

2 What about Carolle and Yves? Listen to the recording and see if you can note down (in English) their likes and dislikes. Carolle and Yves both use the phrase **par contre** (on the other hand).

	Likes	Dislikes
Carolle		
Yves		

ANSWERS P. 170

3 The sound '**ou**' occurred in several words in Conversations 1: **nourriture**, **tout**, **doux**, **beaucoup**, **rouges**. It is not one of the more difficult sounds in French, but it is worth paying it some attention at this stage because some learners try so hard to pronounce the more awkward '**u**' (as in **tu**) correctly that they end up saying **nu** and **vu** for **nous** and **vous**. This can have unfortunate consequences with some words: **beaucoup** means 'a lot', but if you pronounce the second vowel as '**u**' it comes out as **beau cul** – 'beautiful bum'! To save your future blushes, practise repeating after Carolle and Yves on the recording. Carolle will say the words in the left-hand column (which all contain the vowel '**ou**') and Yves will say the words in the right-hand column (which all contain the vowel '**u**').

doux (soft, gentle)
joue (cheek – as in jowl)
nous (we, us, to us)
roue (wheel)
dessous (underneath)
tout (all)
vous (you, to you)

du (some, of the)
jus (juice)
nu (naked)
rue (street)
dessus (on top)
tu (you)
vu (seen)

Raymond BELOT vous fera découvrir les plaisirs
de la table, une cuisine raffinée aux accents du terroir,
avec des produits maison. Quant à Andrée...
laissez-la vous guider dans le choix des vins...!

Salons de réception de 10 à 100 personnes - Parking privé
Réservation: 03 20 90 09 52 → Fermé le dimanche ←
Fax : 03 20 32 70 87
17, rue Roger-Bouvry - 59113 SECLIN
(A1, sortie Seclin - R.N. 25 Sud de Lille)

La Tourelle
BORDEAUX
BLANC
APPELLATION BORDEAUX SEC CONTRÔLÉE
75 cl ℮
Mis en bouteille par
Eugène Reullier
Négociant à Blanquefort - Gironde - France
12% vol.

Ce vin est issu des meilleures provenances du Bordelais.
Il a été sélectionné avec patience,
vé avec passion selon des traditions séculaires.
en bouteille dans la région de production.

COTEAUX D'AIX en PROVENCE
Appellation Coteaux d'Aix en Provence Contrôlée
MISE DANS LA R PRODUCTION
Lou Picassou
75 cl
12 % vol
MIS EN BOUTEILLE PAR
S.I.C.AGRICOLE LES VIGNERONS PROVENCAUX A F-13840
PRODUIT DE FRANCE

CONVERSATIONS

LISTEN FOR...

consistants	substantial
▶ **la triperie**	tripe
▶ **le mélange salé-sucré**	sweet-savoury mix
▶ **les crustacés**	shellfish

Stodge, glorious stodge!

Anna J'adore les plats très consistants, où il y a beaucoup de choses à manger, comme la paëlla, le couscous, les lasagnes, le cassoulet. J'ai horreur de la triperie. J'adore toutes les viandes. J'aime beaucoup les pâtisseries. Je déteste les alcools et les vins.

Sweet and savoury

Guylaine Moi, j'aime beaucoup de choses, sauf le mélange salé-sucré. C'est très difficile de manger la viande et des fruits, par exemple – sinon, j'aime la viande.

Shellfish and white wine

Henri J'aime bien manger et j'aime surtout bien boire. J'aime la viande, bien sûr, mais je préfère le poisson. J'aime aussi les crustacés: les huîtres, les langoustes, les homards ... Avec le crustacé en France on boit du vin blanc.

▶ **la chose** thing
la paëlla paëlla
les lasagnes (f.pl.) lasagne
la pâtisserie (*here*) pastry(-cake)
▶ **salé** savoury, salted
difficile difficult
▶ **par exemple** for example
sinon otherwise
▶ **l'huître** (f.) oyster
▶ **la langouste** crayfish
▶ **le homard** lobster

▶ **j'adore** lit. I adore. **Adorer** is used much more in French than 'to adore' in English.

le couscous is a North African dish which is very popular in France.

- **le cassoulet** is a casserole of beans with goose, pork or mutton.
- **j'ai horreur de la triperie** I can't bear tripe (literally I have horror of the tripe). If **J'ai horreur de** is followed by a masculine singular noun, remember that **de + le = du**, e.g. **J'ai horreur du poulet** I can't bear chicken.
- **le mélange salé-sucré** the mixture of savoury and sweet. French visitors are often appalled at the idea of eating apple sauce, cranberry jelly or pineapple rings with meat.
- **J'aime bien manger et ... bien boire** I like eating well and ... drinking well.

PRACTICE

4

A French guest is coming to stay with you. You have asked her about her likes and dislikes: you'll hear her answer on the recording. Here is a gapped transcript of what she says. Can you fill in the gaps and then answer the question below?

En général, j'aime bien la cuisine anglaise. J'aime toutes les ________________

et à peu près tous les poissons, mais les ________________ me font mal.

J'aime beaucoup les fruits et les ________________, mais je n'aime pas les

________________ et j'ai horreur des ________________. Pour les boissons,

j'aime bien la ________________ anglaise mais je déteste le ________________

What should you avoid giving your guest to eat or drink?

____

____

Answers p. 170

____

5

Read through the first part of the Grammar section on p. 166. Then see if you can complete the sentences below to express some of your own real likes and dislikes. Obviously, there is no one set of correct answers to this exercise.

J'adore ____

J'aime beaucoup ____

J'aime bien ____

J'aime assez ____

Je n'aime pas beaucoup ____

Je n'aime pas ____

Je n'aime pas du tout ______________________________

Je déteste ______________________________

Finally, turn on the recording for this exercise, where Yves will read out this list. Repeat each of the verbs after him and complete the sentence as you have written it out above. For example, when he says **J'adore**…, you may wish to say **J'adore le champagne**.

6 Now you are paying a return visit to the French friend – with your family. You have been asked to let your hostess know if there are things you can't eat or drink, so work out how you will tell her:

a. I don't like pork. ______________________________

b. I can't bear horsemeat. ______________________________

c. Patrick hates eggs. ______________________________

d. Anne doesn't like rice. ______________________________

e. Julie doesn't much like wine. ______________________________

f. Otherwise, we very much like French cooking! ______________________________

____

ANSWERS P. 170

7

On the recording, it is Philippe's turn to give his likes and dislikes. See if you can translate them into French for him. Yves will give correct versions after the pauses.

Choosing French pâtisseries on a Brittany Ferry

CONVERSATIONS

The old town of Senlis

LISTEN FOR...

- **vieille** old
- **romains** Roman
- **moyenâgeuses** medieval

Marie-Lise La ville de Senlis, c'est une ville, heu, intéressante car elle est très vieille. Il y a une cathédrale, il y a des remparts romains, il y a, heu, pas mal de … maisons moyenâgeuses.

- **intéressant(e)** interesting
  des remparts (m.pl.) ramparts
- **vieille** (f.) old.
- **romains** Roman. **Romain(e)** is very easy to confuse with
  roman(e) Romanesque – the style of architecture we call Norman.
- **pas mal de** quite a lot of, e.g. **pas mal de musées** (quite a lot of museums).
- **moyenâgeuses** medieval, from
- **le moyen âge** the Middle Ages.

The rebuilding of Caen

LISTEN FOR...

- **ancienne** (f.) ancient
- **restaurée** (f.) restored
- **une reconstruction** reconstruction, rebuilding

Michel Bien, c'est une ville très ancienne qui a été restaurée et, de l'avis général, bien restaurée, parce que … à la fois il reste, heu, des monuments intéressants, et puis, il y a une reconstruction aussi qui a été bien faite.

de l'avis général in most people's opinion (literally, of the general opinion). Note also

- **à mon avis** in my opinion
- **à votre avis** in your opinion.
- **qui a été restaurée** which has been restored. This past tense will be explained in the later units of the course.

à la fois at one and the same time. Note three words which are all pronounced the same:

- **la fois** time (**une fois** once, **dix fois** ten times)

la foi faith
le foie liver.

une reconstruction a rebuilding. Caen was one of the first towns to be liberated after the Normandy invasion by the Allies in 1944 and was badly damaged in the fighting. The town now houses **le Mémorial**, the award-winning, multi-media Museum for Peace.

qui a été bien faite which has been well done.

Life in La Roche-sur-Yon

LISTEN FOR...

- **agréable** agreeable, pleasant
- **la mer** sea
- **la côte** coast

Denise C'est très calme. Il n'y a pas beaucoup de … de vie, mais la ville est très agréable parce que, en général, les gens sont gentils, sont restés simples, et les commerçants sont très agréables – oui – et la vie n'est pas trop chère encore … enfin, ça peut aller. Le dimanche, les gens ne restent pas à la Roche, parce que la mer est très proche; alors ils passent leur dimanche aux Sables d'Olonne ou bien … sur la côte.

- **la vie** life
- **en général** in general
- **encore** (*here*) yet

- **Il n'y a pas beaucoup de vie** It's not very lively (literally, there is not a lot of life).

sont restés simples have remained unpretentious. (This use of **sont** etc. for the past tense will be covered on p. 228.)

Ça peut aller It's all right (literally, that can go).

- **La mer est très proche** The sea is very near.

ils passent leur dimanche they spend their Sundays.

aux Sables d'Olonne ou bien … sur la côte at les Sables d'Olonne or (somewhere) else on the coast. **Les Sables** translates as Sands. **Ou bien** means 'or else'.

The seaside resort of Soulac-sur-Mer

LISTEN FOR...

fréquenté	frequented
▶ **trop de monde**	too many people
▶ **une plage**	beach
▶ **dangereuse**	dangerous

Claire Maintenant, ça devient un peu trop fréquenté – il y a un peu trop de monde. Enfin, ça reste une plage pas dangereuse, une belle plage de sable, heu, où le climat est agréable, le sable est propre, la mer n'est pas dangereuse, pas trop …

le climat climate
▶ **propre** clean
▶ **ça devient** it's becoming

▶ **trop de monde** too many people (literally, too much of world). Similarly **beaucoup de monde** a lot of people.

PRACTICE

8 You are sitting in a café in a French seaside town. The woman at the next table strikes up a conversation. Answer her questions, following Philippe's prompts. Yves will give correct versions after the pauses.

9 Here is part of a tourist brochure about the town of Le Conquet on the Breton coast. (Because **de + le = du, la ville de + Le Conquet = la ville du Conquet.**) There are plenty of words you won't know, but once again try the technique of reading the whole text through three times. Then see if you can answer the questions on p. 165.

à remarquer dans la ville du Conquet

Les anciennes maisons des XVème et XVIème siècles, et sur le port quelques habitations de pêcheurs aux curieux escaliers extérieurs.

L'Eglise du Conquet a été construite en 1856, avec les matériaux provenant de l'ancienne église de Lochrist. Sa façade accueille quelques statues du XVème dont un "Dieu de pitié".

Le chœur abrite le tombeau de Dom Michel Le Nobletz.

Près de la très belle plage des Blancs Sablons, un vaste et magnifique terrain de camping de 13 hectares. Sur le littoral déchiqueté, sept plages diversement orientées.

~~~

excursions, promenades

Nombreuses promenades, sentiers qui longent le littoral. Randonnées pédestres organisées par l'Office du Tourisme.

Liaisons maritimes avec les îles de Molène et Ouessant.

La plage des Blancs Sablons, 2,5 km de longueur.

Etang de Kerjean. Bois de Trébabu. Presqu'île de Kermorvan.
~~~

a. When was the church of Le Conquet built? ______________________

b. From which other old church did they take the building materials?

____

c. From which century do the statues of the façade date? ______________________

d. What is the French phrase used for 'seven beaches facing in different directions'? ______________________

e. What is the phrase used for 'rambles organised by the Tourist Office'?

____

ANSWERS P. 170

f. What is the expression used for 'sea links'? ______________________

10 You are trying to arrange a holiday house-swap with French contacts, so you are writing to tell them about your town/village. Use the Key words and phrases to help you write out a description. The framework below may be helpful.

Le village/La ville est	petit/petite	Il y a beaucoup de	restaurants
	grand/grande		'pubs'
	calme		magasins
	un centre industriel		monuments
	un centre de culture		
	ancien(ne)	Nous avons	une école
	vieux/vieille		une bibliothèque (library)
	neuf/neuve		un club de tennis
	beau/belle		un cercle anglo-français
	intéressant/intéressante	Nous sommes	près de …
			à X kilomètres de …
Il y a	X habitants		à X minutes de …
	un théâtre		
	un cinéma	C'est une région	agricole
	une piscine (swimming pool)		industrielle
			touristique
	un musée		peu fréquentée par les touristes
	un château du XVIème siècle		
	une église moyenâgeuse		

Obviously there is no one set of correct answers to this exercise, but it is a very useful one because it will mean that you are able in real life to talk about where you come from. It will also prepare you for Exercise 11!

On the recording for this exercise, Yves will ask you questions about the place you come from.

C'est comment? means 'What's it like?'

Distractions are 'sources of entertainment' – anything from a swimming pool to a theatre.

Use the sentences you wrote in Exercise 10 to help you answer in the pauses. There will be no prompts or 'correct answers' this time as the information you give will depend on you – just simulate a normal conversation with Yves.

GRAMMAR AND EXERCISES

Expressing likes and dislikes

To summarise, the range runs:

j'adore (used more than 'I adore' in English)

j'aime beaucoup	I like very much
j'aime bien	I like
j'aime assez	I quite like
je n'aime pas beaucoup	I don't much like
je n'aime pas	I don't like
je n'aime pas du tout	I don't like at all
je déteste/j'ai horreur de	I hate/I can't bear

J'aime (on its own) means 'I like' or 'I love'. Just as in English 'I love you' is actually stronger than 'I love you very much', **Je t'aime** (rather than **Je t'aime beaucoup**) is what you say to the love of your life.

Finally, if you have pet hates, it is a good idea to learn the word for them, so that you know which dishes to avoid. Two common ones are

l'aïl (m.) garlic
les oignons (m.) onions

You can hear both of them pronounced on the recording.

Mon, ma, mes; ton, ta, tes; son, sa, ses

There are three words for 'my' in French:

- If I'm referring to something masculine, the word for 'my' is **mon: mon père, mon verre.**
- If I'm referring to something feminine, the word to use is **ma: ma mère, ma cuisine.**
- However, if the feminine noun begins with a vowel, **mon** is used: **mon amie, mon orange.**
- The third word is **mes**, which is used for all plural nouns: **mes parents, mes enfants, mes filles, mes amies.**

Ton, ta and **tes** (meaning 'your' for a person you call **tu**) follow exactly the same pattern: **ton père, ta mère, ton amie, tes parents, tes amies.**

Son, sa and **ses** also follow this pattern: **son père** means 'his/her father', **sa mère** 'his/her mother', **ses parents** 'his/her parents'.

Adjectives

Turn back to Unit 7 and reread the Grammar section on adjectives on p. 104. It is probably the most densely packed page you have studied in the course so far, so don't be depressed if you haven't mastered it yet.

Irregular adjectives which have occurred in this unit are:

- **beau** (m.), **belle** (f.), **beaux** (m.pl.), **belles** (f.pl.) beautiful, handsome. The masculine singular form used before a vowel sound is **bel**, e.g.
  un bel appartement a beautiful flat
- **doux** (m.), **douce** (f.), **doux** (m.pl.), **douces** (f.pl.) sweet, soft, gentle
- **vieux** (m.), **vieille** (f.), **vieux** (m.pl.), **vieilles** (f.pl.) old. The masculine singular form used before a vowel sound is **vieil**, e.g.
  un vieil ami an old friend

  Vieil is pronounced exactly the same as **vieille.**

12

Here is a list of adjectives that have occurred in the conversations of this unit. They are listed in the same order as the rules in Unit 7. Can you go through those rules and work out the feminine singular form of each of the adjectives?

Masculine singular	*Feminine singular*
général	______
intéressant	______
romain	______
agréable	______
calme	______
proche	______
propre	______
simple	______
fréquenté	______
cher	______
dangereux	______
moyenâgeux	______
ancien	______
gentil	______

ANSWERS P. 170

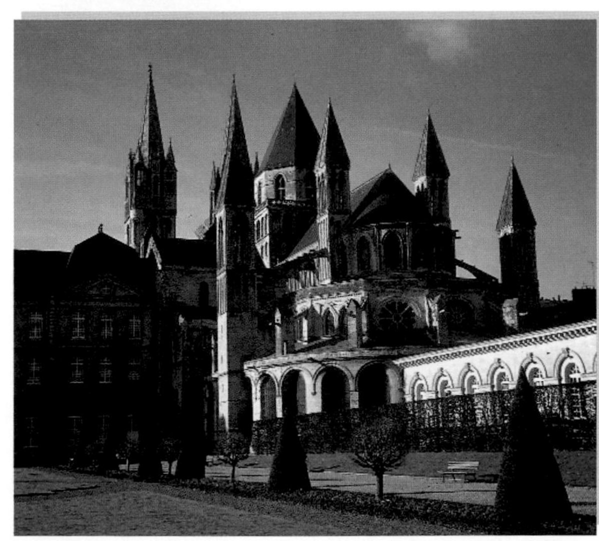

Caen

13

Quelle horreur! Remembering what happens to **de + le** and **de + les**, see if you can translate the following into French (using **avoir horreur de**). If you need to check any part of the verb **avoir**, you'll find it on p. 28.

a. I can't bear cider.

______

b. We can't bear sea-food.

______

c. The children can't bear garlic.

______

d. Charles can't bear onions.

______

e. I can't bear London.

______

f. Emma can't bear the telephone.

______

ANSWERS P. 170

14

Write **Mon**, **Ma** or **Mes**, as appropriate, in each of the gaps:

a. ______ mari est à New York.

b. ______ femme n'aime pas beaucoup Debussy.

c. ______ amie nous invite à déjeuner dimanche.

d. ______ enfants aiment beaucoup manger au restaurant.

e. ______ avion part à 20h15.

f. ______ hôtel est à Saint-Cloud.

g. ______ voiture est au garage.

h. ______ collègues sont très gentils.

ANSWERS P. 170

KEY WORDS AND PHRASES

J'adore la cuisine française	I love (adore) French cooking
Je t'aime	I love you
Dans la nourriture anglaise	In English food
j'aime à peu près tout	I like nearly everything
J'aime beaucoup les fruits	I very much like fruit
les cerises	cherries
J'aime bien les crustacés	I like shellfish
les langoustes	crayfish
les homards	lobsters
Je n'aime pas beaucoup le riz	I don't much like rice
Je n'aime pas les huîtres	I don't like oysters
Je n'aime pas du tout	I don't like at all
le mélange salé-sucré	a sweet-savoury mix
Je déteste les vins doux	I detest sweet wines
– ils me font mal	– they make me ill
J'ai horreur de la triperie	I can't stand tripe
– elle me fait mal	– it makes me ill
le printemps	spring
l'été (m.)	summer
l'automne (m.)	autumn
l'hiver (m.)	winter
C'est très difficile	It is very difficult
par exemple	for example
le cassoulet	casserole of beans and meat
J'aime bien manger et	I like eating well and
surtout bien boire	above all drinking well
C'est une ville ancienne	It is an ancient town
La ville est très vieille	The town is very old
bien restaurée	well restored
la reconstruction	reconstruction
Il y a …	There are …
des remparts romains	Roman ramparts
des maisons moyenâgeuses	medieval houses
le moyen âge	the Middle Ages
En général, c'est intéressant	In general, it is interesting
C'est très agréable	It is very pleasant
A mon avis/à votre avis	In my opinion/in your opinion
La mer est très proche	The sea is very near
On va sur la côte	People go to the coast
C'est une plage propre	It is a clean beach
pas dangereuse	(which is) not dangerous
Ça devient trop fréquenté	It's becoming overcrowded
Il y a trop de monde	There are too many people
Il n'y a pas beaucoup de vie	It's not very lively
La vie n'est pas encore trop chère	The cost of living is not too high yet

Senlis

Senlis is an old town of some 15,000 inhabitants about 30 miles north of Paris. It has a Gothic cathedral and some fine ramparts, some of them Gallo-Roman. There are picturesque old streets and names recalling the town's history, e.g. la Place des Arènes (Amphitheatre Square) and le Rempart des Otages (Hostages' Rampart).

Normandy

There are many attractive old villages in Normandy. It is an ideal region to explore slowly by car. The main places of interest include:

Bayeux

(Pronounced 'Buy-uh', not 'Bay-uh'.) The famous tapestry showing the Norman invasion of 1066 is very well displayed. It is generally known in France as la Tapisserie de la Reine Mathilde because of the tradition that it was worked by Queen Matilda and her ladies-in-waiting.

Mont-St-Michel

France's most popular tourist attraction outside Paris – a dramatic outcrop of rock cut off from the shore at high tide. A chapel built there in the 8th century to mark the appearance of the Archangel Michael grew into a powerful monastery. It was later used by Napoleon as a prison.

Rouen

The old heart of the city is still delightful. The Kings of England were invested as Dukes of Normandy in the Cathedral of Rouen and Joan of Arc was burned at the stake there.

Honfleur

An astonishingly picturesque but still working port surrounded by cobbled streets of slate-hung houses. The 15th-century wooden church of St Catherine, with its unusual double nave following the design of ships' hulls, was built by ships' carpenters to celebrate the expulsion of the English.

La Roche-sur-Yon

La Roche-sur-Yon is a quiet little town of some 48,000 people in the department of la Vendée (south of Brittany). It has a theatre, a museum and a Conservatory of Music and Dramatic Art.

Soulac-sur-Mer

Soulac is a charming little seaside town some 60 miles north-west of Bordeaux near the estuary of the Gironde. It has only about 2000 inhabitants in the winter, but its excellent sandy beaches attract as many holidaymakers as its hotels and camp-sites can accommodate in the summer. A favourite activity for visitors is to hire a bicycle and ride on one of the specially made cycle tracks through the local forest.

AND FINALLY...

15

Do you remember the game where you have to answer questions without saying 'yes' or 'no'? On the recording, Carolle will ask you a string of quick-fire questions about your likes and dislikes: try to answer each as accurately as possible (i.e. with a truthful shade of liking/dislike) without saying **oui** or **non**.

Some extra vocabulary for this activity:

la cuisse de grenouille
frog's leg
la cuisine chinoise
Chinese cooking

ANSWERS

Exercise 2

- ✔ la nourriture française
- ✔ la nourriture anglaise
- ✘ la gelée
- ✘ les vins doux
- ✔ les vins secs
- ✔ le riz
- ✔ les pommes de terre
- ✔ les framboises
- ✔ les cerises
- ✘ les bananes
- ✘ les oranges

Exercise 2

	Likes	Dislikes
Carolle	cheese, eggs, fruit, vegetables	meat, fish, sweet wine
Yves	steak, red wine, French cooking	salads, potatoes, hot dogs

Exercise 4

Here is the full transcript:
En général, j'aime bien la cuisine anglaise. J'aime toutes les viandes et à peu près tous les poissons, mais les crustacés me font mal. J'aime beaucoup les fruits et les légumes, mais je n'aime pas les tomates et j'ai horreur des bananes. Pour les boissons, j'aime bien la bière anglaise mais je déteste le whisky.
You should avoid giving her shellfish, tomatoes, bananas and whisky.

Exercise 6

(a) Je n'aime pas le porc. **(b)** J'ai horreur du cheval. (or Je déteste le cheval.) **(c)** Patrick déteste les œufs. (or Patrick a horreur des œufs.) **(d)** Anne n'aime pas le riz. **(e)** Julie n'aime pas beaucoup le vin. **(f)** Sinon, nous aimons beaucoup la cuisine française!
Note that the articles are necessary in these sentences. Where English has, for example, 'I don't like pork', French has to say **Je n'aime pas <u>le</u> porc**.

Exercise 9

(a) 1856 **(b)** The church of Lochrist **(c)** 15th **(d)** Sept plages diversement orientées **(e)** Randonnées pédestres organisées par l'Office du Tourisme **(f)** Liaisons maritimes

Exercise 12

générale/intéressante/romaine/agréable/calme/proche/propre/simple/fréquentée/chère/dangereuse/moyenâgeuse/ancienne/gentille

Exercise 13

(a) J'ai horreur du cidre. **(b)** Nous avons horreur des fruits de mer. **(c)** Les enfants ont horreur de l'aïl. **(d)** Charles a horreur des oignons. **(e)** J'ai horreur de Londres. **(f)** Emma a horreur du téléphone.

Exercise 14

(a) Mon **(b)** Ma **(c)** Mon **(d)** Mes **(e)** Mon **(f)** Mon **(g)** Ma **(h)** Mes

12 WHERE YOU LIVE AND WHAT THE WEATHER IS LIKE

What you will learn

- expressing your feelings for the place where you live
- discussing the quality of life in the town and in the country
- understanding weather forecasts
- talking about the weather
- something about French attitudes to Paris

Before you begin

Paris and the provinces

One of the most stimulating things about learning another language is discovering those areas of life in which basic assumptions and ways of looking at the world are both similar to and subtly different from our own. An increased sensitivity to these things makes us more adaptable people as we become aware that the categories into which we divide up the world are not the only possible ways of seeing things. The ageing process has been neatly described as 'hardening of the categories', so anything that makes us less rigid must be welcome!

This unit moves into one of these culturally interesting areas as it looks at people's feelings about living in Paris or living in the provinces. Obviously, many of the issues have echoes in our own society and you will be able to reuse much of the language of the unit in explaining why you choose to live where you do. However, there is not in most western countries the absolute contrast between the capital and the rest of the country that there is in French psychology. One needs to be aware that for many French people, moving to Paris signals personal and professional success. To stay in the provinces from choice is a more thorough-going rejection of life in the fast lane than it usually is in Britain.

The weather

Understanding weather forecasts can be quite difficult, even in your own language, so in the real situation you need to use a conscious strategy of listening out for the key words and phrases you will learn in this unit.

Where we say 'It is hot/cold/etc.', French uses the verb **Il fait**:

Il fait chaud It is hot
Il fait froid It is cold
Il fait beau It is fine
Quel temps fait-il? What's the weather like? (literally What weather does it make?)

Pronunciation notes

This unit will give you some practice at the nasal vowels. There is more explanation in Exercise 3.

CONVERSATIONS 

 *Born in Paris*

LISTEN FOR...

- **je suis née** I was born
- **libre** free

Michèle Moi, je suis née à Paris. Paris, c'est mon village natal. C'est beau, et en plus on est libre – on est complètement libre à Paris. C'est une très, très belle ville. Il y a toujours quelque chose à faire et c'est intéressant pour ça.

- **Moi, je suis née** I was born (literally Me, I am born). If a man were speaking, the phrase would have been written
- **Moi, je suis né,** but pronounced exactly the same.

The use of **je suis** to indicate the past with certain verbs will be explained in Unit 15.

en plus moreover

mon village natal the 'village' where I was born.

- **complètement libre** completely free. But for 'free', meaning 'at no cost', use **gratuit.**
- **Il y a toujours quelque chose à faire** There is always something to do.
- **c'est intéressant pour ça** it's interesting because of (literally, for) that.

The anonymity of the big city

LISTEN FOR...

- **anonyme** anonymous
- **personne ne** (+ verb) nobody

Jean-Claude J'adore Paris. Je me sens anonyme. Personne ne me connaît et personne n'a envie de savoir qui je suis.

Je me sens anonyme I feel (myself) anonymous. **Se sentir**, to feel (oneself), is known as a 'reflexive' verb, because its action 'reflects' back on the subject of the verb, i.e. it indicates something one does to oneself. There is more about reflexive verbs in the Grammar section on pp. 182–183. **Se sentir** is also used of health:

▶ **Comment vous sentez-vous?** How are you feeling?
▶ **Je me sens mieux aujourd'hui** I feel better today.

▶ **Personne ne me connaît** Nobody knows me.
▶ **Personne n'a envie de** Nobody wants (from **avoir envie de**, to have a desire to/for). This construction with **personne ne ...** is explained further in the Grammar section on p. 182.

▶ **savoir qui je suis** to know who I am. Remember that **savoir** and **connaître** both mean 'to know', but **savoir** is used for knowing something intellectually – knowing facts – and **connaître** is used for being acquainted – knowing a person or a place. (See p. 120.)

The quality of life

LISTEN FOR...

▶ **les Parisiens**	Parisians
▶ **des salaires**	salaries
▶ **les provinciaux**	people in the provinces
▶ **tendue**	stressed
▶ **le temps de vivre**	the time to enjoy life

Jacques Dans l'ensemble, les Parisiens ont des salaires un peu plus élevés ... que les provinciaux, mais, heu, ils vivent d'une façon ... plus ... tendue. Le temps est très précieux à Paris, alors que ... en province, heu, on a peut-être un peu plus le temps de vivre. La qualité de la vie est peut-être supérieure, heu, en province.

dans l'ensemble overall
ils vivent (from **vivre**) they live
précieux (m.)/**précieuse** (f.) precious
alors que whereas
▶ **la qualité de la vie** the quality of life
supérieure (f.) (*here*) superior, better

un peu plus élevés a bit higher. From the verb **élever**, to raise. (Also used of children: **un enfant bien élevé** is a well brought-up child and **un élève** is a pupil – who is in the course of being brought up.)

les provinciaux people from the provinces.

d'une façon plus ... tendue under more stress (literally, in a more stretched way).

le temps in this case means 'time'. (It can also mean 'weather'.) Note that **temps** is never used in asking the time (remember **Quelle heure est-il?**).

PRACTICE

1 On the recording for this exercise, Yves and Carolle give their opinions on the subject of the relative quality of life in Paris and in a village. You will hear the word **pourquoi?** (why?).

a. Where does Yves think the quality of life is higher? ______________________

b. Why does he think so? ______________________

____

____

c. Which does Carolle prefer? ______________________

d. What reasons does she give? ______________________

ANSWERS P. 186

____

2 See if you can reuse the language from Conversations 1 to answer Yves' questions according to Philippe's prompts. This time, Yves will call you **tu**. His first question will be **Où es-tu né(e)?** Where were you born? Carolle will give correct answers after the pauses.

3 Pronunciation practice: there are three main nasal vowels in French. You have already practised the ones most often spelt '**on**' and '**en**'. In the last recording of Conversations 1, there were examples of the third one, in **Parisiens**, **provinciaux** and **province**. It is most often spelt '**in**'. In speech, the choice of nasal vowel quite often distinguishes between words. On the recording, Philippe, Carolle and Yves will read out the list below. Philippe will say those with the sound '**on**'; Carolle will say those with '**en**' and Yves will say those with '**in**'. Repeat each group of three words after the speakers.

'on'		'en'		'in'	
long	(long)	**lent**	(slow)	**lin**	(linen)
pont	(bridge)	**pan!**	(wham!)	**peint**	(paints)
son	(his/her/its)	**sans**	(without)	**sain**	(healthy)
ton	(your/tone)	**temps**	(weather/time)	**teint**	(colouring)
vont	((they) go)	**vent**	(wind)	**vin**	(wine)

Notes

- Philippe, Carolle and Yves pronounce these vowels in a way that is normal in the northern half of France. In the south, '**en**' is pronounced as '**in**', so that, for example, **Provence** is pronounced **province**!
- There is a fourth nasal vowel, '**un**', but we shall not be doing any work on it as nowadays it is increasingly pronounced the same as '**in**'.

CONVERSATION

Village life

LISTEN FOR...

j'ai vécu longtemps	I lived for a long time
▶ **le bruit**	noise
un rythme de vie	rhythm of life
▶ **des inconvénients**	drawbacks
▶ **une forêt**	forest
des canaux	canals
▶ **des oiseaux**	birds

Guy

Guy Nous habitons dans un village, et même dans un petit village – ce qui est bien agréable. Heu, je peux en parler d'autant plus que j'ai vécu longtemps dans une grande ville, avec la pollution, le bruit, parfois même des problèmes de ... d'agressivité; et là, c'est la verdure, c'est un rythme de vie tellement plus paisible. Bien sûr, il y a des inconvénients: l'alimentation, les médecins, la culture, tout ça se trouve en ville, mais nous vivons au milieu de la verdure, puisque nous sommes exactement au centre d'une forêt, avec des arbres d'un côté, des champs de l'autre, et, tout autour de la maison, des canaux, qui attirent des, des oiseaux comme les hérons, et parfois même, pendant les hivers rudes, les cigognes.

▶ **la pollution** pollution
▶ **même** (*here*) even
l'agressivité (f.) aggression
ce qui (that) which
▶ **parfois** sometimes
tellement so much
▶ **paisible** peaceful
▶ **le milieu** middle
▶ **l'arbre** (m.) tree
▶ **d'un côté** on one side
▶ **de l'autre** on the other
autour de around
attirer to attract
le héron heron
rude hard, rough
la cigogne stork

Le canal de Nantes à Brest

je peux en parler I can speak about it.

d'autant plus que all the more because

j'ai vécu longtemps I lived for a long time. You have not yet learned how to express the past, but this is an irregular past form from the verb **vivre**. There are two verbs 'to live' in French: **habiter**, which has the sense of inhabiting, and **vivre**, which has the sense of being alive. (You may remember **Votre père vit toujours?** Is your father still alive? from Unit 2.) In some contexts, as in this conversation, you could use either verb: Guy had 'spent a lot of his life' in a big city – he had also 'inhabited it for a long time'.

tout ça se trouve en ville all that is to be found in town (literally, finds itself in town). There is more about reflexive verbs like **se trouver** in the Grammar section on pp. 182–183.

PRACTICE

4 Can you name three drawbacks and three advantages of city life, as Guy sees it? If possible, work from the recording rather than the transcript to do this.

Drawbacks: ______________________________

____

Advantages: ______________________________

____

ANSWERS P. 186

5 Now listen to the recording for this activity and see how the speaker feels about living in a village.

Just as **ne** + **personne** means 'nobody', **ne** + **rien** means 'nothing', e.g.
Il n'y a rien à faire le soir There is nothing to do in the evening.
(Again, this will be explained more fully in the Grammar section.)

Which of these statements would the speaker consider true and which false?

a. Le village se situe au milieu d'une forêt. vrai/faux

b. Il y a beaucoup de vie dans ce village. vrai/faux

c. Il y a cinq magasins au centre du village. vrai/faux

d. Il y a un cinéma et un théâtre. vrai/faux

e. Il y a un très bon petit restaurant. vrai/faux

f. Il y a un petit bar. vrai/faux

g. Avant 19h, il y a des bus pour aller en ville. vrai/faux

ANSWERS P. 186

6 A French friend is asking you about the village where you are spending your holiday. Follow Philippe's prompts as you reply. Carolle will give correct versions of your lines after the pauses.

CONVERSATIONS 3

The weather

There are a lot of different terms for weather conditions, but many of them have obvious connections with each other. Study the list below before you listen to the conversations. (For active use, you don't need more than one version of each kind of weather, but it is useful to be able to understand all of them.)

Sunshine
Il fait beau.
Le soleil brille.
Le temps est ensoleillé.

Clouds
Il y a des nuages.
Il fait un temps nuageux.

Rain
Il pleut.
La pluie tombe.
Il fait un temps pluvieux.

Storm
Il y a un orage.
Il fait un temps orageux.

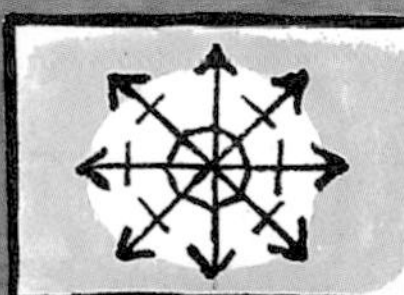

Snow
Il neige.
La neige tombe.

Other vocabulary
une averse a shower
une éclaircie a sunny interval
le brouillard fog

Today's weather: Version 1

LISTEN FOR...

Some of those weather terms as Yves describes today's weather in the different regions of France.

Yves En Bretagne, le temps est nuageux.
Dans le sud-ouest, il y a des orages.
La Côte d'Azur est ensoleillée.
Dans le Massif Central, il y a de la pluie.
Dans les Alpes, il y a de la neige.
Dans la région parisienne, il y a des averses
et dans le Nord de la France, il y a des éclaircies.

- **la Bretagne** Brittany
- **le sud-ouest** the south-west
- **la Côte d'Azur** the Riviera
- **la région parisienne** the Paris area

le Nord de la France is specifically the area around Lille, not the whole northern half of the country.

Today's weather: Version 2

LISTEN FOR...

More weather terms, as Carolle describes exactly the same regional weather in slightly different words.

Carolle En Bretagne, il y a beaucoup de nuages.
Dans le sud-ouest, il fait un temps orageux.
Il fait beau sur la Côte d'Azur.
Dans le Massif Central, il pleut.
Dans les Alpes, il neige.
Dans la région parisienne, il pleut de temps en temps
et dans le Nord de la France, le soleil brille de temps en temps.

- **de temps en temps** from time to time – very confusing, when **le temps** also means 'weather'!

PRACTICE

7 Without looking back at the transcript, listen again to both halves of Conversations 3, following them on the weather map below. Are there any mismatches between what is said on the recording and what is shown on the map?

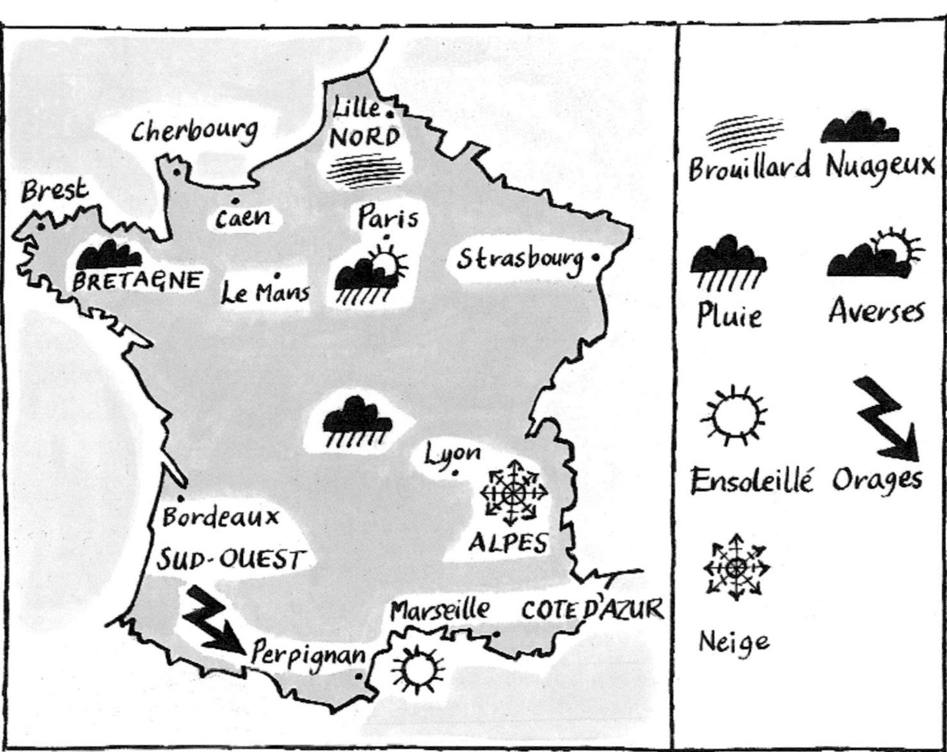

ANSWERS P. 186

8 To help you memorise the vocabulary on weather, complete the sentences in the right-hand column so that they mean the same as the ones in the left.

a.	Il pleut.	Il y a de la ______
b.	Il pleut de temps en temps.	Il y a des ______
c.	Il fait un temps orageux.	Il y a un ______
d.	Le temps est très nuageux.	Il y a beaucoup de ______
e.	Le temps est ensoleillé.	Il fait ______
f.	Le soleil brille de temps en temps.	Il y a des ______

ANSWERS P. 186

9 On the recording, Carolle will ask you five times over **Quel temps fait-il?** (What's the weather like?) Follow Philippe's prompts to give the appropriate answer from the box. Yves will give correct versions after the pauses.

Il fait beau   Il pleut   Il y a des nuages
Il neige   Il y a du brouillard

CONVERSATION 4

A mock weather forecast

LISTEN FOR...

- **la météo** weather forecast

Anna Guylaine, à ton avis, quel temps fera-t-il demain?

Guylaine Je vais te dire la météo de la France. Sur la Bretagne, il est prévu un temps pluvieux, parce qu'il pleut toujours en Bretagne. Dans le sud-ouest, temps nuageux, parce qu'il y a souvent des nuages dans le sud-ouest. Sur la Côte d'Azur, ensoleillé, parce que le soleil brille toujours. Dans le Massif Central, des averses, parce qu'il pleut beaucoup. Dans les Alpes, des éclaircies, entre deux nuages. Dans la région parisienne, brouillard – il y a toujours du brouillard dans la région parisienne. Et dans le Nord de la France, des éclaircies – entre deux flocons de neige!

- **à ton avis** in your opinion
- **entre** between
  le flocon de neige snowflake
- **quel temps fera-t-il demain?** what will the weather be like tomorrow? (literally, what weather will it make tomorrow?) 'What is the weather like today?' is **Quel temps fait-il aujourd'hui? Fera** is an example of the future tense (from the irregular verb **faire**).
- **Sur la Bretagne, il est prévu un temps pluvieux.** lit. Over Brittany, it is forecast a rainy weather.

PRACTICE

10 Without looking back at the transcript, play the last recording (A mock weather forecast) again and see if you can answer the following questions:

What sort of weather does Guylaine predict

a. for Brittany?

____

b. for the South-West?

____

c. for the Riviera?

____

d. for the Massif Central?

____

____

e. for the Parisian region?

____

____

ANSWERS P. 186

11 You have invited Carolle to stay. She telephones from France to ask what the weather is like at different times of the year. Follow Philippe's prompts to answer her questions. Don't forget **Il fait chaud** and **Il fait froid**, which you met in Before you begin. You will also need the expression **en général** (generally). Yves will give correct versions of your part after the pauses.

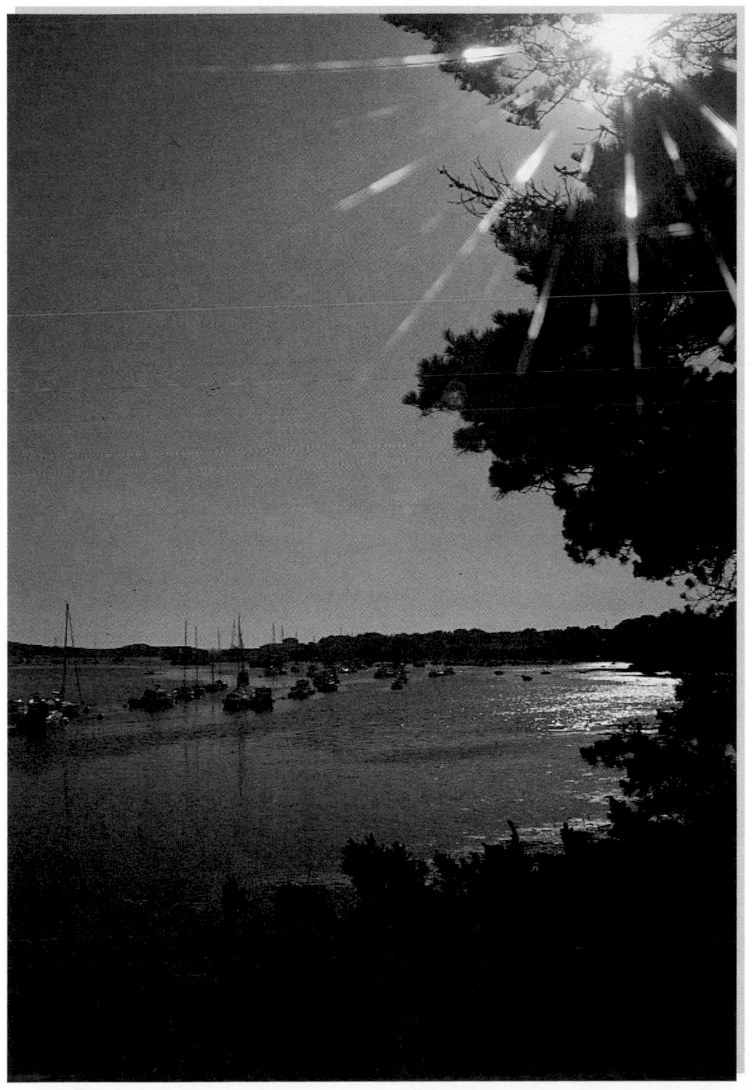

Le soleil brille

GRAMMAR AND EXERCISES

Negatives

Like **ne...pas** (not), most French negatives are made up of **ne** plus another word. Here are some examples:

Personne ne me connaît.
 Nobody knows me.
Je ne connais personne.
 I know nobody/I don't know anybody.
Il ne boit jamais.
 He never drinks.
La vie n'est jamais simple.
 Life is never simple.
Tu ne comprends rien.
 You don't understand anything.
Je ne veux rien.
 I don't want anything.
Il ne travaille que le matin.
 He only works in the morning.
Ce n'est que le début!
 It's only the beginning!

Ne always goes before the verb and the other half of the negative usually goes after it, unless it is the subject of the verb, as in **Personne ne me connaît.**

In speech, the **ne** is very often omitted, but it has to be used in writing.

More about questions

You are by now very used to two ways of asking the kind of questions that can be answered by 'yes' or 'no':

- Just putting a questioning intonation into the voice (in speech only!)
- Putting **Est-ce que** at the beginning of the sentence.

There is a third, more literary, way of forming these questions, which you need to understand if not to use. This is to 'invert' the verb, e.g.

Tu aimes les escargots.
 You like snails.
Aimes-tu les escargots?
 Do you like snails?
Vous parlez français.
 You speak French.
Parlez-vous français?
 Do you speak French?

This way of forming questions is more complicated than the other two so you would do best to stick to **Est-ce que...?** in your own speech and writing.

The words which can introduce questions include: **où?** (where?), **quand?** (when?), **comment?** (how?), **pourquoi?** (why?), **à quelle heure?** (at what time?) and **combien de?** (how much?/how many?). They can be followed by any of the question structures which have just been discussed, so, for example, the question 'Why are you learning French?' could be expressed:

- **Pourquoi vous apprenez le français?** (informal – used in speech only)
- **Pourquoi est-ce que vous apprenez le français?**
- **Pourquoi apprenez-vous le français?**

Again, you are advised to stick to the form with **est-ce que...?**

Reflexive verbs

Tout ça se trouve en ville
 lit. All that itself finds in town

Verbs like **se trouver** are called reflexive verbs because their action reflects back on their subject. Other examples are **se lever**, to get up (lit. to get oneself up) and **se rendre (à)**, to get oneself (to a place). The pronoun is not always **se**: it depends on the subject of the verb. Here is the present tense of the verb **se coucher**, to go to bed:

je me couche	**nous nous couchons**
tu te couches	**vous vous couchez**
il/elle se couche	**ils/elles se couchent**

Another useful reflexive verb is **s'appeler** (lit. to call oneself):

Comment vous appelez-vous?
What is your name?
Je m'appelle Stéphanie
My name is Stephanie

12 Combine the part-sentence on the left with the negative on the right to form a complete sentence, paying particular attention to the word order.

a. Elle aime ne … personne

____

b. Il aime ne … rien

____

c. Nous avons 1000 euros ne … que

____

d. Elle travaille ne … jamais

____

e. Il comprend ne … personne

____

f. Je comprends ne … rien

____

g. Je travaille la nuit ne … que

____

h. Il parle de ses parents ne … jamais

____

ANSWERS P. 186

13 See if you can form questions by combining each of these sentences with the question word given and **est-ce que**. Example:

Elle travaille. Où? **Où est-ce qu'elle travaille?**

a. Il travaille. Comment?

____

b. Ils se rendent à Paris. Quand?

____

c. Elle téléphone à Monsieur Martineau. Pourquoi?

____

d. Vous habitez en France. Où?

____

e. Vous en voulez. Combien?

____

f. Tu te lèves. A quelle heure?

____

ANSWERS P. 186

14 See if you can write out a full sentence giving a negative answer to each of these questions, on the model:

Qui est-ce qu'elle aime? (Personne)
Whom does she love? (Nobody)
Elle n'aime personne.
She doesn't love anybody.

a. Qui est-ce qu'elle voit? (Personne)

____

b. Qu'est-ce qu'il veut? (Rien)

____

c. Quand est-ce qu'il travaille? (Jamais)

____

d. Qu'est-ce que nous faisons ce soir? (Rien)

____

e. Combien de possibilités avons-nous? (Que deux)

____

f. Qui comprend ce texte? (Personne)

____

ANSWERS P. 186

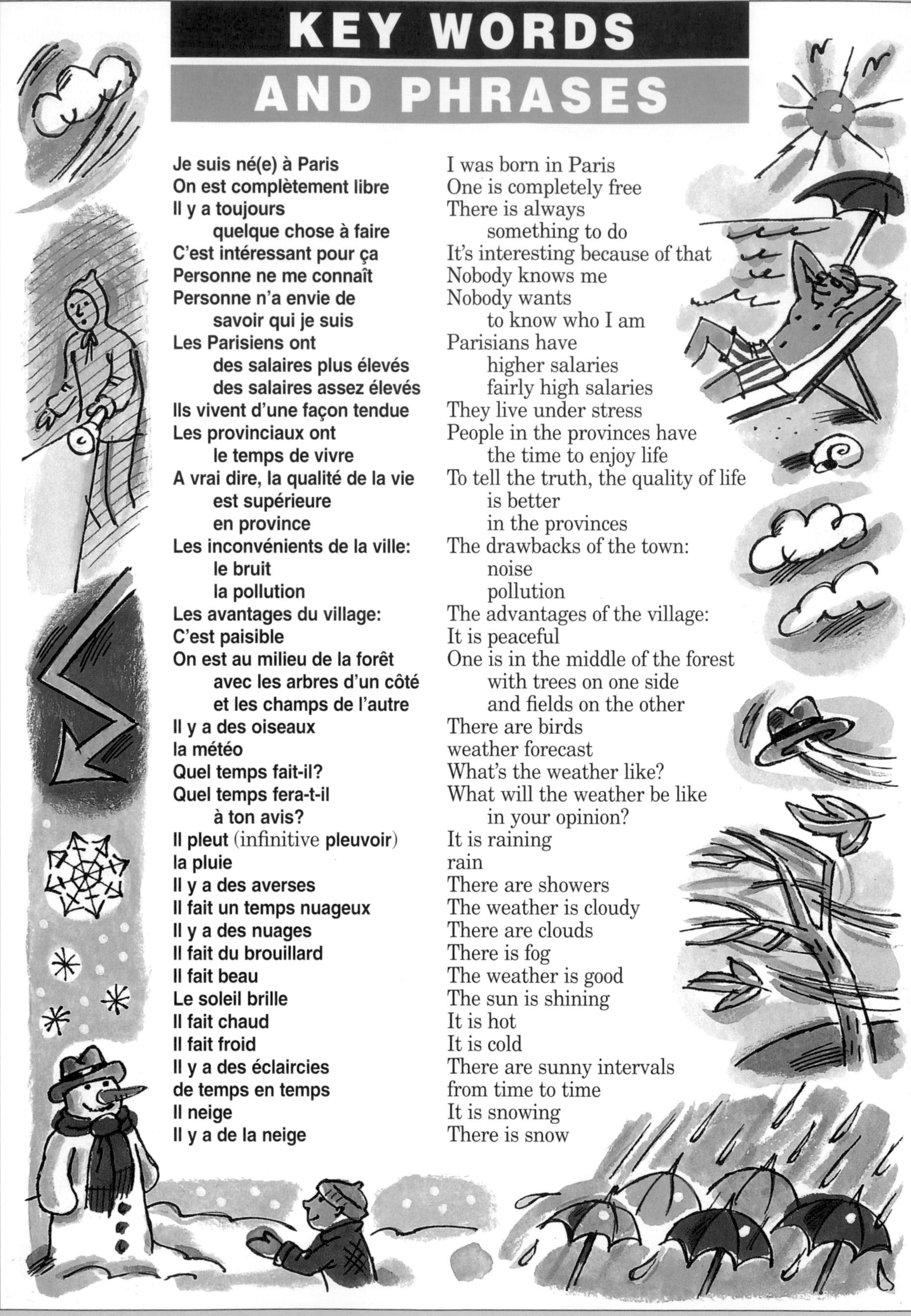

KEY WORDS AND PHRASES

Je suis né(e) à Paris	I was born in Paris
On est complètement libre	One is completely free
Il y a toujours quelque chose à faire	There is always something to do
C'est intéressant pour ça	It's interesting because of that
Personne ne me connaît	Nobody knows me
Personne n'a envie de savoir qui je suis	Nobody wants to know who I am
Les Parisiens ont	Parisians have
des salaires plus élevés	higher salaries
des salaires assez élevés	fairly high salaries
Ils vivent d'une façon tendue	They live under stress
Les provinciaux ont le temps de vivre	People in the provinces have the time to enjoy life
A vrai dire, la qualité de la vie est supérieure en province	To tell the truth, the quality of life is better in the provinces
Les inconvénients de la ville:	The drawbacks of the town:
le bruit	noise
la pollution	pollution
Les avantages du village:	The advantages of the village:
C'est paisible	It is peaceful
On est au milieu de la forêt avec les arbres d'un côté et les champs de l'autre	One is in the middle of the forest with trees on one side and fields on the other
Il y a des oiseaux	There are birds
la météo	weather forecast
Quel temps fait-il?	What's the weather like?
Quel temps fera-t-il à ton avis?	What will the weather be like in your opinion?
Il pleut (infinitive **pleuvoir**)	It is raining
la pluie	rain
Il y a des averses	There are showers
Il fait un temps nuageux	The weather is cloudy
Il y a des nuages	There are clouds
Il fait du brouillard	There is fog
Il fait beau	The weather is good
Le soleil brille	The sun is shining
Il fait chaud	It is hot
Il fait froid	It is cold
Il y a des éclaircies	There are sunny intervals
de temps en temps	from time to time
Il neige	It is snowing
Il y a de la neige	There is snow

DID YOU KNOW?

Paris et la province

Paris is at the heart of French life and French psychology. It is pre-eminent in finance, politics, administration, the arts, education, fashion and commerce. Even in the Overseas Departments and Territories of France, 10,000 or more kilometres away, there is an overwhelming sense that Paris is the centre of the world. Within metropolitan France, there is a complex love-hate relationship between people in the provinces and their capital city: they are immensely and justly proud of its monuments, its art, its music and its theatre, but many feel alienated by the way it has come to dominate the rest of the country and by the **vie de dingue** (rat race) of its inhabitants. People are often resentful of what they perceive as the arrogance of Parisians towards **'les provinciaux'**. On the road, boorish driving will often provoke the comment **'Bien sûr: 75'**, because the 75 on the number-plate indicates that the car was registered in Paris. The way that Parisians speak of the provinces of France as **la province** (singular and undifferentiated) is taken by many as yet another indication of Parisians' sense of superiority: the attitude that what is not Paris is not worth bothering with.

Former indignation in the provinces that **tout passe par Paris**, that is to say that local issues were decided by Parisians who knew nothing about them, was not confined to minority political groups seeking independence for Provence or Brittany. The Parisian stranglehold on decision-making had led to some particularly absurd directives for Overseas Departments with customs, cultures and climates that were generally quite unknown to the Paris bureaucrats. As a response to this situation, partial devolution of local government was introduced under the presidency of François Mitterrand.

The visitor who wants to get to know France must see both Paris and little places in the provinces (which are very different one from another). Paris is beautiful and exciting but (unless you know people in advance) the smaller towns and villages are usually more rewarding in terms of human contact and opportunities to practise the language.

What's on in Paris

Il y a toujours quelque chose à faire à Paris – indeed there is **l'embarras du choix** (an embarrassment of choice). There are several low-price weekly publications, such as *Pariscope*, which are the equivalent of *Time Out*, giving details of theatres, cinemas, restaurants, exhibitions, monuments, walking and boat tours and also some of the less savoury forms of Paris night-life (which cater primarily for British tourists out for a not-so-cheap thrill).

Tourism in Paris

One of the pleasantest ways of seeing a surprisingly large number of the monuments of Paris is by taking a boat trip on the Seine, either on a **bateau mouche** or on a **vedette** (starting point on the tip of the Ile de la Cité under the Pont Neuf).

Guide books to Paris are legion. Two suggestions:

Paris: the Michelin Green Tourist Guide (updated regularly).
Kate Baillie and Tim Salmon, *Rough Guide to Paris*, Rough Guides Ltd (updated regularly).

AND FINALLY...

15 On the recording, Yves is asking you about your town. Follow Philippe's prompts to answer his questions. Carolle will give correct versions after you have had a chance to speak.

France Télécom et le monde est plus proche
Télécarte 120

ANSWERS

Exercise 1

(a) In Paris. **(b)** Salaries are higher and there is a lot to do: theatres, cinemas, museums and restaurants. **(c)** A village. **(d)** It is quiet. You know the people. You are less stressed and you have time to enjoy life.

Exercise 4

Drawbacks of city life: pollution, noise, aggression
Advantages: food supplies, doctors and culture are all in town

Exercise 5

(a) vrai **(b)** faux **(c)** faux **(d)** faux **(e)** faux **(f)** vrai **(g)** vrai (he says there are no buses *after* 7 p.m.)

Exercise 7

The only mismatch is for le Nord, which the map shows as foggy but which the speakers say has sunny intervals.

Exercise 8

(a) pluie **(b)** averses **(c)** orage **(d)** nuages **(e)** beau (*or* chaud) **(f)** éclaircies

Exercise 10

(a) rain **(b)** cloudy weather **(c)** sunshine **(d)** showers **(e)** fog

Exercise 12

(a) Elle n'aime personne. **(b)** Il n'aime rien. **(c)** Nous n'avons que 1000 euros. **(d)** Elle ne travaille jamais **(e)** Il ne comprend personne. **(f)** Je ne comprends rien. **(g)** Je ne travaille que la nuit. **(h)** Il ne parle jamais de ses parents.

Exercise 13

(a) Comment est-ce qu'il travaille? **(b)** Quand est-ce qu'ils se rendent à Paris? **(c)** Pourquoi est-ce qu'elle téléphone à Monsieur Martineau? **(d)** Où est-ce que vous habitez en France? **(e)** Combien est-ce que vous en voulez? **(f)** A quelle heure est-ce que tu te lèves?

Exercise 14

(a) Elle ne voit personne. **(b)** Il ne veut rien. **(c)** Il ne travaille jamais. **(d)** Nous ne faisons rien ce soir. **(e)** Nous n'avons que deux possibilités. **(f)** Personne ne comprend ce texte.

13 MORE ABOUT YOURSELF

What you will learn

- describing your house or flat
- understanding accounts of past events
- talking about the past
- talking about your language learning
- information on intensive language courses
- something about French housing

Before you begin

You are probably frustrated at not knowing how to talk about the past in French. The time has come! In this unit you will be coming to grips with the basic past tense, known as the perfect. (This does not mean 'absolutely wonderful' – it means that the action of the verb has been 'perfected' or completed and so is in the past!) Here is an example:

J'ai travaillé means 'I have worked' or 'I worked'. Its construction is exactly the same as 'I have + worked': **J'ai + travaillé**. 'You have worked' or 'You worked' is **Tu as travaillé**. 'He/she has worked' or 'He/she worked' is **Il/elle a travaillé**. And so on, with the other parts of **avoir**:

Nous avons travaillé
Vous avez travaillé
Ils/elles ont travaillé

The grammatical term for forms like **travaillé** is the past participle.

But first a little revision of vocabulary: can you remember the French for

- the ground floor?
- the bedroom?
- the bathroom?
- the loo?
- the first floor?
- a double bed?
- the shower?

If you couldn't remember some of the words, it might be a good idea to go back and revise Units 4 and 5.

Answers p. 202

Pronunciation notes

This unit will give you some more practice at the sound '**é**'. It will be tied in with the grammar practice, as '**é**' is the most common ending for past participles.

CONVERSATIONS

Michel's apartment

LISTEN FOR...

- **un appartement** flat, apartment
- **pièces** rooms
- **salle de séjour** sitting room

Michel J'ai un appartement de quatre pièces: une pièce au rez-de-chaussée, qui est mon bureau professionnel, et trois pièces au premier étage: salle de séjour et deux chambres.

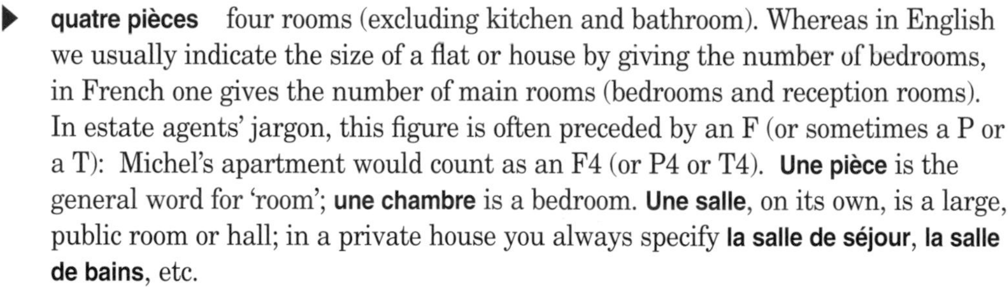

- **quatre pièces** four rooms (excluding kitchen and bathroom). Whereas in English we usually indicate the size of a flat or house by giving the number of bedrooms, in French one gives the number of main rooms (bedrooms and reception rooms). In estate agents' jargon, this figure is often preceded by an F (or sometimes a P or a T): Michel's apartment would count as an F4 (or P4 or T4). **Une pièce** is the general word for 'room'; **une chambre** is a bedroom. **Une salle**, on its own, is a large, public room or hall; in a private house you always specify **la salle de séjour**, **la salle de bains**, etc.
- **mon bureau professionnel** my professional office. **Le bureau** is also used for a study in a house.

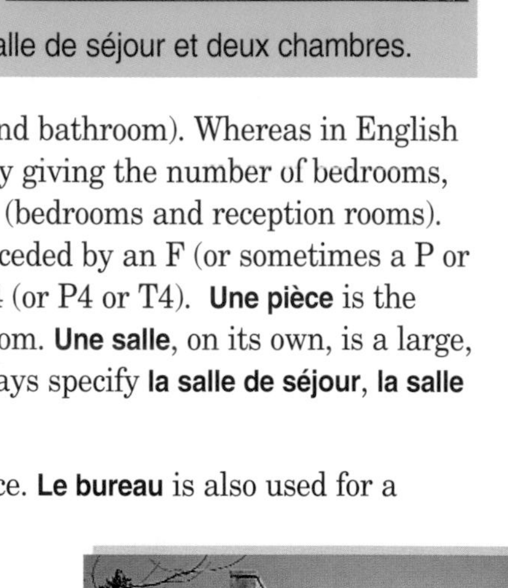

Denise's house

LISTEN FOR...

- **une entrée** entrance hall
- **des placards de rangement** storage cupboards
- **un débarras** junk room

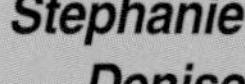

Stephanie Elle est comment, la maison?

Denise Au rez-de-chaussée, il y a une entrée, le bureau de mon mari, deux chambres, une salle d'eau, des toilettes, des placards de rangement, et au premier étage, nous avons la cuisine, la salle de séjour, la salle de bains, trois chambres, un débarras, des toilettes.

- **Elle est comment, la maison?** What's the house like?
- **une salle d'eau** a shower room.

Barbara's house

LISTEN FOR...

- **un pavillon** detached house
- **un grenier** attic
- **une cave** cellar

Barbara Nous avons, heu, un petit pavillon. Nous avons un grand salon où une partie est salon et une partie, salle à manger. Il y a une cuisine. Chacun a sa chambre et il y a aussi la chambre des invités et il y a des salles de bains … Et nous avons aussi un grenier qui, pour le moment, est vide, parce que … il faut le nettoyer – et une cave aussi, où on met des choses … des conserves … certaines choses comme ça.

- **la partie** part
- **la salle à manger** dining room
- **la chambre des invités** guest room

vide empty
la conserve preserve – jam, bottled fruit, etc.
certaines (f.pl.) certain

- **un grand salon** a large sitting room. **Un salon** is the same as **une salle de séjour**. It is also sometimes called **un living** (from the English 'living room').

Chacun a sa chambre Each (of us) has his/her own room.

Il faut le nettoyer We must clean it (literally, it is necessary it to clean). For **le** and **la** when used to mean 'him', 'her' or 'it', see Grammar, p. 150.

Sylvie's bed-sit

LISTEN FOR...

le douzième the twelfth **arrondissement** (borough)
- **un studio** bed-sit

un ciel (*here*) skyscape

Stephanie Où est-ce que tu habites?
Sylvie A Paris, heu, dans le douzième – à un quart d'heure de mon travail.
Stephanie Et tu as un appartement?
Sylvie Un studio, au huitième étage, avec un ciel, quand il fait beau, merveilleux …
Stephanie Un studio, c'est quoi?
Sylvie C'est en général une pièce simplement, mais là j'ai la chance d'avoir une vraie cuisine, et pas un placard qui sert de cuisine, une salle d'eau, qui n'est pas une salle de bains parce qu'il n'y a pas de … de baignoire, et des toilettes.

- **vraie** (f.) real

  sert de (from **servir**) serves as
- **la baignoire** bath-tub

dans le douzième Paris is divided into twenty **arrondissements** (boroughs). They are numbered in a spiral going out from the Ile de la Cité, where the city was originally founded. Generally speaking, the lower the number of the arrondissement, the posher it is as an address. There are some exceptions to this: in particular, **le seizième** is very chic.

à un quart d'heure de mon travail a quarter of an hour away from my work. Similarly, **à 100 kilomètres de Paris** means '100 km from Paris' and **à cinq minutes de chez nous** means 'five minutes from our house'.

avec un ciel, quand il fait beau, merveilleux with a marvellous skyscape when it is sunny. **Le ciel** normally means 'the sky'.

- **j'ai la chance d'avoir...** I have the luck to have...

des toilettes Remember that the word **toilettes** is almost always used in the plural, even when (as in this bed-sit) there is manifestly only one of them.

PRACTICE

1 On the recording for this activity you will hear Marie-Odile talking about her home.

a. Does she live in a house or a flat?

b. How many rooms are there, excluding the kitchen and bathroom?

c. How many bedrooms are there?

d. Which of the following does she have?

ANSWERS P. 202

a study ☐ a cellar ☐ an attic ☐ a junk room ☐

2 A friend has just arrived to stay with you. Imagine that you are showing him round the flat illustrated below, telling him what each of the rooms is (e.g. **Voici la salle à manger**). Follow Philippe's prompts on the recording. Carolle will give correct versions after the pauses.

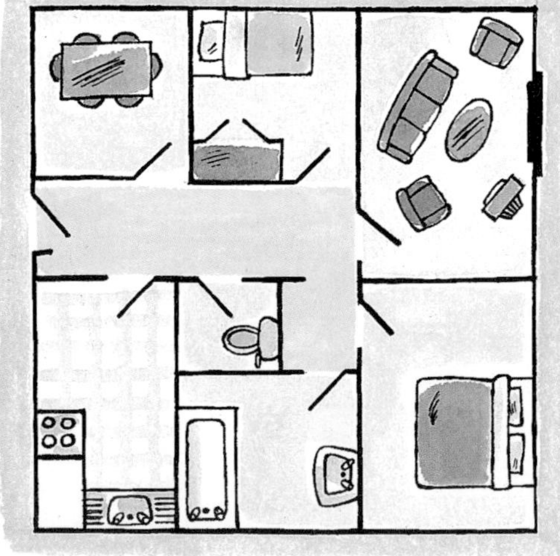

3 Here is part of the registration form from an agency dealing in house exchanges.
✔ or fill in the boxes which apply to your own house/flat.

eau, qtier résid., maison traditionnelle,
au, 4 chbres, cave, gge, beau terrain.
561 € + FA 10,26 %
négo 7.065,25 €. Réf. 6093.

J'habite	en ville	☐	
	dans un village	☐	
	à la campagne	☐	
	sur la côte	☐	
J'ai	une maison	☐	
	un appartement	☐	au ☐ e étage
	un studio	☐	au ☐ e étage
Il y a	une salle à manger	☐	
	un salon séparé	☐	
	un bureau	☐	
Nombre de chambres		☐	
Nombre de salles de bains		☐	

Cadre agréable, calme et verdoyant, beau pavillon trad. (const. 81), tt conf., rdc : séj. de 47 m2 avec insert, cuis. éq., sdb, chbre, bur., gge et cave ; étage : gde mezz. et 2 gdes ch., sdb, beau jard. av. mare sur 1.013 m2.

Nombre de personnes qu'on peut loger confortablement ☐

Il y a	un garage	☐
	un jardin	☐
	une belle vue	☐
	le chauffage central	☐
	une machine à laver	☐
	un lave-vaisselle	☐
	un téléviseur	☐
	une vidéo	☐
	le téléphone	☐
	des vélos	☐

Maison de ville 1 mit., cc fuel, sal./séj., cuis., sdb, 2 ch., cave, terrasse et jardin. Idéal 1ère acquis. 83.850 € + fr. 12,76 % dt hon. négo 4190 €. Réf. 725.

Id. pêche et canotage, belle mais. d'hab. indiv. (1982), gar. et jard. sur 766 m2, séj., cuis. am. en rdc, 3 ch. et sdb à l'ét., surf. hab. 189 m2 env. Px 130.000 € + frais env. 11,02 % dt négo TTC 5.289 €. Réf. 7358.

A moins de 10 km se trouvent
(Less than 10 km away there are situated)

une plage	☐
un lac	☐
une rivière	☐
une piscine	☐
des montagnes	☐
un parc	☐
un musée	☐
un théâtre	☐
un cinéma	☐
un restaurant	☐

Beau pav. de const. trad. ds sect. résid. (semi pl. pied), séj. (26,5 m2 avec insert, cuis., sdb, bur. et 3 ch. au rdc, vaste grenier avec 3 pièces am., belle vér. réc., gge 2 voit., joli jard. (sur 936 m2).

Ctre ville, spécial coup de cœur, mais. av. bcq de cachet, pur style flamand, gde pièce ppal av. coin séj., sal., espace cuis. éq., 2 ch. mansardées dt 1 avec mezz. 73.000 € + frais env. 12,6 % dt négo env. 3.555 € TTC. Réf. 7425.

CONVERSATIONS

Bernadette's experience of learning languages

LISTEN FOR...

▶ **langue**	language
▶ **l'allemand**	German
magnétophones	tape recorders
▶ **l'italien**	Italian

Barbara Qu'est-ce que tu as commencé par faire comme langue?
Bernadette En premier j'ai appris l'allemand, heu, à l'âge de onze ans à l'école – pas de magnétophones à l'époque! Et puis plus tard l'anglais, et puis plus tard j'ai appris aussi l'italien, mais, heu, en vivant en Italie.
Barbara Combien, heu, d'années as-tu habité en Italie?
Bernadette Alors, en Italie, j'ai vécu dix ans, et là j'ai appris l'italien.

en premier in the first place
▶ **plus tard** later on
en vivant (from **vivre**) while living
▶ **en Italie** in Italy

Qu'est-ce que tu as commencé par faire comme langue? What did you start by doing as a language? (i.e. What was the first language you studied?) Note also: **une langue étrangère** (a foreign language) and **la langue maternelle** (mother tongue).

▶ **j'ai appris l'allemand** I learned German. Other languages include: **l'espagnol** (Spanish), **le portugais** (Portuguese), **le russe** (Russian), **le latin** (Latin), **le grec ancien** (Ancient Greek) and **le grec moderne** (Modern Greek). Names of languages do not start with a capital letter in French.

pas de magnétophones à l'époque! no tape recorders at the time!

▶ **as-tu habité?** did you live?

▶ **j'ai vécu dix ans** I lived for ten years (**vécu** is the past participle of the verb **vivre**).

An 18th birthday party

LISTEN FOR...

▶ **une grande fête**	a big party
▶ **on m'a offert**	they gave me
▶ **des cadeaux**	presents

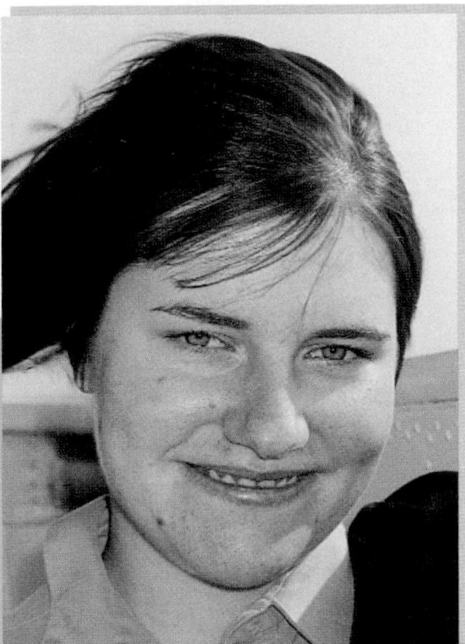

Cécile Le jour de mes dix-huit ans, j'ai fait une grande fête avec mes amis, mes parents et ma famille. Heu, nous nous sommes réunis, heu, le soir même – c'était un samedi – et nous avons mangé, nous avons dansé, nous avons chanté, jusque quatre heures du matin. On m'a offert des cadeaux: on m'a offert une montre, on m'a offert, heu, un bracelet, on m'a offert du parfum et un sac à main.

▶ **la montre** watch
le bracelet bracelet
▶ **le parfum** perfume
▶ **le sac à main** handbag

▶ **j'ai fait une grande fête** I had (lit. I made) a big party.

nous nous sommes réunis we got together. This is from the reflexive verb **se réunir** (to get together). Reflexive verbs form their perfect tense with the verb **être** rather than the verb **avoir**. This will be explained more fully in Unit 15.

le soir même on the very evening (i.e. it was the actual day of her birthday, not just the nearest Saturday).

c'était it was. This is from a different past tense, called the imperfect, which we shall not be covering in this course.

▶ **nous avons mangé** we ate

▶ **nous avons dansé** we danced

▶ **nous avons chanté** we sang

jusque quatre heures du matin until four o'clock in the morning. **Jusqu'à** would be more standard in this construction.

▶ **On m'a offert des cadeaux** People gave me presents. **Offrir** means 'to give' rather than 'to offer'. The perfect tense runs **j'ai offert**, **tu as offert**, **il a offert** … The **m'** is short for **me** (to me).

PRACTICE

Go through the transcripts of Conversations 2 and find the French for:

a. You started ______

b. I learned ______

c. Did you live? (from **habiter**) ______

d. I lived (from **vivre**) ______

e. I made ______

f. We ate ______

g. We danced ______

h. We sang ______

i. They gave me ______

ANSWERS P. 202

On the recording, Yves will tell you his language-learning history. Listen three or four times and see if you can answer the following questions in English:

a. What is Yves' mother tongue?

______

b. At what age did he start Spanish?

______

c. At what age did he start Latin?

______

d. Which language did he study at university?

______

e. How long did he live in Germany?

______

f. In which other country (apart from France) has he lived?

______

ANSWERS P. 202

Read through the transcript of 'An 18th birthday party' once more as you will need to reuse the language from it when Carolle asks you what you did to celebrate your 21st birthday. Philippe will prompt and Yves will give correct replies after the pauses.

CONVERSATION

Déjeuner du matin

by Jacques Prévert, *Paroles,* Éditions Gallimard

LISTEN FOR...

Il a mis (from **mettre**)	He put
Il a tourné (from **tourner**)	He stirred
Il a bu (from **boire**)	He drank
Il a reposé (from **reposer**)	He put down again
Il a allumé (from **allumer**)	He lit
Il a fait (from **faire**)	He made
Il s'est levé (from **se lever**)	He stood up
Il est parti (from **partir**)	He went away
J'ai pleuré (from **pleurer**)	I cried

Il a mis le café
Dans la tasse
Il a mis le lait
Dans la tasse de café
Il a mis le sucre
Dans le café au lait
Avec la petite cuiller
Il a tourné
Il a bu le café au lait
Et il a reposé la tasse
Sans me parler
Il a allumé
Une cigarette
Il a fait des ronds
Avec la fumée
Il a mis les cendres
Dans le cendrier
Sans me parler
Sans me regarder
Il s'est levé
Il a mis
Son chapeau sur sa tête
Il a mis son manteau de pluie
Parce qu'il pleuvait
Et il est parti
Sous la pluie
Sans une parole
Sans me regarder
Et moi j'ai pris
Ma tête dans ma main
Et j'ai pleuré

Jacques Prévert

- **la tasse** cup
- **le sucre** sugar
- **la cuiller** (also spelt **cuillère**) spoon

la cigarette cigarette
le rond ring
- **la fumée** smoke

les cendres (m.pl.) ash
le chapeau hat
le manteau de pluie raincoat
- **la parole** word
- **la main** hand
- **Sans me parler** Without speaking to me. French uses an infinitive here where we use a form of the verb in '-ing'.
- **Sans me regarder** Without looking at me.

Parce qu'il pleuvait Because it was raining. This is another example of the imperfect tense (this time of the verb **pleuvoir**) which you haven't really met yet!

PRACTICE

7 See if you can fill in the missing words from memory. If you can't remember some of them, use the recording rather than the written version of the poem to help you.

Il a ____________________ le café
Dans la tasse

Il a ____________________ le lait
Dans la tasse de café

Il a ____________________ le sucre
Dans le café au lait
Avec la petite cuiller

Il a ____________________

Il a ____________________ le café au lait

Et il a ____________________ la tasse
Sans me parler

Il a ____________________
Une cigarette

Il a ____________________ des ronds
Avec la fumée

Il a ____________________ les cendres
Dans le cendrier

Sans me parler

Sans me regarder

Il s'est ______________________________

Il a ______________________________
Son chapeau sur sa tête

Il a ______________________________ son manteau de pluie
Parce qu'il pleuvait

Et il est ______________________________
Sous la pluie
Sans une parole
Sans me regarder

Et moi j'ai ______________________________
Ma tête dans ma main

Et j'ai ______________________________

8 You are by now very familiar with the poem, so it should not take too much time to learn it properly by heart. It is surprising how often phrases from things that you know by heart come in useful in other contexts – and in this case it is an excellent way of remembering all those past tense forms. Use the recording of the poem to help you learn it, so that you work on your pronunciation at the same time.

9 You are playing a game of Murder and are being interrogated on your every action to see if it was you who poisoned the tea of Madame Lavictime. Philippe will guide your replies and Carolle will give correct versions.

GRAMMAR AND EXERCISES

This is a densely packed Grammar section. Nobody expects you to learn it all off by heart straight away.

The perfect tense of *-er* verbs

The perfect tense of the verb **danser** looks like this:

j'ai dansé	I danced/I have danced
tu as dansé	you danced/you have danced
il a dansé	he danced/he has danced
elle a dansé	she danced/she has danced
nous avons dansé	we danced/we have danced
vous avez dansé	you danced/you have danced
ils ont dansé	they danced/they have danced
elles ont dansé	they danced/they have danced

In the negative, the **ne** and **pas** go either side of the bit of **avoir**:

je n'ai pas dansé
tu n'as pas dansé
il/elle n'a pas dansé
nous n'avons pas dansé
vous n'avez pas dansé
ils/elles n'ont pas dansé

When the verb has an infinitive ending in **-er**, the past participle sounds exactly like the infinitive, but is spelt with an **-é** instead of an **-er** at the end. Here are three more examples:

acheter	to buy	**j'ai acheté**
casser	to break	**j'ai cassé**
commencer	to begin	**j'ai commencé**

The perfect tense of *-re* verbs

The perfect tense of **-re** verbs follows the same pattern, but the regular ending of the past participle is **-u**. (Some **-re** verbs which are irregular in the present tense have regular past participles.)

boire	to drink	**j'ai bu**
croire	to believe	**j'ai cru**
entendre	to hear	**j'ai entendu**
lire	to read	**j'ai lu**
perdre	to lose	**j'ai perdu**
vendre	to sell	**j'ai vendu**

Other verbs with infinitives in **-re** (including a number of irregular verbs) have participles ending in **-i**, **-is** or **-it**:

suivre	to follow	**j'ai suivi**
mettre	to put	**j'ai mis**
prendre	to take	**j'ai pris**
also **apprendre** and **comprendre**:		**j'ai appris**; **j'ai compris**
dire	to say	**j'ai dit**
écrire	to write	**j'ai écrit**
faire	to do, to make	**j'ai fait**

The perfect tense of *-ir* verbs

The standard ending is **-i**:

dormir	to sleep	**j'ai dormi**
finir	to finish	**j'ai fini**

However, some **-ir** verbs have past participles ending in **-u** or **-ert**:

courir	to run	**j'ai couru**
tenir	to hold	**j'ai tenu**
offrir	to give	**j'ai offert**
ouvrir	to open	**j'ai ouvert**

-ir verbs which actually end in **-oir** have past participles ending in **-u**:

pouvoir	to be able	**j'ai pu**
savoir	to know	**j'ai su**
voir	to see	**j'ai vu**
vouloir	to want	**j'ai voulu**

The perfect tense of *être* and *avoir*

être to be **j'ai été**
avoir to have **j'ai eu** (one syllable, pronounced like the **u** in **tu**)

10 To familiarise yourself with the perfect tense, write out the form with **j'ai** for each of the following regular **-er** verbs. The first one has been done for you.

donner to give
j'ai donné

fermer to shut

habiter to live

manger to eat

oublier to forget

parler to speak

passer to spend (time)

penser to think

regarder to look at

téléphoner to telephone

travailler to work

visiter to visit

voyager to travel

The answers are given both on p. 202 and on the recording, where they double as pronunciation practice for the sound '**é**'.

11 Now for **-re** verbs. Replace the infinitives in brackets with the appropriate past participles. You'll need to refer back to the lists in the Grammar section to check the endings.

a. Nous avons [boire] ______ trois bouteilles de vin.
b. J'ai [perdre] ______ 100 euros.
c. Est-ce que tu as [faire] ______ la vaisselle?
d. Ils ont [vendre] ______ la maison.
e. Elles ont [apprendre] ______ l'anglais.
f. Qu'est-ce que vous avez [dire] ______?
g. As-tu [lire] ______ le journal?
h. J'ai [écrire] ______ dix cartes postales.

ANSWERS P. 202

12 Finally, **-ir** verbs, **être** and **avoir**. Can you translate into English this extract from a letter? You can do it in your head or write it out on a piece of paper, as you wish, using the vocabulary at the back of the book to check on any words that you have forgotten. New words are:
un nounours a teddy bear
ravi(e) delighted

J'ai dormi dix heures cette nuit! J'ai donc fini mon petit déjeuner à neuf heures et demie seulement. J'ai voulu acheter un cadeau pour Jean-Louis, parce que c'est son deuxième anniversaire aujourd'hui – je l'ai su hier seulement. Alors j'ai couru aux magasins. J'ai eu de la chance: j'ai tout de suite vu un beau petit nounours pas trop cher. J'ai donc pu l'acheter et je l'ai offert à Jean-Louis à midi. Il a ouvert le paquet tout de suite et il a été ravi. Il a tenu le nounours contre son cœur pendant au moins un quart d'heure!

ANSWER P. 202

KEY WORDS AND PHRASES

Elle est comment, la maison?	What's the house like?
C'est un pavillon	It's a detached house
J'ai … un studio	I have ... a bed-sit
un appartement de six pièces	a six-roomed flat
Il y a …	There are …
le salon/la salle de séjour	the sitting room
le bureau	study
la salle à manger	the dining room
notre chambre	our bedroom
la chambre des invités	the guest room
le débarras	the junk room
Il y a aussi …	There are also …
une entrée	an entrance hall
une cave	cellar
un grenier	attic
des placards	cupboards
une salle d'eau	a shower room
J'ai la chance d'avoir	I have the good fortune to have
une vraie salle de bains	a real bathroom
avec une baignoire	with a bath-tub
J'ai appris le français	I (have) learned French
Tu as appris l'allemand	You (have) learned German
Où as-tu habité?	Where did you live?
Elle a vécu dix ans en Italie	She lived in Italy for ten years
Elle a appris l'italien	She (has) learned Italian
A-t-elle appris d'autres langues plus tard?	Did she learn other languages later on?
On m'a offert	People gave/have given me
des cadeaux	presents
Nous avons fait une grande fête	We (have) had a big party
Nous avons mangé	We ate/have eaten
Vous avez dansé	You (have) danced
Avez-vous chanté?	Did you sing?
Ils ont appris l'espagnol	They (have) learned Spanish
Elles m'ont offert	They gave/have given me
une montre	a watch
du parfum	perfume
un sac à main	a handbag

The whole of the poem **Déjeuner du matin** is also key language for this unit.

DID YOU KNOW?

Housing

Most French city-dwellers live in flats. The block (**l'immeuble**) is watched over by the janitor (**le/la concierge**). Modern blocks usually have a lift (**un ascenseur**), but there are many buildings of four storeys or so which do not. The French equivalent of a council house or flat is **une HLM** (**habitation à loyer modéré** – literally, dwelling with moderated rent). By the doorbell of French houses you will usually find the name of the occupant.

Apprendre le français là où on le parle

Now you have a firm foundation in French, you may be considering building on it by going on a French course in France. The website of the French Embassy in London, www.francealacarte.org.uk, has some information on finding out about courses in France.

The Alliance Française organises trips and accommodation in France combined with lessons. Its Head Office is at 6 Porter Street, London W1U 6DD. Tel. 020 7224 1865; e-mail network@alliancefrancaise.org.uk; website www.alliancefrancaise.org.uk.

If you feel you would like guidance in a choice of school, it is available from CESA Languages Abroad, Pennance Road, Lanner, Cornwall TR16 5TQ. Tel. 01209 211800; fax 01209 211830; e-mail info@cesalanguages.com; website www.cesalanguages.com. They are agents for a number of language schools, which they have vetted. On request, they will send you a user-friendly folder of information about them. When you make your booking, they then charge a very modest administration fee: they recoup most of their costs on a percentage basis from the schools rather than from customers.

Questions to bear in mind when choosing a school include:

- What is your main purpose in going on the course? If your main object is to improve your spoken French, look for course descriptions which stress the oral side.
- How big are the groups in which you would be taught? If you want opportunity to speak in class, under 13 is good and over 20 is bad. Some of the courses organised by French universities consist mainly of lectures given to very large groups of students, which may be fine if you want to learn about, say, French literature, with extensive listening practice, but is far from ideal if you want to speak.
- For how many hours a week would you have classes? Twenty hours or so is generally enough for even the most serious student as you also need to spend time consolidating what you have learned in class.
- What arrangements are made for accommodation? You are likely to make much greater linguistic progress if you stay with a family, because you will be living in French. However, staying in somebody else's home is inevitably something of a gamble and may require considerable reserves of flexibility and tolerance on your part (and on theirs, for that matter).
- What else is included in the cost? Meals? Excursions?
- What are the advantages and disadvantages of the school's locality? Paris has obvious attractions but, if you want to be able to talk to the locals, you would do best to avoid big towns and popular tourist areas.

AND FINALLY...

13

Back to the game of Murder! This time you play the person who discovered the murdered victim. To answer the inspector's questions about what you did this morning, you will need to use the perfect tenses of the verbs

prendre ______________________

faire ______________________

boire ______________________

manger ______________________

entendre ______________________

ouvrir ______________________

voir ______________________

It would help you to make a note of them before you turn on the recording. You will also need the word

le bruit noise

ANSWERS

Before you begin

le rez-de-chaussée/le premier étage/la chambre/un grand lit/la salle de bains/la douche/les toilettes

Exercise 1

(a) a house **(b)** five **(c)** three **(d)** a cellar and an attic

Exercise 4

(a) tu as commencé **(b)** j'ai appris **(c)** as-tu habité? **(d)** j'ai vécu **(e)** j'ai fait **(f)** nous avons mangé **(g)** nous avons dansé **(h)** nous avons chanté **(i)** on m'a offert

Exercise 5

(a) French **(b)** 11 **(c)** 13 **(d)** German **(e)** Nine months **(f)** The USA

Exercise 10

donner	j'ai donné	penser	j'ai pensé
fermer	j'ai fermé	regarder	j'ai regardé
habiter	j'ai habité	téléphoner	j'ai téléphoné
manger	j'ai mangé	travailler	j'ai travaillé
oublier	j'ai oublié	visiter	j'ai visité
parler	j'ai parlé	voyager	j'ai voyagé
passer	j'ai passé		

Exercise 11

(a) bu **(b)** perdu **(c)** fait **(d)** vendu **(e)** appris **(f)** dit **(g)** lu **(h)** écrit

Exercise 12

Remember your version does not have to be word-for-word the same as this:
I slept for ten hours last night! So I finished my breakfast only at half past nine. I wanted to buy a present for Jean-Louis, because it is his second birthday today – I only found out yesterday. (Lit. I knew it only yesterday.) So I ran to the shops. I was lucky: I immediately saw a pretty little teddy bear (that was) not too expensive. So I was able to buy it and I gave it to Jean-Louis at lunch-time (*or* midday/twelve o'clock). He opened the parcel immediately and he was delighted. He held the teddy to his heart for at least a quarter of an hour!

14 TALKING ABOUT THE FUTURE

WHAT YOU WILL LEARN

- understanding what people say about the future
- talking about your own hopes for the future
- talking about your plans
- talking about your daily routine
- something about French leisure activities

BEFORE YOU BEGIN

Every so often in learning a language you meet a construction that smiles at you like a gift because it is so simple – and just like the English. French has a construction for expressing the future which is a direct translation of the English

'I am going' + infinitive   e.g. 'I am going to dance'.

In French, it is

je vais + infinitive   e.g. **Je vais danser**.

(For 'you are going', 'he is going', etc., you just use the other parts of **aller**: **tu vas**, **il va**, etc.)

The main aim of this unit is to build up your confidence at using this structure to talk about the future.

Pronunciation notes

One needs to keep coming back to the sound '**r**', because it is a difficult one for English speakers. It is produced in the back of the throat, unlike the English 'r', which is formed near the front of the mouth. The nearest we come to the articulation of the French '**r**' is when we gargle! You will hear the sound '**r**' in the first recording in such words as

- **devenir journaliste**
  to become a journalist
- **les pays étrangers**
  foreign countries

CONVERSATIONS

Ambitions

LISTEN FOR...

- **des stages** training courses

Jeanne	Qu'est-ce que tu espères faire dans la vie, alors?
Isabelle	J'espère devenir journaliste, faire des reportages dans les pays étrangers sur, heu, l'actualité.
Jeanne	Et qu'est-ce que tu vas faire pour devenir journaliste?
Isabelle	Je vais faire des stages, heu, dans une école à Paris.
Jeanne	Quand ça?
Isabelle	Dans un an ou deux ans, après ma licence à l'université.

Qu'est-ce que tu espères faire dans la vie alors?

- **le reportage** report, article
- **l'actualité** (f.) news, current affairs
  la licence degree
- **qu'est-ce que tu vas faire?** what are you going to do? This construction is explained more fully in the Grammar section on p. 214.
- **Je vais faire des stages** I am going to do some training courses.
- **Quand ça?** When's that?

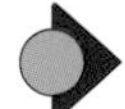

The not-so-liberated woman's ambitions

Cécile	Pour l'année qui vient, j'espère trouver quelqu'un, pour me marier, mais aussi réussir, heu, mon examen.

Pour l'année qui vient For the coming year

- **j'espère trouver quelqu'un pour me marier** I hope to find someone to get married (to). **Se marier** (to get married) is a reflexive verb (see pp. 182–183). 'To marry someone' is 'to get oneself married with someone' in French: **se marier avec quelqu'un**.
- **réussir mon examen** to pass (literally, to succeed) my exam.
- **Passer un examen** is simply to take it, not necessarily to pass it.

PRACTICE

Before going on to these exercises, you should turn to the Grammar section on p. 214 and read the first section, 'Talking about your plans and hopes'.

1 Some of the sentences below are about the past and some about the future. If you write out only the ones about the future in the order in which they are printed, you should produce a text which makes sense!

L'année prochaine, je vais partir trois mois en France.
J'ai passé mes vacances dans les Pyrénées.
Je vais échanger ma maison contre la maison d'un collègue français.
Nous allons aussi échanger nos voitures.
Nous avons loué un gîte dans le village de Saint-Clément.
Il a fait très beau.
Pour moi, ça va être l'occasion de parler français pendant trois mois.
Mon collègue, de son côté, va pouvoir parler anglais.
J'ai beaucoup aimé la région.

____

____

____

____

____

____

You can check your answer by listening to Yves reading out the correct series of sentences on the recording.

2 Instead of saying what you are *going* to do (**aller** + infinitive), you can say what you *hope* to do by using **espérer** + infinitive. In this exercise, Yves will ask you about your holiday plans. You don't want to commit yourself, so answer each of his questions about what you are going to do by saying only that you hope to do whatever it is. Begin each of your answers with **Nous**. For example,

Yves	Vous allez visiter Saint-Malo?
You	Nous espérons visiter Saint-Malo.

Carolle will give a correct version after the pauses.

3 Conversations 1 contained a fine crop of the sound '**r**', so this exercise will give you practice at it – and reinforce at the same time your grasp of the constructions **aller** + infinitive and **espérer** + infinitive.

CONVERSATIONS 

 *Plans for tomorrow*

LISTEN FOR...

- **à l'aube** at dawn
- **faire ma toilette** to get washed and dressed
- **aller chercher** to go and fetch
- **emmener** to take (someone somewhere)

Christian Alors, demain matin, je vais me lever comme d'habitude à l'aube. Je vais, heu, faire ma toilette. Je vais aller chercher, heu, un collègue qui habite pas très loin d'ici. Je vais, heu, l'emmener à son travail avant de regagner le mien, qui se trouve, heu, dans la même ville mais à environ cinq kilomètres.

- **comme d'habitude** as usual
  environ approximately
- **je vais me lever** I'm going to get up. See pp. 182–183 and p. 214 for reflexive verbs.
- **je vais aller chercher un collègue** I'm going to go and fetch a colleague. **Chercher** means 'to look for', but **aller chercher** means 'to go and fetch', e.g. **Allez chercher votre manteau** (Go and fetch your coat). Similarly, **venir chercher** means 'to come and fetch', e.g. **Tu peux venir me chercher à la gare?** (Can you come and fetch me from the station?)
- **pas très loin d'ici** not very far from here.
- **l'emmener** to take him. Remember that **le** (or, here, **l'**) can mean 'him' or 'it' as well as 'the'.

avant de regagner le mien before getting back to mine (i.e. my work). French uses **avant de** + an infinitive where we say 'before …ing', e.g.
Il faut faire des stages avant de devenir journaliste (It is necessary to do training courses before becoming a journalist).
Le mien (mine) refers to **mon travail.** The feminine form is **la mienne,** e.g. **Votre fille est plus grande que la mienne** (Your daughter is taller than mine).

Changing jobs

LISTEN FOR...

un lieu de travail	place of work
▶ **être responsable**	to be in charge
▶ **une maison de quartier**	community centre
▶ **se rencontrer**	to meet each other
se distraire	to enjoy oneself

Christian A la rentrée donc, heu, je vais changer de lieu de travail. Je vais en effet passer d'un travail d'un côté de la ville à un lieu de travail de l'autre côté de la ville.

Jeanne Et qu'est-ce que vous allez faire dans ce nouveau lieu de travail?

Christian Je vais être responsable d'une, heu, maison de quartier, qui est le … le centre d'animation du quartier – un lieu où toutes les personnes peuvent se rencontrer pour, heu, y trouver différents services administratifs, sociaux, médicaux – pour discuter, pour, heu, boire un verre – ou se distraire.

en effet in fact, indeed
différents (m.pl.) different, various
administratifs (m.pl.) administrative
sociaux (m.pl.)/**social** (m.sing.) social
médicaux (m.pl.)/**médical** (m.sing.) medical
▶ **discuter** to chat

▶ **à la rentrée** when I get back after the holiday (literally, at the return). **La rentrée** is the name given both to the period when everyone returns from their summer holidays and to the beginning of term.

d'un côté … de l'autre côté on one side … on the other side. This is also used for 'On the one hand … on the other hand'.

responsable means 'responsible', of course. **Le/la responsable** is 'the person responsible' or 'the person in charge'.

le centre d'animation the social centre. Literally, **animation** means 'putting life into something'; the leader of a group is often known as **l'animateur** and the verb for what s/he does is **animer**.

▶ **boire un verre** to have a drink (lit. to drink a glass). You should also learn the expression

▶ **prendre un pot** (pronounced 'po'), which means the same thing and is used rather more frequently when people suggest going for a drink, e.g. **On va prendre un pot?** Shall we go for a drink?

- **se rencontrer** to meet each other. Most reflexive verbs indicate what people do to themselves, but some can indicate what they do to each other, e.g. **Nous nous détestons** means 'We detest each other', rather than 'We detest ourselves' and **Elles s'écrivent** means 'They write to each other', rather than 'They write themselves'.
- **se distraire** to enjoy themselves. Note also **une distraction**, which means 'an amusement' or 'something to do'.

PRACTICE

4 Below is a brief account of a supermum's routine for tomorrow morning. Complete the gaps with the correct phrase:

Je vais faire/Je vais les emmener/Je vais arriver/ Je vais me lever/ Je vais aller chercher/Je vais prendre

____

à sept heures moins le quart.

____

ma toilette.

____

le petit déjeuner avec les enfants.

____

les enfants d'une amie.

____

à l'école avec les miens.

____

ANSWERS P. 218 à mon bureau vers neuf heures.

5 Here is a newspaper summary of some of the things to do in Cannes on a particular Thursday and Friday in June. (**Échecs** – literally 'failures' – is the French name for chess ... you can see the connection with 'check'.)

Pour vous distraire

Aujourd'hui jeudi

Antiquités :

De 16 à 22 heures, sur le marché couvert Forville. Le rendez-vous des antiquaires (argenterie, bibelots, meubles, étains, vêtements rétro, livres etc) 50 exposants. Tous les jours.

Danse :

Au Palais Croisette (Noga Hilton), à 21 heures, la Compagnie "No comment" Bruno Vandelli présente "Histoire parallèle", création 94. Prix des places : 14 et 10€. Réservations à la billetterie du Palais : 04.92.98.62.77.

Echecs :

Tous les jours (sauf le dimanche) à Cannes Echecs (11, avenue Saint Louis - proche parking Vauban- tel 04.93.39.41.39), parties amicales, parties blitz, cours, tournois.

Demain vendredi

Musique :

A 20 heures, vendredi musical du Martinez. A partir de 20 heures, duo de harpes.

Récital :

A 21 heures, au grand auditorium du Palais, gala des municipaux avec Nicole Croisille. Réservations : 04.92.98.62.77.

Les expositions

Art Jonction :

Au Palais des Festivals (Hall des Expositions) de 15 à 23 heures. Art Jonction International (Marché international d'art contemporain). Environ 80 galeries venant de 12 pays présentent un large panorama de l'art contemporain. Jusqu'au 6 juin.

Musée de la mer, fort de l'île Sainte-Marguerite :

— Expositions permanentes (prisons d'Etat, fresques de Jean Le Gac…) et expositions temporaires de photographies axées sur des thématiques liées au monde méditerranéen, tous les jours, sauf mardi et jours fériés, de 10 h 30 à 12 heures et de 14 heures à 16 h 30.

— Jusqu'au 13 juin, exposition de photos de Giuseppe Cavalli, Luigi Ghirri, Bernard Guillot, Douglas Keats, Claude Nori, Françoise Nunez, Carlos Perez-Siquier, Bernard Plossu et Joachim Vallet.

Musée de la Castre :

Ouvert de 10 heures à 12 heures et de 14 heures à 17 heures, sauf mardi et jours fériés. Expositions permanentes (collections ethnologiques et archéologiques, peinture régionale, donation Damien…).

Musée-Chapelle Bellini, parc Fiorentina, avenue de Vallauris. Collection Emmanuel et Lucette Bellini. Ouvert de 14 heures à 17 heures du lundi au vendredi et sur rendez-vous. Téléphone : 04.93.38.61.80.

Here is an extract from a letter in which a visitor to Cannes says which of those things she is planning to do over the next two days. See if you can fill in the gaps with the appropriate words from the box.

visiter	vais	aller	pouvoir	dormir	espère

Ce matin, je ______________ jouer aux échecs à Cannes Échecs. L'après-midi, je vais ______________ le Salon d'antiquités sur le marché Forville. Et puis le soir, à 21 heures, j' ______________ voir 'Histoire parallèle' au Palais Croisette. Demain, je vais sans doute ______________ jusqu'à midi. L'après-midi, je vais ______________ au Musée de la mer pour voir une exposition de photos. Et puis j'espère ______________ prendre des billets pour le récital de Nicole Croisille.

ANSWERS P. 218

6 Now it's your turn to talk about your plans, which are also based on the newspaper cutting in Exercise 5. On the recording, Philippe will prompt you and Yves will give correct versions of your lines after the pauses.

CONVERSATION 3

As well as the construction **aller** + infinitive, French has a 'proper' future tense. You don't need to use it yourself just yet, but you do need to understand it when you hear it. This conversation will introduce you to it and then it will be explained in the Grammar section.

Holiday plans

LISTEN FOR...

j'irai	I shall go
l'Hérault	the department around Montpellier
mon beau-frère	my brother-in-law/stepbrother
ma belle-sœur	my sister-in-law/stepsister
des balades	walks
plein d'histoires	lots of stories

Nathalie Au mois d'août, j'irai passer mes vacances dans l'Hérault. C'est une région que je ne connais pas du tout. J'irai avec mon beau-frère, ma belle-soeur et leurs enfants. Nous allons probablement nous baigner tous les jours. Nous irons faire des balades en montagne, profiter des musées et des choses à visiter. J'espère qu'il y aura beaucoup de soleil. Comme ça, on pourra profiter du mois de vacances et rentrer à la maison avec des photos et plein d'histoires à raconter.

- **leurs** (pl.) their
- **la montagne** mountain
- **profiter de** profit from, take advantage of
- **comme ça** that way (lit. like that)

l'Hérault Note the use of the article before the name of a department. You should also use it when you refer to British counties (which are all treated as masculine): **J'habite dans le Kent.**

mon beau-frère can mean either 'my brother-in-law' or 'my stepbrother'. Similarly, **le beau-père** can be either 'father-in-law' or 'stepfather' and **la belle-mère** either 'mother-in-law' or 'stepmother'.

- **Nous allons probablement nous baigner** We shall probably bathe. From the reflexive verb **se baigner**, to bathe (oneself). Here, the infinitive is **nous baigner** rather than **se baigner** because it means 'to bathe ourselves' rather than 'to bathe oneself'. There is more about this in the Grammar section on p. 214.

▶ **des choses à visiter** of the things to visit. This construction with **à** is useful: **C'est à voir** (It is worth seeing), **Quelque chose à boire** (Something to drink), **C'est difficile à dire** (It is difficult to say).

il y aura there will be (the future of **il y a**).

on pourra we'll be able to.

Nous irons We shall go.

avec des photos with photos. Note that 'photographs' is **des photographies**. **Un photographe** is a photographer.

plein d'histoires à raconter lots of stories to tell.

PRACTICE

Important:
You should turn to the Grammar section on p. 214 and read 'The future tense' before going on to these exercises.

7 Here is a set of horoscopes. (Any resemblance between them and real life is purely coincidental!)

☆ **BÉLIER (21-3/20-4)** ☆
Travail: Vous réussirez dans un projet important.
Amour: Vous découvrirez des charmes nouveaux chez votre partenaire.

☆ **TAUREAU (21-4/21-5)** ☆
Travail: Une meilleure relation avec vos collaborateurs vous facilitera la vie.
Amour: L'amour sera doux.

☆ **GÉMEAUX (22-5/21-6)** ☆
Travail: Vous aurez beaucoup de travail, mais aussi beaucoup de réussite.
Amour: Vous apprendrez à mieux comprendre et à mieux aimer votre partenaire.

☆ **CANCER (22-6/22-7)** ☆
Travail: Hélas! vous perdrez votre travail.
Amour: Votre partenaire vous consolera.

☆ **LION (23-7/23-8)** ☆
Travail: Vous partirez à l'étranger: tout ira très, très bien.
Amour: Vous rencontrerez l'homme/la femme de votre vie.

☆ **VIERGE (24-8/23-9)** ☆
Travail: Un nouveau projet deviendra très intéressant.
Amour: Un vieil ami/une vieille amie reprendra contact avec vous … tout est possible!

☆ **BALANCE (24-9/23-10)** ☆
Travail: Vous trouverez une solution à vos problèmes financiers.
Amour: Vous aimerez et on vous aimera.

☆ **SCORPION (24-10/22-11)** ☆
Travail: Votre travail vous intéressera énormément: vous vivrez jour et nuit au bureau.
Amour: Votre partenaire vous quittera.

☆ **SAGITTAIRE (23-11/21-12)** ☆
Travail: Votre travail deviendra financièrement plus intéressant.
Amour: Vous aimerez, tous les deux, comme des adolescents qui aiment pour la première fois.

☆ **CAPRICORNE (22-12/20-1)** ☆
Travail: Les choses n'iront pas bien: vous serez très tendu.
Amour: Là non plus, vous n'aurez pas de chance.

☆ **VERSEAU (21-1/18-2)** ☆
Travail: On vous donnera la possibilité de faire un stage. Si vous acceptez, votre vie sera transformée … en bien.
Amour: Là aussi, votre vie changera, mais vous ne regretterez rien.

☆ **POISSONS (19-2/20-3)** ☆
Travail: Vos efforts seront récompensés.
Amour: Oui! Oh oui!

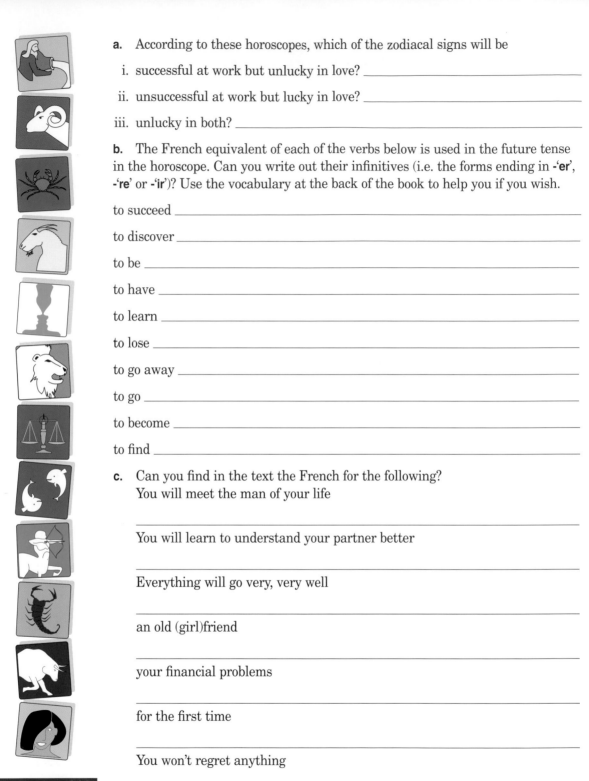

a. According to these horoscopes, which of the zodiacal signs will be

i. successful at work but unlucky in love? ______

ii. unsuccessful at work but lucky in love? ______

iii. unlucky in both? ______

b. The French equivalent of each of the verbs below is used in the future tense in the horoscope. Can you write out their infinitives (i.e. the forms ending in **-'er'**, **-'re'** or **-'ir'**)? Use the vocabulary at the back of the book to help you if you wish.

to succeed ______

to discover ______

to be ______

to have ______

to learn ______

to lose ______

to go away ______

to go ______

to become ______

to find ______

c. Can you find in the text the French for the following?

You will meet the man of your life

______

You will learn to understand your partner better

______

Everything will go very, very well

______

an old (girl)friend

______

your financial problems

______

for the first time

______

You won't regret anything

______

ANSWERS P. 218

8 Carolle is looking forward to a dream holiday (**des vacances de rêve**) visiting the French Polynesian islands of Tahiti and Mooréa. Listen to her on the recording as many times as you like and see if you can answer the following questions:

a. In which month is Carolle taking her holiday?

b. How long does the flight (**le vol**) to Tahiti take?

c. What is the time difference between Paris and Tahiti?

d. How many stars does the hotel have?

e. What does Carolle say they can do every day?

f. How do they intend to make the trip around the island (**le tour de l'île**)?

g. How far from Tahiti is Mooréa?

h. Why is Carolle so confident that the weather will be good all the time?

ANSWERS P. 218

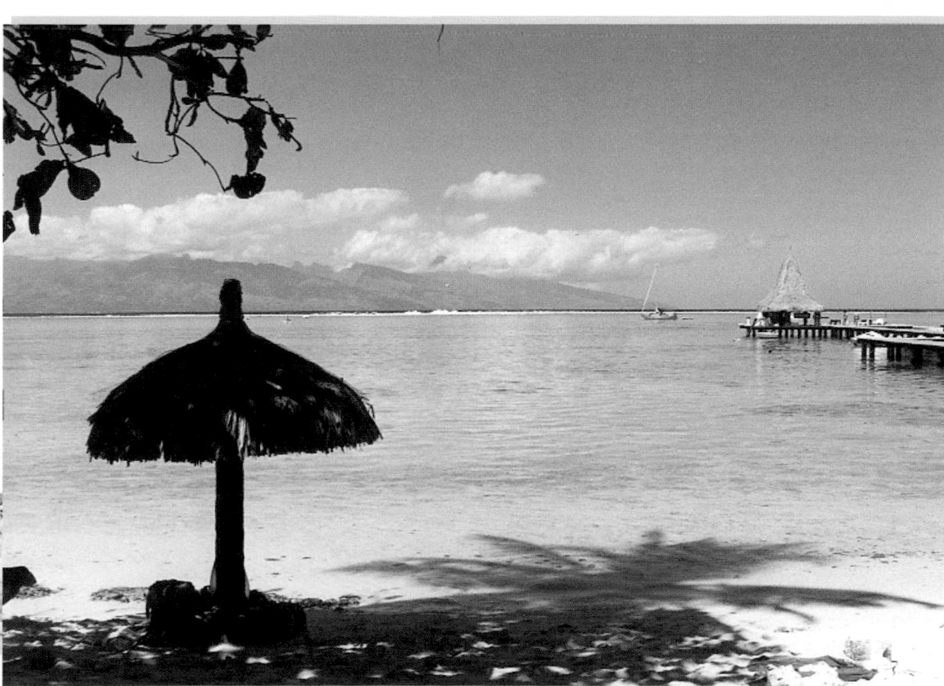

GRAMMAR AND EXERCISES

Talking about your plans and hopes

In this unit, you are learning to talk about the future using the construction: a part of **aller** + infinitive. For example,

je vais + danser I am going + to dance

Here are some more examples, to help familiarise you with the pattern:

Nous allons partir à six heures
We are going to leave at six o'clock
Est-ce que tu vas venir avec nous?
Are you going to come with us?
Il ne va pas réussir son examen
He is not going to pass his exam
Ils ne vont pas comprendre
They are not going to understand

Note that, in the negative, **ne** and **pas** go either side of the part of **aller**.

'I hope to do something' follows exactly the same pattern as 'I am going to do something': **J'espère** + infinitive. For example,

J'espère + danser I hope + to dance
J'espère partir en Australie
I hope to leave for Australia
Nous espérons nous baigner
We hope to bathe

Note the difference in the way the accents slope: the longer sound **'è'** is used in **espère** because it is the last full syllable of the word; the sharper **'é'** is used when there is another full syllable following.

The future tense

The construction **aller** + infinitive is the simplest way of expressing the future and it would be sensible for you to stick to it for the time being. However, you do need to *understand* the 'proper' future tense when you hear it. The endings of the future tense are the same as those of the present tense of the verb **avoir**: **-ai**, **-as**, **-a**, **-ons**, **-ez**, **-ont**.

These endings are tacked onto a stem which is most often derived from the infinitive.

- With **-er** and **-ir** verbs, the whole of the infinitive is the stem, so that you have such forms as **je travaillerai**, **tu habiteras**, **vous finirez** and **ils partiront**.
- With **-re** verbs, the stem is the infinitive minus the final **-e**, for example, **il prendra**, **nous vendrons**.
- Some of the commonest verbs have irregular stems in the future tense – though they all have regular endings. Here are the main ones:

être: **je serai**, **tu seras**, **il/elle sera**, **nous serons**, **vous serez**, **ils/elles seront**
avoir: **j'aurai**, **tu auras**, **il/elle aura**, **nous aurons**, **vous aurez**, **ils/elles auront**
aller: **j'irai**, **tu iras**, **il/elle ira**, **nous irons**, **vous irez**, **ils/elles iront**
faire: **je ferai**, **tu feras**, **il/elle fera**, **nous ferons**, **vous ferez**, **ils/elles feront**
pouvoir: **je pourrai**, **tu pourras**, **il/elle pourra**, **nous pourrons**, **vous pourrez**, **ils/elles pourront**

More about reflexive verbs

You may care to refresh your memory on reflexive verbs by looking at pp. 182–183 again. The infinitive of a reflexive verb, as you find it in a dictionary, includes the word **se**: e.g. **se marier**, **se lever**, **se coucher** (to go to bed), **se trouver**, **se situer**, **se rencontrer**, **se distraire**. However, **se** means 'oneself', 'himself', 'herself', 'itself' or 'themselves'. It does *not* mean 'myself', 'yourself' or 'ourselves' – you have to use other pronouns for those, even when they are part of the infinitive. To take the verb **se marier** (to get married) as an example:

je vais me marier	**nous allons nous marier**
tu vas te marier	**vous allez vous marier**
il/elle va se marier	**ils/elles vont se marier**

You can repeat these forms after Yves on the recording – as well as helping you get the hang of the infinitives of reflexive verbs, it is another chance to practise the sound **'r'**!

9 Build up your confidence in recognising the two ways of expressing the future by going through the list of sentences below and indicating whether each one is in the past, the present or the future.

a. Je vais téléphoner à ma mère.
past/present/future

b. J'ai compris l'essentiel du texte.
past/present/future

c. Je prendrai l'avion au départ de Roissy.
past/present/future

d. Ils fermeront le magasin à sept heures.
past/present/future

e. J'aime voyager de nuit.
past/present/future

f. J'ai eu une bonne surprise ce matin.
past/present/future

g. Tu seras riche!
past/present/future

h. Il deviendra président de l'association.
past/present/future

i. Elle va devenir ambassadeur.
past/present/future

j. Vous comprenez ma situation.
past/present/future

k. Vous aurez une voiture de location.
past/present/future

l. Nous ferons le ménage.
past/present/future

m. Nous finissons notre petit déjeuner.
past/present/future

ANSWERS P. 218

10 Write out these sentences replacing the 'proper' future tense with the construction **aller** + infinitive, on the model

Il travaillera à Paris.
Il va travailler à Paris.
or
Les enfants ne viendront pas.
Les enfants ne vont pas venir.

a. Je partirai à Tahiti avec mon mari. ____________________

____

b. Nous prendrons l'avion. ____________________

____

c. Les enfants resteront chez mes parents. ____________________

____

d. Le soleil brillera tous les jours. ____________________

____

e. Nous louerons une voiture. ____________________

____

f. Nous ferons le tour de l'île. ____________________

____

g. Vous ne viendrez pas avec nous? ____________________

____

ANSWERS P. 218

11 Using the **aller** + infinitive construction, put each of the following into the future, on the model:

Je me baigne. *Je vais me baigner.*

a. Tu te maries avec elle.

____

b. Ils se rencontrent au bar.

____

c. Vous vous levez à l'aube.

____

d. Nous nous trouvons à Caen.

____

e. Elle se baigne.

____

f. Je me distrais au cinéma.

____

g. La nouvelle banque se situe là.

____

ANSWERS P. 218

KEY WORDS AND PHRASES

J'espère devenir journaliste	I hope to become a journalist
Qu'est-ce que tu espères faire?	What do you hope to do?
Elle espère se marier	She hopes to get married
Nous espérons faire des balades en montagne	We hope to go for walks in the mountains
Vous espérez faire des reportages	You hope to write (lit. make) articles
Elles espèrent réussir leur examen	They (f.) hope to pass their exam
Je vais faire ma toilette	I'm going to get washed and dressed
Tu vas te lever	You're going to get up
comme d'habitude	as usual
à l'aube	at dawn
Il va passer un examen	He is going to take an exam
Nous allons partir à l'étranger	We are going to go abroad
Vous allez { boire un verre / prendre un pot	You're going to have a drink
Ils vont se rencontrer	They're going to meet
Je vais aller chercher un collègue pour l'emmener à son travail	I'm going to go and fetch a colleague to take him to his work
Il va être responsable d'une maison de quartier	He will be in charge of a community centre
comme ça	that way/like that
Quand ça?	When's that?
à la rentrée	after the holiday
Nous allons discuter de l'actualité	We're going to chat about current affairs
Nous allons profiter des choses à visiter	We're going to take advantage of the things to visit
Nous allons nous baigner	We're going to bathe

DID YOU KNOW?

Leisure activities

A much-loved French national pastime is the weekly gamble on the horses. Betting does not take place in special betting shops but in cafés and bars with the sign PMU. Every Sunday, many families place a bet on horses running in a race called **le tiercé**, in which you have to guess the first three past the post. The largest amount of money is won by people who have predicted the first three in the right order, smaller amounts by those who have the right horses, but in the wrong order.

Le loto national, the national lottery, is another popular pastime. The winnings vary: they are always high, but even higher on particular occasions such as Christmas, 14 July, Mothers' Day and, surprisingly, Friday 13th.

The most popular team sports are soccer (**le football**) and rugger. (**Le rugby** is the great game in the south-west.) Organised competition in both games is avidly followed by fans all over the country. Cycling is another favourite and the Tour de France, which takes place in the summer and lasts for three weeks, is the most important sporting event of the year. The day's winner wears **le maillot jaune** (the yellow jersey) and large prizes are to be won.

La pêche (fishing), **la chasse** (hunting), **le ski** (skiing), **la voile** (sailing), **la planche à voile** (wind-surfing) and **boules** (French bowls) are other favourite activities. The game of **boules** or **pétanque** consists of first throwing **le cochonnet** (the jack) and then trying to throw your bowls as near as possible to it. Proper **boules** are made of metal, with different traceries on them to identify one from another, but you can buy coloured wooden or plastic ones quite cheaply for playing on the beach or at a camp-site.

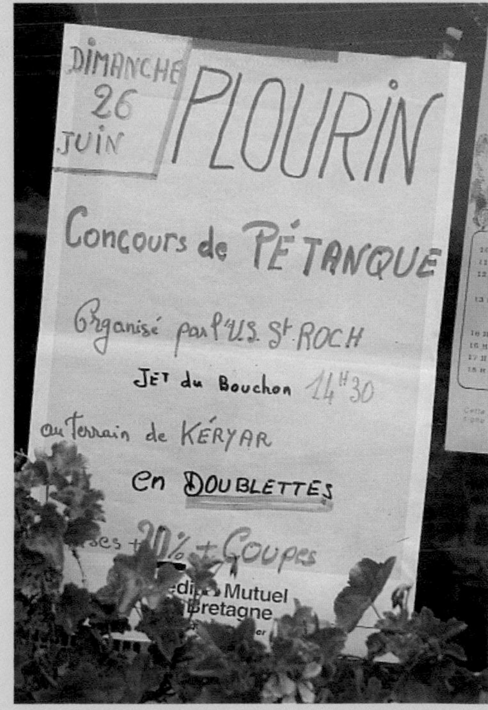

AND FINALLY...

12 It's New Year's Day – **le Jour de l'An** – and time for making resolutions! Philippe will suggest some to you – see if you can put them into French. Yves will give correct versions after the pauses.

ANSWERS

EXERCISE 4

Je vais me lever à sept heures moins le quart. Je vais faire ma toilette. Je vais prendre le petit déjeuner avec les enfants. Je vais aller chercher les enfants d'une amie. Je vais les emmener à l'école avec les miens. Je vais arriver à mon bureau vers neuf heures.

EXERCISE 5

vais/visiter/espère/dormir/aller/pouvoir

EXERCISE 7

(**a**) i. Scorpio ii. Cancer iii. Capricorn (**b**) to succeed: réussir; to discover: découvrir; to be: être; to have: avoir; to learn: apprendre; to lose: perdre; to go away: partir; to go: aller; to become: devenir; to find: trouver (**c**) Vous rencontrerez l'homme de votre vie/Vous apprendrez à mieux comprendre votre partenaire/Tout ira très, très bien/une vieille amie/vos problèmes financiers/pour la première fois/Vous ne regretterez rien

EXERCISE 8

(**a**) July (**b**) 20 hours (**c**) 12 hours (Carolle says that when it is noon in Paris it is midnight in Tahiti)
(**d**) Four (**e**) Bathe (**f**) In a hired car (**g**) 15 km
(**h**) She says there is never any rain in July

EXERCISE 9

(**a**) future (**b**) past (**c**) future (**d**) future (**e**) present (**f**) past (**g**) future (**h**) future (**i**) future (**j**) present (**k**) future (**l**) future (**m**) present

EXERCISE 10

(**a**) Je vais partir à Tahiti avec mon mari. (**b**) Nous allons prendre l'avion. (**c**) Les enfants vont rester chez mes parents. (**d**) Le soleil va briller tous les jours. (**e**) Nous allons louer une voiture. (**f**) Nous allons faire le tour de l'île. (**g**) Vous n'allez pas venir avec nous?

EXERCISE 11

(**a**) Tu vas te marier avec elle. (**b**) Ils vont se rencontrer au bar. (**c**) Vous allez vous lever à l'aube. (**d**) Nous allons nous trouver à Caen. (**e**) Elle va se baigner. (**f**) Je vais me distraire au cinéma. (**g**) La nouvelle banque va se situer là.

15 TALKING ABOUT WHERE YOU HAVE BEEN

WHAT YOU WILL LEARN

- describing past journeys
- describing past holidays
- describing past leisure activities
- how to keep up your French

BEFORE YOU BEGIN

You may be feeling a little breathless by this last unit of the course. The last two units have covered a great deal of ground, enabling you to talk about both the past and the future. This unit looks at the different way of forming the perfect tense which is used for certain verbs of motion. Don't feel disheartened because you haven't mastered it all: it takes time to learn and to become confident at using different tenses. All this course is setting out to do is to introduce you to them so that your conversation is not completely restricted to the present tense. The practice which leads to fluency and accuracy will need to come after you have finished *Breakthrough French*, but the course will have given you the grounding to make that possible.

So far, almost all the verbs you have met in the perfect tense have formed that perfect with the verb **avoir** (e.g. **j'ai travaillé**, **vous avez fait**). In this unit you will tackle the verbs of motion which form their perfect tense with **être** instead of **avoir**.

For example, in the first conversation, Isabelle says

je suis partie	I left
on est allé	we went
je suis retournée	I returned
je suis restée	I stayed

(which must count as a verb of non-motion!)

and Brigitte says

nous sommes partis	we left
nous sommes arrivés	we arrived
nous sommes allés	we went

Pronunciation notes

In the early stages of language learning, your speech is inevitably staccato: you … say … one … word … at … a … time. Part of developing fluency is learning to say words in groups, as native speakers do. As a general rule (frequently broken by native speakers), French puts the stress on the final syllable of a word or a group of words. So, for example, in the phrase **au bord de la mer** (beside the sea/at the seaside) it is the word **mer** which should be stressed. There will be more about this in Exercise 9.

CONVERSATIONS

A trip to England

LISTEN FOR...

Place-names: **Boulogne, Douvres** (Dover), **Maidstone, Londres, le Kent**

Isabelle Alors je suis partie, heu, par, heu, Boulogne et j'ai pris le car-ferry jusqu'à Douvres. On est allé jusqu'à Maidstone. Je suis restée une semaine à Maidstone. Après, je suis allée à Londres. J'ai visité Londres ... les musées: j'ai vu un peu toutes les curiosités de la ville. Et puis, je suis retournée dans le Kent.

la curiosité place of interest

- **je suis partie** I left. Many French people, like Isabelle, pronounce **je suis** as one syllable (something like 'shwee').
- **le car-ferry** The meaning is not difficult to guess when you see it written, but English words pronounced **à la française** can be difficult to catch.
- **On est allé** We went.
- **je suis restée** I remained. **Rester** does not mean 'to rest'.
- **je suis retournée** I returned.

Sailing to Morocco

LISTEN FOR...

au Maroc to Morocco
en voilier in a sailing boat
▶ **en bateau** in a boat
faire escale to put into port
des vents winds

Brigitte Heu, je suis allée au Maroc en voilier. Nous sommes partis de France, heu, à la fin de juillet en bateau et nous sommes arrivés, heum, cinq jours plus tard en Espagne. Nous sommes repartis mais nous avons dû faire escale, heu, une centaine de kilomètres plus loin, de nouveau en Espagne. Et ... de là nous avons réussi à avoir des vents plus favorables et ... nous sommes allés directement à Casablanca au Maroc.

de nouveau once again
de là from there

- **nous sommes arrivés** we arrived.
- **nous sommes repartis** we left again.
- **nous avons dû** we had to. This is the perfect tense of the verb **devoir** (to have to).

faire escale to put into port. **Une escale** is also the word used when an aeroplane makes a stop-over.

- **une centaine** about 100.

nous avons réussi à avoir des vents plus favorables we succeeded in having more favourable winds.

PRACTICE

1 Without looking back at the full transcripts, play Conversations 1 again and see if you can write in the gaps below the correct verbs from the boxes.

A trip to England

j'ai pris **je suis retournée** **Je suis restée** **On est allé** **J'ai visité** **je suis partie** **j'ai vu**

Alors , ________________ heu, par, heu, Boulogne et ________________ le car-ferry jusqu'à Douvres. ________________ jusqu'à Maidstone. ________________ une semaine à Maidstone. Après, je suis allée à Londres. ________________ Londres … les musées: ________________ un peu toutes les curiosités de la ville. Et puis, ________________ dans le Kent.

Sailing to Morocco

Nous sommes partis **Nous sommes repartis** **nous sommes allés** **nous sommes arrivés** **nous avons réussi** **je suis allée**

Heu, ________________ au Maroc en voilier. ________________ de France, heu, à la fin de juillet en bateau et ________________ , heum, cinq jours plus tard en Espagne. ________________ mais nous avons dû faire escale, heu, une centaine de kilomètres plus loin, de nouveau en Espagne. Et … de là ________________ à avoir des vents plus favorables et ________________ directement à Casablanca au Maroc.

ANSWERS P. 232

2 For this exercise, you will need to reuse some of the verbs that you wrote into the gaps in Exercise 1. On the recording, Yves will ask you some questions about a recent trip to France. Philippe will suggest answers in English – see if you can put them into French. Carolle will come in with correct versions after the pauses.

3 Have you noticed how the spelling of the past participle changes when the perfect is formed with **être**? Isabelle said **Je suis partie**, but Brigitte said **Nous sommes partis**. Isabelle said **On est allé**, but Brigitte said **Je suis allée** and **Nous sommes allés**. Before you read on any further, pause for a minute and see if you can work out any logical explanation for this variation.

Now turn to p. 228 and read the explanation in the Grammar section.

When you have done that, see if you can write the correct forms of the perfect tense in the speech balloons below. The verbs to use are given to the left of the drawings.

a. aller

Je .... au cinema hier soir.

b. rester

Moi, je .... à la maison.

c. partir

Nous .... au Canada.

Nous .... à l'école à neuf heures.

Je .... tout de suite.

Nous .... au 2e étage de la Tour Eiffel.

ANSWERS P. 232

e. venir

f. monter

d. arriver

CONVERSATIONS

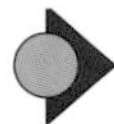

What Barbara did yesterday

LISTEN FOR...

▶ **nous avons un peu joué**	we played a bit
▶ **on a nagé**	we swam
on avait soif	we were thirsty
un court de tennis	a tennis court
▶ **le bois**	the wood

Barbara Heu, hier – nous avons un peu joué à la maison avec, heu, nos voisins. Après, heu, nous sommes allés ensemble à la piscine. On a joué, on a nagé, on a fait des courses. Après, heu, on est allé boire une petite boisson parce que … on avait soif. Et après, heu, on a essayé d'avoir un court de tennis, mais on n'a pas pu. Alors, nous avons pris nos vélos … nous avons fait un grand tour dans le bois … et … puis après, heu, on est rentré à la maison.

- ▶ **hier** yesterday
- ▶ **le voisin** neighbour
- ▶ **ensemble** together
- ▶ **la boisson** drink

on a fait des courses (*here*) we had races. Its more usual meaning is 'we did some shopping'. Note also

▶ **la natation** swimming.

on avait soif we were thirsty (literally, one had thirst). **Avait** (had) is in the imperfect tense. This is a descriptive past tense which is beyond the scope of this course. You should remember the present tense:

▶ **j'ai soif, on a soif.** Being hungry is also expressed with the verb **avoir**:

▶ **j'ai faim, on a faim.** So are being cold and being hot:

▶ **j'ai froid, on a froid; j'ai chaud, on a chaud.**

▶ **on a essayé** we tried (from the verb **essayer**).

mais on n'a pas pu but we couldn't (get a tennis court). In connection with tennis, note the constructions

▶ **jouer au tennis** (i.e. a sport) but

▶ **jouer du piano** (i.e. an instrument).

▶ **un grand tour** (*here*) a long ride. **Un tour** can be used for any sort of outing, on foot or by transport. The word has all sorts of other meanings as well – it is interesting to look it up in the dictionary.

The boss's motorcycle accident

LISTEN FOR...

▶ **il a eu un accident (de moto)**	he had a (motorcycle) accident
▶ **il s'est cassé le coude**	he broke his elbow
▶ **on l'a conduit à l'hôpital**	they took him to hospital
▶ **c'était une catastrophe**	it was a catastrophe

Jean-Claude Et ton patron? Tu m'as dit qu'il a eu un accident …

Michèle Ah oui, en ce moment c'est la mode! Il a eu un accident de moto. Alors, il est tombé; il s'est cassé le coude, en plusieurs morceaux; on l'a conduit à l'hôpital et on l'a opéré tout de suite.

Jean-Claude Et sa moto?

Michèle Elle est complètement cassée. Enfin, c'était une catastrophe, quoi!

▶ **il a eu un accident** he has had an accident. **Il a eu** is from the perfect of the verb **avoir**. A car accident is **un accident de voiture**.

▶ **Il s'est cassé le coude** He broke his elbow. The French construction is literally 'He to himself broke the elbow'. If you are unlucky, you might need to say

▶ **Je me suis cassé le bras** I have broken my arm

▶ **Je me suis cassé la jambe** I have broken my leg

en plusieurs morceaux in several pieces

▶ **on l'a conduit à l'hôpital et on l'a opéré tout de suite** he was taken to hospital and operated on immediately. French often uses **on** ('one took him to hospital') where English uses a passive ('he was taken to hospital'). **Conduit** is from the verb **conduire**, to drive or to take by car.

enfin in short.

quoi literally, what? Here it is used to finish the exclamation and has no particular meaning.

PRACTICE

4 Match up each of the words and phrases on the left with the one closest in meaning from the right-hand column.

a.	la maison	i.	la forêt
b.	on	ii.	nous
c.	nager	iii.	prendre un pot
d.	boire une petite boisson	iv.	retourner
e.	le vélo	v.	le pavillon
f.	le bois	vi.	la bicyclette
g.	rentrer	vii.	se baigner

ANSWERS P. 232

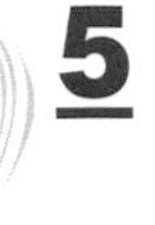

5 In the conversation printed below, Bernadette tells her husband what Barbara and her sister did yesterday.
Notice the forms of the verbs, which are all in the perfect tense:
elles ont ... and **elles sont ...** referring to the daughters and
ils ont ... and **ils sont ...** referring to the group of boys and girls.

Jean-Claude Qu'est-ce que les filles ont fait hier?
Bernadette Elles sont allées prendre un pot avec les enfants des voisins. ☐
Ils ont essayé d'avoir un court de tennis, mais ils n'ont pas pu. ☐
Ils ont joué ensemble un peu à la maison. ☐
Puis ils sont partis dans le bois à vélo... ☐
Et ils sont allés à la piscine. ☐

You will notice that Bernadette does not mention the activities in the same order as Barbara did in Conversations 2. Without looking back at the transcript of the conversations, play the recording of Barbara again and number the boxes above in the order in which she says things happened.

ANSWERS P. 232

6 You have been looking after some children over half-term. Reuse the language from Conversations 2 to tell Carolle what you did with them each day. You can use either **nous** or **on** for 'we': Yves will be using **nous** when he gives correct versions after the pauses.

CONVERSATION 

 *Work and play*

LISTEN FOR...

en tant que caissière	as a check-out assistant
un mobile-home	(pronounced **à la française!**)
du sable chaud	of the warm sand
▶ **pour bien s'amuser**	to have a lot of fun

Cécile Le premier mois de vacances, au mois de juillet, donc, j'ai travaillé dans un supermarché, en tant que caissière, et le deuxième mois, au mois d'août, je suis allée me reposer avec mes parents dans un mobile-home, au bord de la mer. Les vacances au bord de la mer se sont très bien passées: j'ai pu profiter du temps, du soleil, de la mer, du sable chaud, et puis, tous les soirs nous allions en discothèque, avec mes amis et ma sœur, pour danser, pour chanter, pour heu, pour heu, pour bien s'amuser, pour bien se détendre avant de, de reprendre les, les cours.

▶ **me reposer** to rest (myself). Remember that **rester** means to stay/remain, *not* to rest.

▶ **au bord de la mer** beside the sea.

▶ **Les vacances … se sont très bien passées** The holiday … went very well. From the verb **se passer**, to happen (e.g. **J'espère que tes vacances se passent bien**, I hope your holiday is going well).

nous allions we used to go. This is another example of the imperfect tense, which is used to describe how things were or what used to happen.

▶ **se détendre** to relax.

▶ **avant de reprendre les cours** before going back to college (literally, before taking up classes again).

PRACTICE

7 On the recording, Yves is asking Carolle about her holiday in Anjou, the area around Angers.

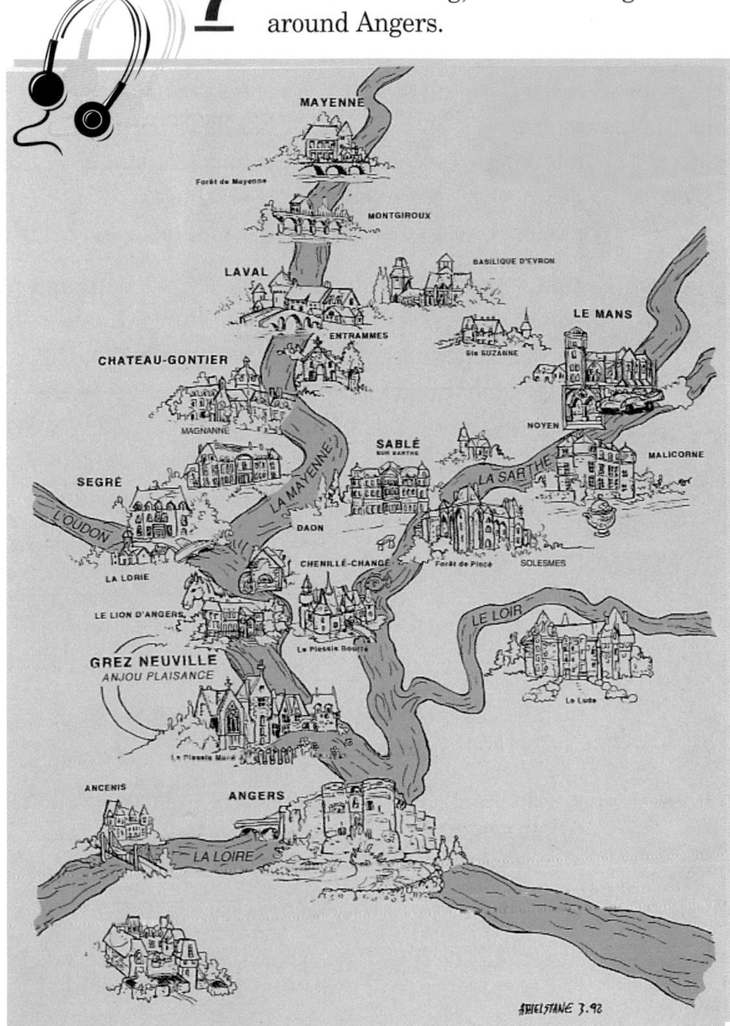

a. Did Carolle hire

- ☐ a gîte?
- ☐ a boat?
- ☐ a caravan?

b. Did she go

- ☐ with friends?
- ☐ with family?
- ☐ alone?

c. Does she say boating is

- ☐ energetic?
- ☐ boring?
- ☐ relaxing?

d. On which river are the places she mentions (see map):

- ☐ la Mayenne?
- ☐ la Sarthe?
- ☐ la Loire?

e. Tick the things Carolle says they did:

- ☐ see pretty villages
- ☐ stay on board all the time
- ☐ visit châteaux
- ☐ drink champagne
- ☐ go for country walks
- ☐ play ball
- ☐ go to restaurants

ANSWERS P. 232

8 In this exercise, you will be giving an account of your own holiday in and near Angers. Philippe will prompt you and Carolle will give correct versions after the pauses on the recording. All but one of the verbs you will need to use form their perfect tense with the verb **être**: e.g. **je suis allé(e)**, **nous sommes parti(e)s**. The one exception is the verb **louer** (to hire), which forms its perfect in the usual way with **avoir**: **j'ai loué**, **tu as loué**, etc.

9 Make sure you have read the note on pronunciation on p. 219 before you turn on the recording for this exercise, which will give you practice at pronouncing groups of words.

GRAMMAR AND EXERCISES

The perfect with *être*

A few verbs, mainly verbs of motion, form their perfect tense with **être** instead of **avoir**. So, for example, 'he went' or 'he has gone' is **il est allé**. The whole of the perfect tense of **aller** looks like this:

je suis allé(e)	**nous sommes allé(e)s**
tu es allé(e)	**vous êtes allé(e)(s)**
il est allé	**ils sont allés**
elle est allée	**elles sont allées**

When the perfect is formed with **être** like this, the past participle behaves like an adjective: it is feminine if the person it refers to is feminine and plural if it refers to more than one person. So a man would write **je suis allé**, but a woman would write **je suis allée** (which sounds exactly the same in speech). In **vous êtes allé(e)(s)**, both the **e** and the **s** are bracketed, because **vous** can be used for one masculine person (**vous êtes allé**) *or* one feminine person (**vous êtes allée**) *or* a group including males (**vous êtes allés**) *or* an all-female group (**vous êtes allées**).

In the negative, **ne** and **pas** are put either side of the bit of **être**, e.g.
il n'est pas allé, elles ne sont pas allées.

Here is the full list of verbs which form their perfect tense with **être**. They are principally verbs expressing motion of the whole body. You need to learn the whole list because there are plenty of other verbs which also express motion of the whole body but which form their perfect in the usual way with **avoir**, e.g. **marcher** (to walk): **j'ai marché** and **nager** (to swim): **j'ai nagé**.

Infinitive		*Perfect*
aller	to go	**je suis allé(e) etc.**
venir	to come	**je suis venu(e)**
arriver	to arrive	**je suis arrivé(e)**
partir	to leave	**je suis parti(e)**
entrer	to enter	**je suis entré(e)**
sortir	to go out	**je suis sorti(e)**
monter	to go up	**je suis monté(e)**
descendre	to go down	**je suis descendu(e)**
rester	to stay	**je suis resté(e)**
tomber	to fall	**je suis tombé(e)**
retourner	to return	**je suis retourné(e)**
naître	to be born	**je suis né(e)**
mourir	to die	**il est mort/elle est morte**

Mort/morte is the only one of these past participles where there is a difference in pronunciation between the masculine and the feminine: in the masculine the **t** of **mort** is not pronounced: in the feminine **morte** it is pronounced.

In addition, all compounds of these verbs form the perfect with **être**. These compounds include:

revenir	to come back
repartir	to go away again
rentrer	to go back in or go home

All reflexive verbs (see pp. 182–183 and p. 214) also form their perfect with **être**. Here is the perfect of the verb **se lever**, to get up:

je me suis levé(e)	**nous nous sommes levé(e)s**
tu t'es levé(e)	**vous vous êtes levé(e)(s)**
il s'est levé	**ils se sont levés**
elle s'est levée	**elles se sont levées**

Again, in the negative, **ne** and **pas** go either side of the bit of **être**, e.g.

je ne me suis pas levé(e)
tu ne t'es pas levé(e)
il ne s'est pas levé
elle ne s'est pas levée
nous ne nous sommes pas levé(e)s
vous ne vous êtes pas levé(e)(s)
ils ne se sont pas levés
elles ne se sont pas levées

Note: One verb which does *not* form its perfect tense with **être** is the verb 'to be': **être** itself. As you saw in Unit 13, the perfect of **être** is formed with **avoir**: **j'ai été** (I have been), **nous avons été** (we have been), etc.

10 To familiarise yourself with the forms of the perfect with **être**, write down the correct one for each of the pairs below. For example,

Il + tomber **Il est tombé.**

So that you don't have to put in brackets for alternatives, assume that ambiguous pronouns such as **je** are masculine for this exercise.

a. Il + arriver

b. Elle + entrer

c. Nous + venir

d. Je + rester

e. Tu + descendre

f. Il + naître

g. Elle + mourir

h. Elles + sortir

i. Ils + monter

ANSWERS P. 232

11 Write out each of these in the negative. Example:

Il est monté dans le train.
Il n'est pas monté dans le train.

a. Nous sommes rentrés.

b. Le bébé est né à la maison.

c. Elle est allée à Paris.

d. Vous êtes arrivés à Orly?

e. Il est mort à Verdun.

f. Ils sont partis à Genève.

g. Tu es venue à la maison.

ANSWERS P. 232

12 The reflexive verbs **se coucher**, **se trouver**, **se baigner**, **se rencontrer** and **se marier** all follow the pattern of **se lever**, which is set out on p. 228. See if you can use those verbs to translate the sentences below into French. This time, where there is ambiguity, assume that the persons concerned are all female.
Example:
I got up at midday.
Je me suis levée à midi.
It is **levée** because we are assuming that the speaker is female.

a. I got married in September.

b. She got up at six o'clock.

c. He went to bed at midnight.

d. We went for a swim this morning.

e. We found ourselves in Lille.

f. They met in Rouen.

g. Did you (**tu**) get married in France?

ANSWERS P. 232

KEY WORDS AND PHRASES

Je suis parti(e) en bateau	I left by boat
Je suis resté(e) une semaine à …	I stayed in … for a week
Nous sommes arrivés	We arrived
une centaine de kilomètres	about 100 kilometres
plus loin	further on
Nous avons dû repartir	We had to leave again
Hier, nous sommes allé(e)s	Yesterday, we went
à la piscine	to the swimming pool
On a nagé, on a joué	We swam, we played
On a fait de la natation	We went swimming
Nous avons pris nos vélos	We took our bikes
On a fait un tour dans le bois	We had a ride in the wood
ensemble	together
Nous avons joué au tennis	We played tennis
Nous avons joué du piano	We played the piano
J'ai soif, on a soif	I'm thirsty, we're thirsty
J'ai faim, on a faim	I'm hungry, we're hungry
J'ai froid, on a froid	I'm cold, we're cold
J'ai chaud, on a chaud	I'm hot, we're hot
Il a eu un accident (de moto)	He had a (motorcycle) accident
Il s'est cassé le coude	He broke his elbow
On l'a conduit à l'hôpital	They took him to hospital
Je me suis cassé la jambe/le bras	I have broken my leg/my arm
Je suis allé(e) au bord de la mer	I went to the seaside
pour me reposer	to have a rest
pour me détendre	to relax
pour m'amuser	to have fun
avant de reprendre les cours	before going back to college
J'en ai profité	I took advantage of it
Les vacances	The holiday
se sont très bien passées	went very well
C'était très agréable	It was very pleasant

LOOKING FORWARD

Congratulations on working all the way through the course! You should now be able to cope with most of the situations that are likely to come your way in a French-speaking country, particularly if you get people to help you by asking them:

Qu'est-ce que ça veut dire?
What does that mean?
Pouvez-vous répéter, s'il vous plaît?
Can you repeat, please?
Pouvez-vous parler plus lentement, s'il vous plaît?
Can you speak more slowly, please?

You never finish learning a language; that is one of the exciting – and frustrating – things about it. Even if you decide that you really do not need to reach a higher level than you now have, you should realise that you forget a language very quickly if you don't keep practising it.

It is partly a question of recalling the actual words that you have met, but also of making sure that you retain the ability to switch into French mode. If you keep on doing even a few minutes of French quite frequently, the whole French package will stay close to the surface of your mind. It is like making sure that you are keeping a software package loaded on your computer so that you can dip into it when you need to do so.

You can keep your French ticking over by revising the material from this course, perhaps playing the recordings in the car. Take every opportunity to use your language when you speak to French people so that you develop your speaking and listening skills. You may have the opportunity to correspond with French people you have met on holiday. You can make a point of watching French films on television.

You can also read in French. We have different reading modes in our own language: depending on the reason we are reading a text, we can skim through it for information or we can read it slowly and carefully, making sure we understand every word. We have a tendency to think that this slow careful reading is the only valid kind when we come to a foreign language, as though we are somehow cheating if we skim. Not at all! Both are skills which we need to develop – it is as useful to have two (or more) reading modes in French as it is in English.

A very good way into reading is by working with parallel texts. You can either use books which are published with the French on one page and the English translation facing it, or you can make up your own parallel texts, perhaps with technical literature which is of interest to you, by using the French and the English versions alongside each other. Try to make a practice of reading the French through once more afterwards: it is very satisfying to find that you can now understand it without having to keep stopping and looking words up.

If you want to make further progress with the language, you can then move on to a higher level of course, perhaps (and this is, naturally, a totally unbiased suggestion!) **Breakthrough French 2** by Stephanie Rybak and then **Breakthrough French 3** by Jenny Ollerenshaw and Stephanie Rybak, both published by Palgrave Macmillan.

AND FINALLY...

13

You ask Yves about his holiday on the island of Guadeloupe in the West Indies. *Note:* **Est-ce que** is used with the perfect tense in exactly the same way as with the present. If you were talking to a man you called **vous**, you might ask:

Est-ce que vous êtes parti pendant les vacances?
Est-ce que vos vacances se sont bien passées?
Est-ce que vous vous êtes reposé?
Qu'est-ce que vous avez fait?
Est-ce que vous vous êtes baigné?
Quand est-ce que vous êtes rentré?

In this exercise, you will need to ask Yves those questions, but addressing him as **tu** (e.g. **Est-ce que tu t'es reposé?**). Spend a few moments working out your questions before you turn on the recording.

ANSWERS

EXERCISE 1

A trip to England
je suis partie/j'ai pris/on est allé/je suis restée/j'ai visité/j'ai vu/je suis retournée
Sailing to Morocco
je suis allée/nous sommes partis/nous sommes arrivés/nous sommes repartis/nous avons réussi/nous sommes allés

EXERCISE 3

(a) suis allée **(b)** suis resté **(c)** sommes partis **(d)** sommes arrivées **(e)** suis venu **(f)** sommes montés

EXERCISE 4

(a) v **(b)** ii **(c)** vii **(d)** iii **(e)** vi **(f)** i **(g)** iv

EXERCISE 5

Elles sont allées prendre un pot avec les enfants des voisins.	3
Ils ont essayé d'avoir un court de tennis, mais ils n'ont pas pu.	4
Alors, ils ont joué ensemble un peu à la maison.	1
Puis ils sont partis dans le bois à vélo…	5
Et ils sont allés à la piscine.	2

EXERCISE 7

(a) a boat **(b)** with friends **(c)** relaxing **(d)** la Mayenne **(e)** see pretty villages, visit châteaux, go for country walks (**des balades à la campagne**) and go to restaurants.

EXERCISE 10

(a) Il est arrivé. **(b)** Elle est entrée. **(c)** Nous sommes venus. **(d)** Je suis resté. **(e)** Tu es descendu. **(f)** Il est né. **(g)** Elle est morte. **(h)** Elles sont sorties. **(i)** Ils sont montés.

EXERCISE 11

(a) Nous ne sommes pas rentrés. **(b)** Le bébé n'est pas né à la maison. **(c)** Elle n'est pas allée à Paris. **(d)** Vous n'êtes pas arrivés à Orly? **(e)** Il n'est pas mort à Verdun. **(f)** Ils ne sont pas partis à Genève. **(g)** Tu n'es pas venue à la maison.

EXERCISE 12

(a) Je me suis mariée en septembre. **(b)** Elle s'est levée à six heures. **(c)** Il s'est couché à minuit. **(d)** Nous nous sommes baignées ce matin. **(e)** Nous nous sommes trouvées à Lille. **(f)** Elles se sont rencontrées à Rouen. **(g)** Est-ce que tu t'es mariée en France?

REVIEW SECTION

You have covered a great deal of ground in working through the course: it would be very surprising if you could remember everything you have learned! To help you review and consolidate the language you have met, there are fifteen extra speaking exercises – one corresponding to each unit – at the end of the last cassette.

Before you tackle each of these exercises, go back and test yourself on the Key words and phrases from the relevant unit. Then repeat aloud any that you had forgotten until you are confident that you now know them.

Exercise 1

The words learned at the very beginning of a language course are often the ones we have most difficulty in pronouncing correctly later on, because we originally learned them with the foreign accent of a beginner. **Bonjour** and **bonsoir** cause particular problems because they have both the nasal '**on**' (not '**onn**') and the sound '**r**'.

This exercise gives you a chance to hone your pronunciation of the Key words and phrases from Unit 1.

Exercise 2

This exercise gives you a chance to go over the kind of conversation you are likely to have with someone you meet for the first time.

Exercise 3

You are in a café, ordering snacks and drinks. You'll need to start by asking **Qu'est-ce que vous avez à manger?**

Exercise 4

You are at the reception desk in a hotel trying to book a room for tonight.

Exercise 5

You are in a tourist office, asking for a town plan and then getting directions.

Exercise 6

You are about to go to France. A French friend will be meeting you off the plane, so you telephone her to give her all the details. You will need to give her the flight number (**le numéro du vol**). It is **Vol AF 947**, which the French say as 'nine hundred and forty-seven' rather than 'nine four seven', so you had better prepare that one in advance.

Exercise 7

You are shopping for food and wine in a village store.

Exercise 8

You are splashing out on a new swimming costume! Your first line in this exercise will be:

Je cherche un maillot de bain. I'm looking for a swimming costume.

EXERCISE 9

You are in a travel agency in Lille enquiring about travel to London. You'll find that you get a good deal on the train going through the Tunnel if you book fifteen days in advance (**à l'avance**).

EXERCISE 10

You are ordering a meal in a restaurant where the dish of the day turns out to be a casserole cooked to their own recipe: **un ragoût maison**. Health warning: doing this exercise may make you hungry!

EXERCISE 11

You are on the phone telling a French friend what to expect when he comes to stay with you.

EXERCISE 12

Carolle asks you whether you prefer to live in town or in the country.

EXERCISE 13

In this exercise, Yves asks you whether you have lived in France. You will need to use the verb **louer** (to rent).

EXERCISE 14

Carolle asks you what you are going to do during the holiday; you tell her about your forthcoming trip to the island of la Réunion in the Indian Ocean.

EXERCISE 15

Yves is asking you about your recent holiday in Tahiti and Bora Bora. (In French both names are pronounced with the stress on the last syllable of each word.)

Voilà!

C'est tout!

Félicitations!

Au revoir!

GRAMMAR SUMMARY

This section

- gives definitions of parts of speech like NOUN and ADJECTIVE
- gives basic rules for how they are used in French
- tells you where in the book you will find further explanations
- goes further into some points which are not covered in detail elsewhere in the course

VERBS

A VERB expresses action or being,
e.g. The man *goes*; I *am*; Mary *hates* football.

The INFINITIVE is the form of the verb which in English begins with *to*,
e.g. *to go*; *to be*; *to hate*.

The SUBJECT of a verb is the person or thing performing the action of the verb,
e.g. *the man* goes; *I* am; *Mary* hates football.

The OBJECT of a verb is the person or thing on the receiving end,
e.g. Mary hates *football*; John loves *it*; Mary loves *John*.

There are three main groups of regular verbs in French:

1. those with infinitives ending in **-er**, e.g. **travailler, habiter** (see p. 28)
2. those with infinitives ending in **-re**, e.g. **vendre, attendre** (see p. 58)
3. those with infinitives ending in **-ir**, e.g. **finir, choisir** (see p. 150)

Some of the main irregular verbs are given on pp. 12, 28, 42, 74, 120 and 137.

PRESENT

The French present tense corresponds to two kinds of present tense in English. So, for example, **je travaille** can be translated as either *I work* or *I am working*, depending on the context. Similarly, both *I speak* and *I am speaking* would be translated by **je parle**.

FUTURE

To express the future, use the construction which is a direct equivalent of the English construction 'to be going + to do', e.g. *I am going to speak* is **Je vais parler** and *We are going to leave at six o'clock in the morning* is **Nous allons partir à six heures du matin**.

Unit 14 has more about this construction, along with an introduction to the formal future tense (e.g. **je parlerai; nous partirons**) which you need to understand if not to use.

PAST The main tense for expressing past events is the perfect. It is explained in Units 13 and 15. As with the present, this one French tense is equivalent to two different tenses in English, so **j'ai fini** means both *I have finished* and *I finished* and **vous avez travaillé** can be translated as either *you have worked* or *you worked.*

Most verbs form their perfect by using the appropriate part of **avoir** and a form called the past participle, e.g. **j'ai fini**; **vous avez travaillé**. Examples of English past participles are: *walked*; *taken*; *held*. In English as in French, they combine with the verb *to have* to form the perfect tense, e.g. *I have walked*; *you have taken*; *they have held*. A list of French past participles is given on pp. 198–199.

In the negative, the **ne** and **pas** go either side of the bit of **avoir**, so you have **je n'ai pas fini**; **vous n'avez pas travaillé.**

Some verbs form their perfect with the present tense of **être** rather than **avoir**, e.g. **je suis entré(e), elle est arrivée; nous sommes sorti(e)s**. With **être**, the past participle behaves like an adjective and 'agrees' with the subject of the verb. So a man would write **je suis entré** but a woman would write **je suis entrée**. All reflexive verbs (see pp. 182–183, 214) form their perfect tense with **être**, e.g. from the verb **se rencontrer**: **nous nous sommes rencontré(e)s**. See Unit 15 for further explanation and a list of the other verbs which form their perfect tense with **être**.

Nouns and articles

> A NOUN is the name of a person or thing, e.g. *James, child, dog, book.*
>
> French ARTICLES are the equivalents of *the*, *a*, *an* and *some*.

All French nouns are masculine or feminine. The word for *the* is **le** before a masculine singular noun (e.g. **le taxi**), **la** before a feminine singular noun (e.g. **la voiture**) and **l'** before any singular noun beginning with a vowel sound (e.g. **l'autobus**). Before any plural noun the word for *the* is **les** (e.g. **les avions**).

The word for *a* or *one* is **un** before a masculine singular noun (e.g. **un ami**) and **une** before a feminine singular noun (e.g. **une amie**).

Some before a masculine singular noun is **du** (e.g. **du vin**); before a feminine singular noun it is **de la** (e.g. **de la bière**); before any singular noun beginning with a vowel sound it is **de l'** (e.g. **de l'eau**) and before any plural noun it is **des** (e.g. **des bouteilles**).

We often leave out the article in English but you must use one in French (e.g. *Love is blind* is **L'amour est aveugle** and *I'd like coffee* is **Je voudrais du café**).

Most nouns form their plural by adding an **-s**. Note the following three groups of exceptions:

1. Those ending is **-s**, **-x** or **-z** in the singular remain unchanged in the plural, e.g.

le fils	*son*	**les fils**	*sons*
le choix	*choice*	**les choix**	*choices*
le nez	*nose*	**les nez**	*noses*

2. Those ending in **-eau** or **-eu** in the singular add an **-x** to form their plural, e.g.

le tableau	*picture*	**les tableaux**	*pictures*
le cheveu	*a single hair*	**les cheveux**	*hair*

(Where we talk about someone's hair, the French logically talk of their 'hairs'.)

3. Most of those ending in **-al** in the singular have their plural in **-aux**, e.g.

le cheval	*horse*	**les chevaux**	*horses*
le journal	*newspaper*	**les journaux**	*newspapers*

One common exception to this rule is

le festival **les festivals**

Adjectives

An ADJECTIVE describes a noun or pronoun, e.g. *big, beautiful, green, intelligent.*

In French, an adjective 'agrees' with the noun or pronoun it describes. In other words, it has a masculine ending when describing something masculine, a feminine ending when describing something feminine and a plural ending when describing something plural, e.g.

Georges est grand.	*Georges is tall.*
Marie est grande.	*Marie is tall.*
Ils sont grands.	*They* (m.) *are tall.*
Marie et Anne sont grandes.	*Marie and Anne are tall.*

The feminine singular of an adjective is usually formed by adding an **-e** to the masculine singular (as in **grand/grande**). Plurals are usually formed by adding an **-s**. The main exceptions to this basic pattern are given on pp. 104 and 166.

Possessive adjectives

POSSESSIVE ADJECTIVES are words such as *my*, *your* and *his.*

For **mon, ma, mes** (*my*), **ton, ta, tes** (*your*) and **son, sa, ses** (*his/her/its*) see p. 166. For **notre, nos** (*our*) and **votre, vos** (*your*), see p. 136. The word for *their* is **leur** in the singular, e.g. **leur père**; **leur maison**, and **leurs** in the plural, e.g. **leurs enfants**; **leurs livres**.

Adverbs

> An ADVERB is a word which modifies the action of a verb. English examples are: *well*, *quickly*, *angrily*, *smoothly*.

Most adverbs are formed by adding **-ment** to the feminine of the adjective:

lent(e)	▶	**lentement**	*slowly*
rapide	▶	**rapidement**	*rapidly*
immédiat(e)	▶	**immédiatement**	*immediately*
facile	▶	**facilement**	*easily*
difficile	▶	**difficilement**	*with difficulty*
doux/douce	▶	**doucement**	*gently, sweetly*
heureux/heureuse	▶	**heureusement**	*happily*

Adjectives ending in **-ent** give adverbs ending in **-emment**. Adjectives ending in **-ant** give adverbs ending in **-amment**. These two endings are both pronounced the same (with the second-last syllable as an '**a**'). Examples:

évident(e)	▶	**évidemment**	*evidently*
violent(e)	▶	**violemment**	*violently*
constant(e)	▶	**constamment**	*constantly*
indépendant(e)	▶	**indépendamment**	*independently*

Some of the commonest French adverbs are irregular: **bien** (*well*), **mal** (*badly*), **vite** (*quickly*), **souvent** (*often*).

Prepositions

> A PREPOSITION is a word or phrase which goes before a noun or pronoun to show its relation to another part of the sentence. English prepositions include *before*, *under*, *in front of*, *until*, *without*, *on*, *by*, *except for*. A list of common French prepositions is given on p. 74.

Le and **les** change their form when used with the prepositions **de** or **à** (or prepositions like **près de** or **jusqu'à** which end in **de** or **à**):

de + le	▶	**du**	**Je viens du café.**
de + les	▶	**des**	**Le café est près des magasins.**
à + le	▶	**au**	**On va au cinéma.**
à + les	▶	**aux**	**Il est aux États-Unis.**

Pronouns

A PRONOUN is a word that stands instead of a noun,
e.g. Mary loves Fred – she loves him.
The cars damaged the lawn – they damaged it.
In these examples, *she* and *they* are called 'subject pronouns' because they replace the subject. Similarly, *him* and *it* are direct object pronouns because they replace the direct object of the verb.

Some verbs take an indirect object rather than a direct object, e.g. He speaks to them, not [He speaks them].

Here are the main subject, direct object and indirect object pronouns in French. The usual position for all of them is before the verb.

Subject	*Direct object*	*Indirect object*
je (*I*)	**me** (*me*)	**me** (*to me*)
tu (*you*)	**te** (*you*)	**te** (*to you*)
il (*he / it*)	**le** (*him / it*)	**lui** (*to him*)
elle (*she / it*)	**la** (*her / it*)	**lui** (*to her*)
nous (*we*)	**nous** (*us*)	**nous** (*to us*)
vous (*you*)	**vous** (*you*)	**vous** (*to you*)
ils (*they*)	**les** (*them*)	**leur** (*to them*)
elles (*they*)	**les** (*them*)	**leur** (*to them*)

Examples:

Il la voit. — *He sees her / it.*
Il lui parle. — *He speaks to him / to her.*
Je les connais. — *I know them.*
Je leur envoie une lettre. — *I am sending a letter to them.*

Y — **Y** means **there, to there** or **to it**. Examples:

Paul va à Paris aujourd'hui. — *Paul is going to Paris today.*
Moi, j'y vais jeudi. — *I'm going (there) on Thursday.*
J'y travaille. — *I work there.*
Tu y vas quelquefois? — *Do you go there sometimes?*

EN — As well as being a preposition meaning *in*, **en** can be a pronoun meaning: *of it* or *of them*. Here are some examples:

Qui veut du gateau? — *Who wants some cake?*
Jacques, tu en veux? — *Jacques, do you want some (of it)?*

Vous avez combien d'enfants? — *How many children do you have?*
J'en ai trois. — *I have two (of them).*

The *of it / of them* is often not used in English sentences like this, but you have to use **en** in French.

Numbers

1	**un**
2	**deux**
3	**trois**
4	**quatre**
5	**cinq**
6	**six**
7	**sept**
8	**huit**
9	**neuf**
10	**dix**
11	**onze**
12	**douze**
13	**treize**
14	**quatorze**
15	**quinze**
16	**seize**
17	**dix-sept**
18	**dix-huit**
19	**dix-neuf**
20	**vingt**
21	**vingt et un**
22	**vingt-deux**
23	**vingt-trois**
24	**vingt-quatre**
25	**vingt-cinq**
26	**vingt-six**
27	**vingt-sept**
28	**vingt-huit**
29	**vingt-neuf**
30	**trente**
31	**trente et un**
32	**trente-deux**
40	**quarante**
41	**quarante et un**
42	**quarante-deux**
50	**cinquante**
51	**cinquante et un**
52	**cinquante-deux**
60	**soixante**
61	**soixante et un**
62	**soixante-deux**
70	**soixante-dix**
71	**soixante et onze**
72	**soixante-douze**
73	**soixante-treize**
74	**soixante-quatorze**
75	**soixante-quinze**
76	**soixante-seize**
77	**soixante-dix-sept**
78	**soixante-dix-huit**
79	**soixante-dix-neuf**
80	**quatre-vingts**
81	**quatre-vingt-un**
82	**quatre-vingt-deux**
83	**quatre-vingt-trois**
90	**quatre-vingt-dix**
91	**quatre-vingt-onze**
92	**quatre-vingt-douze**
93	**quatre-vingt-treize**
94	**quatre-vingt-quatorze**
95	**quatre-vingt-quinze**
96	**quatre-vingt-seize**
97	**quatre-vingt-dix-sept**
98	**quatre-vingt-dix-huit**
99	**quatre-vingt-dix-neuf**
100	**cent**
101	**cent un**
102	**cent deux**
103	**cent trois**
150	**cent cinquante**
200	**deux cents**
201	**deux cent un**
202	**deux cent deux**
299	**deux cent quatre-vingt-dix-neuf**
300	**trois cents**
333	**trois cent trente-trois**
1000	**mille**
1.000.000	**un million**

1st, 2nd, 3rd etc. are expressed:

premier/première
deuxième (or **second(e)**)
troisième
quatrième
cinquième
sixième
septième
huitième
neuvième
dixième
onzième
douzième
...
vingtième
centième
millième

VOCABULARY

Many words have more than one meaning, depending on the context in which they are used. You will have to look them up in a dictionary to find the full range of possibilities as this list of vocabulary is largely restricted to the sense of the words as they are used in the course.

m. = masculine, f. = feminine, pl. = plural

Adjectives:

- **blanc(he)** means that the masculine form is **blanc** and the feminine **blanche**.
- where only one form is given (e.g. **jeune**), it is used for both the masculine and the feminine.

A

à at, to
  à 10 km 10 km away
acheter to buy
d' **accord** fine, OK
actualité (f.) current developments; (usually pl.) current affairs, news
adresse (f.) address
adorer to adore
âge (m.) age
agence (f.) **de voyages** travel agency;
  agence postale 'sub-sub-post office'
agent (m.) **de voyages** travel agent
il s' **agit de** it concerns
agneau (m.) lamb
agréable nice, pleasant
agressivité (f.) aggression
agricole agricultural
aider to help
aïl (m.) garlic
aimer to like, to love
air (m.) air, appearance
alimentation (f.) food
allemand(e) German
aller to go
aller/aller simple (m.) single (ticket)
aller et retour (m.) return (ticket)
allo/allô hello
allumer to light
alors then, well
  alors que whereas
américain(e) American
amour (m.) love
s' **amuser** to enjoy oneself
an (m.) year
  le jour de l'an New Year's Day
ananas (m.) pineapple
ancien(ne) ancient, former
andouille (f.) chitterlings sausage
anglais(e) English; often used for British
animateur (-trice) (f.) presenter, leader
animation (f.) life, activities
animer liven up, present
année (f.) year
anniversaire (m.) birthday, anniversary
anonyme anonymous
août August
appartement (m.) flat, apartment
s' **appeler** to be called
apporter to bring
apprendre to learn
après after
après-midi (m. or f.) afternoon
arbre (m.) tree
arrêt (m.) **de bus** bus-stop
arrivée (f.) arrival
arriver to arrive
ascenseur (m.) lift, elevator
aspirine (f.) aspirin
assez quite, fairly, enough
assiette (f.) plate
assis(e) sitting
  place assise seat
assorti(e)s various, matching
assurance (f.) insurance
attirer to attract
aube (f.) dawn
auberge (f.) inn
aujourd'hui today
aussi also
d' **autant plus que** especially as
auto (f.) car
autobus (m.) bus
automne (m.) autumn, fall
autour de around
autre other
avant (+ noun) before
  avant de (+ infinitive) before
avec with
averse (f.) shower (of rain)
aveugle blind
avion (m.) aeroplane
avis (m.) opinion
avoir to have
avril April

B

baguette (f.) French stick (of bread)
se **baigner** to bathe
baignoire (f.) bath-tub
balade (m.) walk, ramble, ride
banlieue (f.) suburb
bas (m.) stocking
  en bas at the bottom
bateau (m.) boat
beau, bel (m., used before vowel), **belle** beautiful, handsome
  il fait beau it is fine, sunny
beaucoup a lot, very much
beau-frère (m.) brother-in-law,

stepbrother
belle-sœur (f.) sister-in-law, stepsister
besoin (m.) need
avoir besoin de to need
bibliothèque (f.) library
bien well; **ou bien** or else; **bien sûr** of course
bière (f.) beer
bifteck (m.) steak
billet (m.) ticket
bistro(t) (m.) pub/bar serving food
blanc(he) white
bleu(e) blue
bleu marine navy blue
bœuf (m.) beef, ox
boire to drink
bois (m.) wood
boisson (f.) drink
boîte (f.) box, can
bon(ne) good
bonjour good-day, hello
bonsoir good evening, hello
bord (m.) edge
boucherie (f.) butcher's shop
bouilli(e) boiled
boulanger (-ère) baker
boulangerie (f.) bakery
braisé(e) braised
bras (m.) arm
brasserie (f.) large café serving food
briller to shine
britannique British
brouillard (m.) fog
bruit (m.) noise
brushing (m.) blow-dry
brut (m.) dry (of sparkling drinks)
bureau (m.) office, study, desk

C

ça that
cabine téléphonique (f.) telephone booth
cabinet (m.) **de toilette** washing facilities
cadeau (m.) present
caisse (f.) cash desk, payment office
calme quiet
campagne (f.) country
canal (m.) canal, channel
canard (m.) duck
carotte (f.) carrot
carte (f.) card, map, 'à la carte menu'
carte de crédit credit card
carte postale postcard
carte téléphonique telephone card
carterie (f.) card-shop
casser to break
cassis (m.) blackcurrant, blackcurrant liqueur
cassoulet (m.) casserole of beans with goose, pork or mutton
ce, cet (m., used before vowel), **cette, ces** this/that, these/those
ce qui which (lit. that which)
ceinture (f.) belt
cela that
célibataire (adj. or noun, m. or f.) single, unmarried, bachelor
cendre (f.) ash
centaine (f.) about 100
centre-ville (m.) town-centre
cerise (f.) cherry
c'est it is, this is
chacun(e) each
chambre (f.) bedroom, chamber
chance (f.) luck
changer to change
chanter to sing
charcuterie (f.) delicatessen selling mainly cooked pork products
chasse (f.) hunt, hunting, flush (WC)
chaud(e) hot
avoir chaud (of person) to be hot
il fait chaud it is hot
chauffage (m.) central heating
chaussette (f.) sock
chaussure (f.) shoe
chemise (f.) shirt
chemisier (m.) blouse
chèque (m.) **de voyage** traveller's cheque
cher, chère dear, expensive
chercher to look for, to fetch
cheval (m.) horse
chèvre (f.) goat; (m. – short for **fromage de chèvre**) goat-cheese
chez at the house of
chinois(e) Chinese
chocolat (m.) chocolate
choisir to choose
chômage (m.) unemployment
chose (f.) thing
cidre (m.) cider
ciel (m.) sky, heaven, skyscape
cigogne (f.) stork
cimetière (m.) cemetery
circuler to move around, (of traffic) to flow
citron (m.) lemon
clair(e) light, clear
clé/clef (f.) key
climat (m.) climate
cochonnet (m.) piglet, (in **boules**) jack
à la cocotte casseroled
code (m.) **postal** post-code
cœur (m.) heart
avoir mal au cœur to feel sick
coiffeur (-euse) hairdresser
coiffure (f.) hair-do
salon (m.) **de coiffure** hairdressing salon
collaborateur (-trice) co-worker
collant (m.) tights
combien how much, how many
comme as, like, in the way of
commencer to start
comment how
Comment? What?
C'est comment? What's it like?
commerçant(e) shopkeeper
compartiment (m.) compartment
complet (-ète) full, complete
complètement completely
comprendre to understand, to include
comprimé (m.) tablet
compris(e) included
comptable (m. or f.) accountant
compter to count
concierge (m. or f.) caretaker
conduire to drive
confirmer to confirm
confortable comfortable
confortablement comfortably
connaître to know, to be acquainted with

conserve (f.) preserve, tinned food
consistant(e) substantial, stodgy
contourner to go round
contre against
  par contre on the other hand
correspondance (f.) mail, (transport) connection
côte (f.) coast, chop
  avec de grosses côtes (knitting) with wide ribbing
à côté de next to
d' un côté on one side, on the one hand
se coucher to go to bed, to lie down
coude (m.) elbow
coupe (f.) cut, cup
couper to cut
courir to run
cours (m.) course, class
course (m.) errand, race
  faire les courses to go shopping
court (m.) **de tennis** tennis court
cravate (f.) tie
crème (f.) cream
crêpe (f.) pancake
crêperie (f.) pancake-house
croire to believe
croque-madame (m.) toasted cheese and ham sandwich with an egg on top
croque-monsieur (m.) toasted cheese and ham sandwich
crustacé (m.) shellfish
cuiller/cuillère (f.) spoon
cuisine (f.) cooking, kitchen
cuisiné cooked
cuisinier, (-ère) cook
cuisse (f.) thigh
  cuisse de grenouille frog's leg
cuit(e) cooked
  bien cuit (of meat) well done
curiosité (f.) curiosity, place of interest

D

dangereux (-euse) dangerous
dans in
danser to dance
de of, from
débarras (m.) junk room
début (m.) beginning
décembre December
découvrir to discover
délicieux (-euse) delicious
demain tomorrow
demander to ask for
demi(e) half
  demi-sec (of sparkling drinks) sweetish (lit. half-dry)
dent (f.) tooth
départ (m.) departure
  au départ de ex, leaving from
derrière behind
descendre to go down, get off
désirer to desire, to wish for
se détendre to relax
détester to detest
deuxième second
devant in front of
devenir to become
devoir to be under an obligation to (do something)
  je dois I ought, I should, I must, I have to
diarrhée (f.) diarrhoea
difficile difficult
dimanche (m.) Sunday
dinde (f.) turkey
dire to say, to tell
discuter to discuss, to argue
se distraire to enjoy oneself
donc so, then
donner to give
dormir to sleep
dos (m.) back
douche (f.) shower
doute (m.) doubt
doux, douce sweet, gentle
tout droit straight on
droite right
du, de la, de l', des of the, some
dû past participle of **devoir**
durer to last

E

eau (f.) water
échec (m.) failure; (pl.) chess
éclaircie (f.) sunny interval
écolier (-ère) schoolchild
écrire to write
en effet indeed
également equally, too
église (f.) church
électricien (m.) electrician
élevé(e) brought up, raised, high
élève (m. or f.) pupil
emmener to take (somebody somewhere)
emploi (m.) employment
employé(e) employee
en in
encolure (f.) (of garment) neck
encore again, still, yet
  encore une fois once again
enfant (usually m.) child
enfin at last, well
enseignement (m.) teaching
ensemble together
  dans l'ensemble overall
ensoleillé(e) sunny
ensuite then, next
entendre to hear
  entendu agreed (lit. heard)
entre between
entrée (f.) entry, entrance hall; (at table) traditionally the course served between the starter and the meat, today used confusingly sometimes of the starter and sometimes of the main course
à l' envers backwards
envie (f.) desire
  avoir envie de to want to
épicerie (f.) grocer's shop
escale (f.) stop-over
escargot (m.) snail
espagnol(e) Spanish
essayer to try
est-ce que indicates a yes/no question
et and
établissement (m.) establishment
étage (m.) floor, storey
étais, était was (imperfect of **être**)
États-Unis (m.pl.) United States
été (m.) summer; (also past participle of **être**)
étoile (f.) star
être to be
éviter to avoid
exactement exactly

examen (m.) exam
excuser to excuse
  excusez-moi excuse me
par **exemple** for example
extra brut (of sparkling drinks) extremely dry
extra sec (of sparkling drinks) dry to medium dry

F

en **face de** opposite
facile easy
façon (f.) way
  de toute façon in any case
faim (f.) hunger
  avoir faim to be hungry
faire to do, to make
il **faut** it is necessary
faux, fausse false
félicitations (f. pl.) congratulations
femme (f.) woman, wife
  femme au foyer housewife
  femme d'affaires businesswoman
  femme de ménage cleaning lady
fermer to shut
fête (f.) party, celebration, feast, public holiday
  fête nationale national holiday, Bastille Day (14 July)
ficelle (f.) string, thin loaf
filet (m.) fillet
fille (f.) girl, daughter
fils (m.) son
fin (f.) end
financier (-ère) financial
finir to end
fleur (f.) flower
fleuriste (m. or f.) florist
flocon (m.) flake
foi (f.) faith
foie (m.) liver
fois (f.) time
  à la fois at the same time
foncé(e) dark
fonctionnaire (m. or f.) civil servant, administrator
forêt (f.) forest
foulard (m.) scarf
framboise (f.) raspberry
français(e) French
fréquenté(e) frequented, crowded
frère (m.) brother
frit(e) fried
  frites (f.) French fries!
froid(e) cold
  avoir froid (of person) to be cold
  il fait froid it is cold
fromage (m.) cheese
fruit (m.) (piece of) fruit
  fruits de mer seafood
fumée (f.) smoke
fumer to smoke

G

galette (f.) savoury pancake
gare (f.) station
  gare SNCF railway station
  gare routière bus station
garçon (m.) boy, waiter
gauche left
gazeux (-euse) fizzy
gelée (f.) jelly
général(e) general
gens (pl., usually m.) people
gentil(le) nice, kind
gigot (m.) leg (of lamb)
glace (f.) ice, ice cream
gorge (f.) throat
goûter to taste, to have tea
grand(e) big, large, tall
  grand magasin (m.) department store
grandir to grow taller
grand-mère (f.) grandmother
grand-parent (m.) grandparent
grand-père (m.) grandfather
grand-place (f.) main square
gras(se) fatty, greasy, plump
gratuit(e) free (of charge)
grec, grecque Greek
  grec ancien, grec moderne Ancient Greek, Modern Greek
grenier (m.) attic
grenouille (f.) frog
grillé(e) grilled
gros(se) fat, large
grossir to grow fat

H

As some words beginning with 'h' are deemed to begin with a vowel sound and some (a minority) to begin with a consonant, the definite article is given with each of the nouns in this section.

habiter to live in
l' **habitude** (f.) habit
  comme d'habitude as usual
haut(e) high
  en haut on top, high up
hein meaningless filler-word
hélas alas
l' **heure** (f.) hour, time
hier yesterday
l' **histoire** (f.) story, history
l' **hiver** (m.) winter
l' **HLM** (m. or f.) = **habitation à loyer modéré** council house/flat
le **homard** (m.) lobster
l' **homme** (m.) man
  homme d'affaires businessman
l' **hôpital** (m.) hospital
l' **horaire** (m., most often used in pl.) time, timetable
l' **horreur** (f.) horror
  avoir horreur de not to be able to bear (something)
l' **hôtel** (m.) **de ville** town hall
l' **huître** (f.) oyster
hygiénique hygienic
  papier (m.) **hygiénique** toilet paper
l' **hypermarché** (m.) hypermarket

I

ici here
  par ici over here
idéal(e) ideal
  idéal (m.) the ideal
il y a there is, there are
illimité(e) unlimited
imperméable (m.) raincoat
inclinable reclining
inconvénient (m.) drawback
industriel(le) industrial
inférieur(e) lower, inferior
infirmier (-ère) nurse
ingénieur (m.) engineer
intéressant(e) interesting

invité(e) guest
inviter to invite
italien(ne) Italian

J

jamais (and **ne … jamais**) never
à jamais for ever
jambe (f.) leg
jambon (m.) ham
janvier January
jaune yellow
jeudi (m.) Thursday
jeune young
jour (m.) day
le jour de l'an New Year's Day
jouer to play (**de** + musical instrument, **à** + game/sport)
journal (m.) newspaper
juin June
jupe (f.) skirt
jupon (m.) petticoat
jus (m.) juice
jusqu'à until, as far as
juste just, right, tight

K

kilométrage (m.) 'mileage'
kir (m.) white wine with blackcurrant liqueur

L

la the, her, it
là there
lac (m.) lake
laisser to leave
lait (m.) milk
lait-fraise (m.) strawberry milk-shake
langouste (f.) crayfish
langue (f.) language, tongue
langue étrangère foreign language
langue maternelle mother tongue
laver to wash
se laver to wash (oneself)
laverie (f.) **automatique** laundrette
lave-vaisselle (m.) dishwasher
le the, him, it
légume (m.) vegetable
lentement slowly
lessive (f.) washing, washing powder
lettre (f.) letter
leur their, to them
lever to lift
se lever to get up
librairie (f.) bookshop
libre free
libre-service (m.) self-service shop
licence (f.) university degree
lieu (m.) place
lire to read
lit (m.) bed
livre (m.) book; (f.) pound
location (f.) hire
loger to accommodate
loin far
longtemps for a long time
louer to hire
lundi (m.) Monday

M

ma my
machine (f.) **à laver** washing machine
Madame Mrs, Madam
Mademoiselle Miss
magasin (m.) shop
magnétophone (m.) tape recorder
mai May
maigrir to grow thinner
maillot (m.) **de bain** swimming costume
main (f.) hand
maintenant now
mairie (f.) town hall
mais but
maison (f.) house, firm
mal (m.) pain, evil; (adverb) badly
avoir mal to have a pain
faire mal to hurt
mal de tête headache
pas mal not bad (can = pretty good!)
pas mal de quite a lot of
manteau (m.) coat
marché (m.) market
mardi (m.) Tuesday
mari (m.) husband
marié(e) married
marine navy
Maroc (m.) Morocco
marron brown
mars March
matin (m.) morning
me me, to me
mécanicien (m.) mechanic
médecin (m.) doctor
médicament (m.) medicine
mélange (m.) mixture
même same, even
mer (f.) sea
merci thank you
mercredi (m.) Wednesday
mère (f.) mother
Messieurs-dames ladies and gentlemen
météo (f.) weather forecast
métro (m.) tube, underground
mettre to put
midi midday, noon
mien(ne) mine
mieux better
le/la mieux the best
milieu (m.) middle
minuit midnight
mise (f.) **en plis** (hair) set
modèle (m.) style, type
moi me, I
moins less
mois (m.) month
mon, ma, mes my
monde (m.) world
trop de monde too many people
Monsieur Mr, Sir
montagne (f.) mountain
monter to go up
montre (f.) watch
morceau (m.) piece
moto (f.) motorbike
mouchoir (m.) handkerchief
mourir to die
moyen (m.) way, means, average
moyen(ne) average, middling
moyen âge (m.) Middle Ages
moyenâgeux medieval
mûr(e) ripe
musée (m.) museum

N

nager to swim
naissance (f.) birth
naître to be born
natal(e) of birth
natation (f.) swimming
nationalité (f.) nationality
nature 'as nature intended', plain
  thé (m.) **nature** tea without milk or lemon
ne … pas not
nettoyer to clean
né(e) born
neige (f.) snow
neiger to snow
Noël (m. or f.) Christmas
noir(e) black
nom (m.) name, surname
nombre (m.) number
non no
non-fumeurs no smoking
nord (m.) north
notre, nos our
nounours (m.) teddy bear
nourriture (f.) food
nouveau (-elle) new
novembre November
nuage (m.) cloud
nuageux (-euse) cloudy
nuit (f.) night
numéro (m.) number, figure

O

octobre October
œuf (m.) egg
offrir to offer, to give
oie (f.) goose
oignon (m.) onion
oiseau (m.) bird
on one/we/they
orage (m.) storm
orageux (-euse) stormy
oreille (f.) ear
ou or
  ou … ou either … or
où where
oublier to forget
ouest (m.) west
oui yes
ouvert(e) open
ouvrir to open

P

pain (m.) bread
paisible peaceful
pamplemousse (m.) grapefruit
panneau (m.) sign
pantalon (m.) trousers
papier (m.) paper
Pâques (m. sing. or f. pl) Easter
par by, through
parc (m.) park
parce que because
pardon sorry, excuse me
parfait(e) perfect
parfois sometimes
parfum (m.) perfume
parisien(ne) Parisian
parole (f.) word
partenaire (m. or f.) partner
partie (f.) part
partir to leave, to go off
  à partir de from
pas (m.) step
  ne … pas not
passer to pass, to spend (time), to take (an exam)
pâtisserie (f.) pastry, cake, cake-shop
pavillon (m.) detached house
payer to pay
pays (m.) country, area
pêche (f.) fishing, peach
pendre to hang
penser to think
Pentecôte (f.) Pentecost, Whitsun
perdre to lose
père (m.) father
personne (f.) person
  ne … personne nobody
petit(e) small
  petit pain (m.) bread roll
petite-fille (f.) granddaughter
petit-fils (m.) grandson
peu (m.) little
  un petit peu a little bit
  à peu près more or less
pharmacie (f.) chemist's
pharmacien (m.) pharmacist
photographe (m. or f.) photographer
photographie (f.) photograph
pièce (f.) room, coin, part
pied (m.) foot
piscine (f.) swimming pool
placard (m.) cupboard
plage (f.) beach
plan (m.) map, plan
planche (f.) **à voile** windsurfing
plat (m.) dish
  plat du jour dish of the day
plat(e) flat; (of mineral water) still
plateau (m.) tray, platter
plein(e) full
  plein de full of, lots of
pleurer to cry
pleuvoir to rain
plombier (m.) plumber
pluie (f.) rain
plus more, plus
  en plus as well, moreover
plusieurs several
pluvieux (-euse) rainy
poché(e) poached
à point (of meat) medium
poisson (m.) fish
poissonnerie (f.) fishmonger's
pomme (f.) apple
  pomme de terre potato
pont (m.) bridge
porc (m.) pork
portail (m.) gate
portugais(e) Portuguese
possibilité (f.) possibility, option
pot (m.) pot, drink
poulet (m.) chicken
pour for
  pour cent per cent
pourquoi why
pouvoir to be able to
précieux (-euse) precious
préférer to prefer
premier (-ère) first
prendre to take
prénom (m.) forename
près de near to
pressé(e) in a hurry
pression (f.) draught (beer)
prévoir to foresee, to predict
prier to beseech
  je vous en prie please don't mention it
printemps (m.) spring
problème (m.) problem
prochain(e) next

à la prochaine! till our next meeting!
proche near
produit (m.) product
professeur (m.) teacher
profiter (de) to take advantage (of)
promotion (f.) special offer
propre clean, own
puis then
pull (m.) pullover

Q

quai (m.) platform, quay
qualité (f.) quality
quand when
quart (m.) quarter
quartier (m.) district
maison (f.) **de quartier** community centre
que what, which
ne ... que only
quel(le) which
à quelle heure? at what time?
quelque chose something
quelquefois sometimes
quelques a few
qu'est-ce que ...? what ...?
quitter to leave
ne quittez pas hang on, please
quoi what

R

raconter to tell, to recount
ragoût (m.) stew
rangement (m.) storage
rapide fast
ravi(e) delighted
réceptionniste (m. or f.) receptionist
rechercher to seek
regagner to get back to
regarder to look at
règle (f.) rule
en règle in order
régler to pay
relier to link
remparts (m. pl.) ramparts
rencontrer to meet (someone)
se rencontrer to meet (each other)
rendez-vous (m.) meeting, appointment
rendre to give back, to render
se rendre à to get oneself to (a place)
renseignements (m. pl.) information
rentrée (f.) start of term, beginning of school year
rentrer to go home, to go back in
repartir to leave again
répéter to repeat
reportage (m.) report, news story
reposer to put down again
se reposer to rest
reprendre to take back, to take up again
réseau (m.) network
réserver to reserve, to book
responsable responsible; (m. or f.) the person responsible
restaurer to restore
rester to stay, to remain
retourner to return
retraite (f.) retirement, retreat
se réunir to get together
réussir to succeed, to pass (an exam)
réussite (f.) success
revenir to come back
au revoir goodbye
rez-de-chaussée (m.) ground floor
rien (and **ne ... rien**) nothing
rillettes (f. pl.) potted meat
rivière (f.) river
riz (m.) rice
robe (f.) dress
romain(e) Roman
rond(e) round
rose pink
rôti(e) roast
rouge red
rouler to roll, (of traffic) to move
route (f.) road
Royaume-Uni (m.) United Kingdom
rude rough, crude
rue (f.) street
russe Russian
rythme (m.) rhythm

S

sable (m.) sand
sac (m.) bag
sac à main handbag
sachet (m.) little bag, packet, sachet
saignant(e) bleeding; (of meat) rare
saint-pierre (m.) (fish) John Dory
saison (f.) season
salade (f.) salad, lettuce
salaire (m.) salary
salé(e) salty, savoury
salle (f.) room
salle à manger dining room
salle communale village hall
salle de bains bathroom
salle d'eau shower-room
salle de séjour living room
salon (m.) sitting room, salon
samedi (m.) Saturday
sans without
saucisse (f.) sausage
saucisson (m.) salami
sauf except for
saumon (m.) salmon
savoir to know
sec, sèche dry
sèche-cheveux (m.) hair dryer
séjour (m.) stay
salle (f.) **de séjour** sitting room
sel (m.) salt
gros sel coarse grain salt
semaine (f.) week
sentir to feel, to sense, to smell
se sentir to feel (well/ill etc.)
séparé(e) separated
septembre September
servir to serve
seul(e) alone, only
shampooing (m.) shampoo
short (m.) shorts
si if
siège (m.) seat
s'il vous plaît please
simple simple, straightforward, unpretentious
simplement simply
sinon if not, otherwise
se situer to be located
slip (m.) underpants
sœur (f.) sister

soif (f.) thirst
soir (m.) evening
soleil (m.) sun
Sopalin (m.) (trade name for) kitchen paper
sorte (f.) sort
sortir to go out, to take out
souhaiter to wish for
sous under
soutien-gorge (m.) bra
souvent often
stade (m.) stage, stadium
stage (m.) training course
station-service (f.) service station
studio (m.) bed-sit, studio
sucre (m.) sugar
  sucré(e) sweet
sud (m.) south
Suisse (f.) Switzerland
  suisse Swiss
  petit suisse (m.) small cream cheese
suivre to follow
supérieur(e) superior, upper
supermarché (m.) supermarket
suppositoire (m.) suppository
sur on
sûr(e) sure
en **sus** in addition, extra

T

tabac (m.) tobacco, tobacconist's shop
taille (f.) size, waist
tant so much
  en tant que as, in the capacity of
tard late
tartiner to spread, to butter
tasse (f.) cup
te you, to you
télécarte (f.) phonecard
téléviseur (m.) television set
télévision (f.) television
tellement so much
temps (m.) time, weather
  de temps en temps from time to time
tendre to hold out, to stretch (something)
  tendu(e) stressed
tenir to hold
tennis (m.) tennis, tennis court
terminer to end
tête (f.) head
thé (m.) tea
tiens! exclamation of interest
timbre (m.) stamp
toilettes (f. pl.) toilet
  faire sa toilette to wash and dress
tomate (f.) tomato
tomber to fall
ton, ta, tes your
toujours always, still
tour (m.) trip, tour, walk; (f.) tower, tower-block
touristique touristic
tourner to turn
Toussaint (f.) All Saints' Day
tout(e) all
  tout de suite immediately
traiteur (m.) caterer
  chez le traiteur at the delicatessen
travail (m.) work
travailler to work
traverser to cross
très very
triperie (f.) tripe
trop too, too much
  trop de too much (of)
trouver to find
  se trouver to find oneself, to be situated

U

uniquement only

V

vacances (f. pl.) holiday
vaisselle (f.) washing up, crockery
vanille (f.) vanilla
à la **vapeur** steamed
veau (m.) veal, calf
végétarien(ne) vegetarian
vélo (m.) bicycle
vendre to sell
vendredi (m.) Friday
venir to come
vent (m.) wind
verre (m.) glass
vers towards; (of time) around
vert(e) green
veste (f.) jacket
vêtement (m.) garment
viande (f.) meat
vide empty
vie (f.) life
vieillir to grow old
vieux, vieil (m. before vowel), **vieille** old
ville (f.) town, city
vin (m.) wine
visiter to visit
visuel(le) visual
voici here is, here are
voilà there is, there are, that's right, 'there you are', (concluding) 'that's it, then'
voile (f.) sailing
voilier (m.) sailing boat
voir to see
voisin (m.), **voisine** (f.) neighbour
voiture (f.) car
vos, votre your
vouloir to want
voyager to travel
vrai(e) real, true
  vraiment really, truly

Y

y a-t-il? is there?, are there? (question form of **il y a**)
yaourt (m.) yoghurt

INDEX